Evolutionary Theory
and
Cognitive Therapy

Paul Gilbert, PhD, FBPsS, received his degree from Edinburgh University in 1980 and in the same year qualified with the British Psychological Society as a clinical pyschologist. He has written extensively in the areas of shame, social anxiety and mood disorder. Dr. Gilbert also has published, with Professor Birchwood, work on psychosis. More recently he has been developing psychological therapies for deep shame and self-attacking within a cognitive framework, which is called Compassionate Mind Training.

Evolutionary Theory
and
Cognitive Therapy

Paul Gilbert, PhD, FBPsS, Editor

 Springer Publishing Company

Copyright © 2004 by Springer Publishing Company, Inc.

Springer Publishing Company, Inc.
536 Broadway
New York, NY 10012-3955

Acquisitions Editor: Sheri W. Sussman
Production Editor: Sara Yoo
Cover design by Joanne E. Honigman

04 05 06 07 08 / 5 4 3 2 1

Library of Congress Cataloging-in-Publication Data

Evolutionary theory and cognitive therapy / (edited by) Paul Gilbert. — 1st ed.
    p. cm.
  Expanded from a special issue of the Journal of Cognitive Psychotherapy.
  Includes bibliographical reference and index.
  ISBN 0-8261-2187-X (alk. paper)
  1. Cognitive therapy. 2. Evolution (Biology) I. Gilbert, Paul.
RC489.C63E96 2004
616.89'142—dc22   2004010748

Printed in the United States of America by Integrated Book Technology.

Contents

Contributors

Kent G. Bailey, PhD
Virginia Commonwealth University
Richmond, Virginia

Max Birchwood, PhD
University of Birmingham
Birmingham Mental Health Services
Trust, England

Sarah Byrne, PhD
University of Birmingham
Birmingham Mental Health Services
Trust, England

Leslie S. Greenberg, PhD
York University
Toronto, Canada

Nina Heinrichs, PhD
University of Braunschweig
Braunschweig, Germany

Stefan G. Hofmann, PhD
Boston University
Boston, Massachusetts

Robert L. Leahy, PhD
American Institute for Cognitive
    Therapy
Weill-Cornell University Medical
    Center
New York, New York

Giovanni Liotti, PhD
Scuola di Specializzazione
Psicoterapia Cognitiva APC, Roma

Alan Meadon, PhD
University of Birmingham
Birmingham Mental Health Services
Trust, England

David A. Moscovitch, PhD
Boston University
Boston, Massachusetts

Angela Nelson, PhD
University of Birmingham
Birmingham Mental Health Services
Trust, England

Peter Trower, PhD
University of Birmingham
Birmingham Mental Health Services
Trust, England

Introduction: Evolution Theory and Cognitive Therapy

Paul Gilbert

The chapters of this book were all commissioned for a special edition of *Journal of Cognitive Psychotherapy: An International Quarterly* in 2002 (with a chapter by Byrne et al, published the following year). Robert Leahy, the then editor of the journal, proposed the idea of exploring how cognitive therapy and theory might be informed by evolution theory and offered me an opportunity to edit that issue. This was an exciting project for a number of reasons. When Beck (1996) reflected on cognitive theory he noted some of the challenges to its theoretical and empirical basis that have emerged over the last 30 years. He argued that while the concepts of schematic and cognitive processing remain valid and offer insights into the vulnerability, onset and recovery from disorders, our understanding of how such operations are performed in the brain has developed rapidly. Indeed, because cognitive therapy has always been evidence-based, determined not to get caught up in esoteric theorizing as some other therapies had, it was keen to stay close to, and develop with, basic psychological science. In the last years, of course, psychological science has raced ahead with (for example) new methods for exploring non-conscious processing (Haidt, 2001), linking neurosciences with cognition (Schwartz & Begley, 2002) and understanding the evolved underpinnings for some of our feeling and ways of thinking (Gilbert, 1989; Buss, 2003). Indeed, the last 30 years has revealed much about how the brain evolved to process information, the nature of affect processing, and differences in systems for conscious, slow and reflective processing versus fast, immediate unconscious processing (Haidt, 2001; Panksepp, 1998).

The challenges of evolution theory

The increasing recognition that the human brain has evolved over a long period of time with specific competencies for attending to and processing information has generated new challenges for cognitive theory. Some of the challenges include the following:

Genes: Genes influence differences between people and facilitate types of learning, temperament and dispositions to emotional distress (Plomin & Crabbe, 2000). However, it is phenotypes that are of interest to therapists. Phenotypes are emergent from genetic disposition shaped by experiences. Linking genes to experience-built phenotypic outcomes is difficult however and there are major debates on this matter (e.g., see Li, 2003, Lickliter & Honeycutt, 2003). To offer one example, monkeys with the short version of the 5-HT transport gene are highly reactive to early stresses and vulnerable to anxiety, depression and aggression. However, Suomi (1997, 1999) has shown that if at-risk infants are cross-fostered to highly responsive mothers, their developmental outcomes can be significantly altered; these monkeys can do *exceptionally* well in their groups. The point is that some people can develop fear schema easier and more powerfully than others but phenotypes can be changed by learning. Indeed, behavioral therapies that focus on giving people direct experience with feared stimuli, and enabling desensitization, have been extraordinarily successful. Understanding more about phenotypes, individual differences, how these show up in cognitive systems, and tailoring learning experiences to their phenotypes, may aid our therapeutic effectiveness (Plomin & Crabbe, 2000). Those working in the tradition of dialectical behavior therapy for borderline personality disorder often make assumptions regarding emotional phenotypic vulnerabilities in their patients— that is, that these patients have particular vulnerabilities in affect regulation coded in physiological systems (Linehan, 1993). It is these vulnerabilities that inform therapy and process.

Motivation: There is increasing awareness of the importance of innate preparedness for schema formation. Obvious examples are innate mechanisms underpinning *motivations* to form attachments (Bowlby, 1980); for in-group/out-group formation and the need to belong (Baumeister & Leary, 1995), and seeking sexual partners and alliances (Buss, 2003). Humans are not born "aimless" but are biologically prepared to become social beings: learning from, and maturing under the influence of, other social beings. We are set up to form certain kinds of schema of self and others. There is good evidence that our early experiences shape our phenotypes for different styles of social relating, e.g., secure in our attachments, anxious, avoidant or disorganized (Cassidy & Shaver, 1999). The link between motivational process and cognition remains vague in cognitive theory with, at times, motives being seen as products of cognitions (Gilbert, 1992). Although core beliefs help to *organize* how we experience and engage with our motives, certain motives (e.g., for food, love, sex and safeness) are also part of our evolved nature. Those with psychopathic difficulties, for example, may have problems in being motivated to care for others or be emotionally moved by the distress of others (Miller, & Eisenberg, 1988).

Physiological maturation. Influences on the physiological maturation of the brain begin in the womb. Immediately postbirth the infant is highly reactive to social stimuli. Indeed, babies are born to be highly sensitive to social cues and to be influenced by the minds of others. New evidence suggests that the signals of voice tone, facial expressions, holding and stroking all impact on the infant's developing brain. This is called intersubjectivity (Trevarthen & Aitken, 2001) and intersubjectivity can influence subtle interactions between the mind of the therapist and patient.

There is a major concern now that so powerful are early experiences in shaping our brain (Schore, 2002) that children exposed to serious neglect, trauma and abuse might suffer subtle forms of brain damage (Teicher, 2002). Understanding these effects will clearly influence therapy and our understanding of what people need in order to learn new ways to self-regulate and come to terms with early trauma. Indeed, cognitive therapists are beginning to explore how to develop therapies that impact on specific memory systems (Brewin, 2003) help mature new neuropathways and processing systems, such as for self-compassion (Gilbert & Irons, in press; Lee, in press), and experience emotional validation (Leahy, in press).

Cognitive biases. One of the strongest claims of cognitive therapy is that distress is linked to cognitive biases, which in turn are linked to core beliefs. Therapy can be aimed to alter both cognitive biases and core beliefs. However, there is also increasing evidence that the human mind comes with built-in tendencies for *biased information processing* especially in areas that are self-serving and/or protective/defensive (Gilbert, 1998ab; Leahy, this volume; Tobena, Marks, & Dar, 1999). Biases can increase under stress, partly linked to the stress state itself and the effects of cortisol on attention. To think and behave logically (or even morally) rather than with prejudice (especially in interpersonal contexts) is often a skill we have to learn and mature rather than a natural function of our minds.

Cognitive competencies. We know that humans differ fundamentally from other primates in their *evolved cognitive competencies.* There are at least three types of "self-and-other focused" cognitive competencies that are key to *human* ways of thinking and can be used in a variety of situations and for social relating (Chiappe, 2000). These are: symbolic self-other representations (Sedikides & Skowronski, 1997), theory of mind, which concerns our abilities to derive theories about what others know, are thinking, intending or feeling (Byrne, 1995; Nickerson, 1999), and meta-cognition (Wells, 2000). The frontal cortex (the maturation of which is highly influenced by social experiences) is especially important for these socially focused competencies and allows for our more basic social motives and emotions to be organized, planned, inhibited and choreographed in new ways than they are for other animals (Goldberg, 2002). Suddendoff & Whitten (2001) call the human mind a *collating mind* because of the way we can use symbols, engage in pretend play, run simulations, create fantasises, and bring together multiple domains of knowledge, styles of reasoning and meta-representations to bear on an issue. Our core beliefs emerge for these competencies for they influence how we build models of self and the world, how we reason about them, and how we allocate attributions for things happening.

Problems can arise in each of these. For example, the way we "language," symbolize and narrate "self and other," can involve biases of meaning that are culturally reinforced (Heath, Bell & Sternberg, 2001). Problems in theory of mind may show up in how people *are able* to reason and use competencies for working out what others may think or intend. Autism and some forms of psychosis can involve problems in theory of mind competencies. It is also evident that humans can make many mistakes in their assumptions about what other people know, feel, and intend, compared to what they know, feel and intend themselves (Nickerson, 1999). This has implications for how people form beliefs about what others think about them. We also use our theory of mind competencies to create a variety of fantasy relationships (Bering, 2002).

Wells (2000) has shown how meta-cognitive processing needs to be added to standard cognitive therapy and therapy. Our thoughts and feelings about our thoughts and feelings are key sources of distress. We can become anxious of becoming anxious. We may label anxiety as something understandable and acceptable or as bad, and evidence of personal weakness or dangerous. Meta-cognitions can also allow us to *de-couple* emotions from actions. If we are anxious our automatic tendency might be to run away but if we believe we can overcome our fear by facing up to it then we may not do as our emotions push us to. We might feel hungry but in order to lose weight and be slim or healthy, we may not act on the desire to eat. We might become celibate for spiritual beliefs and values. We can also deliberately set out to train our minds—something animals cannot do. Indeed, new cognitive therapies are exploring ways to help people use meta-cognitive abilities (Wells, 2000). Some meta-cognitive therapies have grown from western and eastern hybrids of *mindfulness* training. Here the aim is not to try to change the *content* of one's thinking but one's relationship to it. One seeks to develop an attitude of acceptance and non-judgmentally "being with" one's thoughts. (Segal, Williams & Teasdale, 2002). In many ways this helps people to deal with the urgencies of their evolved (often limbic) brains, which are entrained to the hassles of daily life, and pushing for action. Mindfulness is now being built into many forms of psychotherapy, and does not preclude efforts to help people also change attentional focus, re-evaluate, refocus and reattribute (Schwartz & Begley, 2002)

Non-conscious processing. There is little doubt that helping people change their conscious processing and core beliefs can be immensely helpful. However, this does not mean we can ignore the growing evidence for nonconscious processing. It is in fact quite easy to stimulate or prime implicit affect via subliminal and other routes and fool people (lead them to incorrect cognitions) as to the reasons for their emotions (Baldwin, & Fergusson, 2001; Haidt, 2001). Indeed, it has been known for a long time that people can arrive at decisions about situations, and generate reasons for their feelings, or moral issues but cannot articulate exactly how they reasoned to get there (Haidt, 2001). Some of the early cognitive descriptions that linked emotion with cognition, whilst once useful heuristic for clinical work, are now giving ways to richer more complex models (Dalgleish & Power, 1997; Teasdale, 1999; Lambie, & Marcel, 2002). New models of the role or emotions and nonconscious processes, and their impact on conscious cognitions, are appearing constantly.

The evolutionary focus. Beck has always argued for the importance of understanding evolved mental mechanisms underpinning cognitive processes. For example, he argued that depression is mediated through innate mechanisms regulating attachment and defeat (Beck, 1987, 1999). In their important book on anxiety, Beck, Emery and Greenberg (1985) outlined how various forms of schema and cognitive processes activate innate defensive processes such as fight, flight, freeze, faint and demobilization. In 1990, Beck and colleagues argued that personality disorders represented problems in the over- or under-development of basic evolved strategies (Beck, 1999). Given the importance that cognitive therapy has always placed on the scientific understanding of mental functioning and processes rooted in our evolved design, this volume brings together leading contributors to what is emerging as a field of evolutionary approaches to psychopathology.

Outline

The opening chapter explores some of the central evolutionary concepts that may have implications for cognitive theory and practice. It will discuss concepts of evolved strategies, which are designed to fit social niches and how these are coordinated through psychobiological response systems for detecting and responding to threat/punishment and safeness/reward. The latter part of the chapter will focus on working with self-criticism and shame, and the value of developing inner compassion. In chapter 2, Bailey discusses how humans have evolved within the contexts of certain types of relationships. As a result we have evolved cognitive systems for assessing degree of kinship (both biological and psychological). This has important implications for therapy because therapists can be sought out to act like "kin," and patients can have a variety of assumptions about the availability and degree of investment a therapist will make in them. This can create conflicts that need addressing. In chapter 3, Greenberg, well-known for his work in emotion, explores the way emotions evolved as basic information and instructional mechanisms that inform and push animals into certain behaviors. Many emotional systems evolved long ago and Greenberg outlines how, by directly interacting with emotional systems, therapy can provide avenues for cognitive restructuring new feelings and new meaning.

Section II focuses on specific problems using an evolutionary-cognitive theory approach. In chapter 4, Leahy explores a fundamental strategic orientation closely related to those outlined in chapter 1. Leahy's work focuses on the evolved dimensions of optimism and pessimism. He reviews the evidence on how these strategies are linked to approach-avoidance, and underpin various types of social behavior such as sexual behavior, attachment and cooperation. Leahy also explores the implications for therapy. The theme of risk, threat and threat processing is further developed by Hofmann, Moscovitch and Heinrichs in chapter 5 on fear and anxiety. They explore the evolutionary mechanisms for fear and anxiety, and how these mechanisms affect cognitive factors, which play an important role in various phobias including social phobia. These authors also consider how evolutionary approaches to fear and anxiety can aid the development of cognitive therapy techniques.

In chapter 6, Liotti offers a fascinating and important account of the way evolved mechanisms, to construe attachment relationships, can come to function in a disorganized way. This occurs when the attachment objects (e.g., parents) are seen as both potential sources of safeness but also threats. Common in borderline disorder, attachment representations are coded in conflicting ways in both the defense and safeness systems. Liotti explores important therapuetic interventions using this approach. The distressing problem of psychosis has recently been subject to a lot of cognitive therapy interest and work. In chapter 7, Byrne, Trower, Birchwood, Meaden and Nelson offer a fascinating exploration into the nature and treatment of command hallucinations in psychosis. Using the evolutionary model (that has suggested that some forms of self-evaluations evolved from social ones) they explore the power and dominant-subordinate interactions between the voice hearer and his/her voice. They then outline therapeutic interventions based on this model. These show considerable promise for working with this type of difficulty.

Evolutionary approaches to psychopathology are relatively new and not without controversy. Nonetheless, it is hoped that this collection of chapters will stimulate interest, debate and research, all of which will help to inform our therapeutic interventions and advance. It is also a tribute to Beck's pioneering insights and work on the thoughts and beliefs of our evolved minds.

References

Baldwin, M.W., & Fergusson, P. (2001). Relational schemas: The activation of interpersonal knowledge structures in social anxiety. In W.R Crozier & L.E Alden (Eds.), *International handbook of social anxiety: Concepts, research and interventions to the self and shyness* (pp. 235–257). Chichester: J. Wiley.

Baumeister, R.F., & Leary, M.R. (1995). The need to belong: Desire for interpersonal attachments as a fundamental human motivation. *Psychological Bulletin, 117*, 497–529.

Beck, A.T. (1987). Cognitive models of depression. *Journal of Cognitive Psychotherapy: An International Quarterly, 1*, 5-38.

Beck, A.T. (1996). Beyond belief: A theory of modes, personality and psychopathology. In P. Salkovskis (Ed.), *Frontiers of cognitive therapy* (pp. 1–25). New York: Oxford University Press.

Beck, A.T. (1999). Cognitive aspects of personality disorders and their relation to syndromal disorders: A psycho-evolutionary approach. In, C.R Cloninger (Ed.), *Personality and psychopathology* (p 411–430). Washington D.C: American Psychiatric Association.

Beck, A.T., Emery, G., & Greenberg, R.L. (1985). *Anxiety disorders and phobias: A cognitive approach.* New York: Basic Books.

Beck, A.T., Freeman, A., & Associates (1990). *Cognitive therapy of personality disorders.* New York: Guilford.

Bering, J. M. (2002). The existential theory of mind. *Review of General Psychology, 6*, 3–34.

Bowlby, J. (1980). *Loss: Sadness and depression. Attachment and Loss, (Vol. 3).* London: Hogarth Press.

Brewin, C. R. (2003). *Post-traumatic stress disorder: Malady or myth?* New Haven: Yale University Press.

Buss, D.M. (2003). *Evolutionary psychology: The new science of mind (Second Edition).* Boston, Massachusetts: Allyn and Bacon.

Byrne, R.W. (1995). *The thinking ape.* Oxford: Oxford University Press.

Cassidy. J., & Shaver, P.R. (1999). *Handbook of attachment: Theory, research and clinical applications.* New York: Guilford Press.

Chiappe, D.L. (2000). Metaphor, modularity and the evolution of conceptual integration. *Metaphor and Symbol, 15*, 137–158.

Dalgleish, T. & Power, M.J. (1997), *Handbook of cognition and emotion.* Chichester, UK: John Wiley & Sons Ltd.

Gilbert, P. (1989). *Human nature and suffering.* Hove: Lawrence Erlbaum Associates.

Gilbert, P. (1992). *Depression: The evolution of powerlessness.* Hove: Lawrence Erlbaum Associates Ltd. And New York: Guilford.

Gilbert, P. (1998a). Evolutionary psychopathology: Why isn't the mind better designed than it is? *British Journal of Medical Psychology, 71,* 353–373.

Gilbert, P. (1998b). The evolved basis and adaptive functions of cognitive distortions. *British Journal of Medical Psychology, 71,* 447–463.

Gilbert, P., & Irons, C. (in press). Focused therapies and compassionate mind training for shame and self-attacking. In P. Gilbert (Ed.), *Compassion: Conceptualizations, research and use in psychotherapy.* London: Brunner-Routledge.

Goldberg, E. (2002). *The executive brain: Frontal lobes and the civilized mind.* New York: Oxford University Press.

Haidt, J. (2001). The emotional dog and its rational tail: A social intuitionist approach to moral judgment. *Psychological Review, 108,* 814–834.

Heath, C., Bell, C., & Sternberg, E. (2001). Emotional selection: The case of urban legends. *Journal of Personality and Social Psychology, 81,* 1028–1041.

Lambie, J.A., & Marcel, A.J. (2002). Consciousness and the varieties of emotion experience: A theoretical framework. *Psychological Review, 109,* 219–259.

Leahy, R. (in press) A social-cognitive model of validation. In P. Gilbert (Ed.), *Compassion: Conceptualizations, research and use in psychotherapy.* London: Brunner-Routledge.

Lee, D. (in press) The perfect nurturer: A model to develop a compassionate mind within the context of cognitive therapy. In P. Gilbert (Ed.), *Compassion: Conceptualizations, research and use in psychotherapy.* London: Brunner-Routledge.

Li, S.C. (2003). Biocultural orchestration of developmental plasticity across levels: The impact of biology and culture in shaping the mind and behavior across the life span. *Psychological Bulletin, 129,* 171–194.

Lickliter, R., & Honeycutt, H. (2003). Developmental dynamics: Toward a biologically plausible evolutionary psychology. *Psychological Bulletin, 129,* 819–835 (plus peer commentary, pp. 836–872).

Linehan, M. (1993). *Cognitive behavioral treatment of borderline personality disorder.* New York: Guilford.

Miller, P.A., & Eisenberg, N. (1988) The relation of empathy to aggressive behaviour and externalizing/antisocial behavior. *Psychological Bulletin, 103,* 324–344.

Nickerson, R.S. (1999). How we know—and sometimes misjudge—what others know: Inputting one's own knowledge to others. *Psychological Bulletin. 125,* 737–759.

Panksepp, J. (1998). *Affective neuroscience.* New York: Oxford University Press.

Plomin, R., & Crabbe, J. (2000). DNA. *Psychological Bulletin, 126,* 806–828.

Schore, A.N (2002) Dysregulation of the right brain: A fundamental mechanism of traumatic attachment and the psychopathologies of posttraumatic stress disorder. *Australian and New Zealand Journal of Psychiatry, 36,* 9–30.

Schwartz, J. M., & Begley, S. (2002). *The mind and the brain: Neuroplasticity and the power of mental force.* New York: Regan Books.

Sedikides, C., & Skowronski, J.J. (1997). The symbolic self in evolutionary context. *Personality and Social Psychology Review, 1,* 80–102.

Segal, Z., Williams, J.M.G., & Teasdale, J. (2002). *Mindfulness-based cognitive therapy for depression: A new approach to preventing relapse.* London: The Guilford Press, London.

Suddendoff, T., & Whitten, A. (2001). Mental evolution and development: Evidence for secondary representation in children, great apes and other animals. *Psychological Bulletin, 127,* 629–650.

Suomi, S.J. (1997). Early determinants of behavior: Evidence from primate studies. *British Medical Bulletin, 53,* 170–184.

Suomi, S.J. (1999). Attachment in rhesus monkeys. In J. Cassidy & P.R Shaver (Eds.), *Handbook of attachment: Theory, research and clinical applications* (pp. 181–197) New York: Guilford Press.

Teasdale, J.D. (1999). Emotional processing: Three modes of mind and the prevention of relapse in depression. *Behaviour Research and Therapy, 37,* 29–52.

Teicher, M.H. (2002). Scars that won't heal: The neurobiology of the abused child. *Scientific American, 286*(3), 54–61.

Trevarthen, C,, & Aitken, K. (2001). Infant intersubjectivity: Research, theory, and clinical applications. *Journal of Child Psychology and Psychiatry, 42,* 3–48.

Tobena, A., Marks, I., & Dar, R. (1999). Advantages of bias and prejudice: An exploration of their neurocognitive templates. *Neuroscience and Behavioral Reviews, 23,* 1047–1058.

Wells, A. (2000). *Emotional disorders and metacognition: Innovative cognitive therapy.* Chichester, UK: John Wiley & Sons Ltd.

Part One

Specific Orientations

Chapter 1

Evolutionary Approaches to Psychopathology and Cognitive Therapy

Paul Gilbert

M any now accept that humans did not arrive on this planet *de novo* but are products of millions of years of evolution of the mammalian line. Moreover, the history of our evolution is recorded in our genes and reflected in our physical forms and basic psychology. The implications of this are only just beginning to impact on the psychological sciences (Barrett, Dunbar, & Lycett, 2002; Buss, 1999) and there is much debate about these implications (e.g., Collins, Maccoby, Steinberg, Heatherington, & Bornstein, 2000). The same is likely to be true when we take the evolutionary lens to the theories informing our cognitive therapies. This chapter begins by first outlining some of the basic issues in evolution theory, as noted in the preface, and then explores how they may be relevant to cognitive therapy.

Evolution is the process by which biological change in structural forms, competencies and functions, occurs. Although the idea that species can change over time had been around before Darwin set off on his historic travels aboard the Beagle in 1839, it was Darwin's great insight that the engine of change comes from the fact that all individual members of all species are exposed to problems in the struggle to survive and reproduce. Those with traits and abilities that give advantage in this struggle, be it escaping predators, finding food, or securing breeding opportunities, will out-reproduce those who are less competent and will thus pass on those traits. The driving force for species variation is therefore selective pressure, which became known as the theory of change by *natural selection*. Hence, over time, different environments can advantage or disadvantage genetically coded traits and abilities (e.g., white fur in cold snowy climates, running speed) and get passed on to subsequent generations. Note, however, that if you survive to a ripe old age but leave no offspring, then any genes that may underpin such good fortune die with you. However, if you help your relatives survive and reproduce, then to the extent that they carry genes in common with you, those genes are passed to succeeding generations. This became known as inclusive fitness (Buss, 1999; Hamilton, 1964).

According to evolutionary psychology many of our basic mental mechanisms are the result of *distal* pressures (meaning selective pressures operating in the past and over the long term). We have the potential abilities and competencies that we do because they solved problems and aided reproductive fitness in eons passed. For example, without adequate attachment and care infants die, and so (unlike fish, for example) humans are innately oriented to form early attachments and respond to their presence or absence. Humans, then, are not *tabulae rasae* but come into the world in some way prepared and equipped with mental mechanisms that are necessary for them to learn to live as humans (e.g., learn a language, respond to mother's love, participate in group activities).

Those who are less enamored with evolutionary psychology focus more on the processes of learning: the *proximate* factors (factors that operate during an individual's life)—that is, the social and cultural shapers of human psychology rather than the more innate and prepared. However, most now agree that it is *the interaction* between evolved dispositions, learning, and sociocultural contexts that creates the complexity of the human mind and is a source of many common forms of psychopathology (Gilbert, 1995; McGuire & Troisi, 1998; Nesse, 1999). This is also known as the *genotype-phenotype* interaction (Barrett, Dunbar, & Lycett, 2002). Phenotypes are the way traits (genotypes and potentials) are expressed by virtue of how they have been shaped by experience. For example, we have a genotype for learning an aural language but how well we learn, what we learn, and the actual way we use language (the phenotype) are dependent on experience. Recent work has shown that different environments can actually turn genes "on and off." This is partly because different genes underpin the development and operation of different strategies and competencies to fit different niches, a theme we touch on below. For a fascinating and highly readable account of the way the environment—including internal physiological processes like cortisol—can have gene-controlling effects, see Ridley, 2000.

Evolutionary Concepts and Psychopathology

There have been a growing number of developments in applying evolutionary concepts to psychopathology (Gilbert, 1989, 1995, 1998a, 1998b; Marks, 1987; McGuire & Troisi, 1998; Nesse, 1999) and psychotherapy (Gilbert & Bailey, 2000). Before we proceed to explore this avenue there are a number of key points to keep in mind, some of which may seem counterintuitive.

1. Although passing genes to the next generation is key to evolution, animals are not directly motivated to increase their genes in succeeding generations. This is partly because success at passing on genes is an outcome that no animal could calculate. Hence, animals are motivated to engage in behaviors (such as acquiring certain types of resources, forming alliances, finding sexual partners and having offspring/children) that they can monitor. When done competently these tasks would, in the normal course of events, lead to "fitness." Partly because of our human evolved abilities for goal planning and metarepresentations of our behaviors, we can develop beliefs about what will make us happy or not. Hence humans have potentially great flexibility in how we enact different motivational dispositions in that, for example, we can desire sex but use contraception; or choose to "make money," acquire status, and forgo reproduction; or in the pursuit of "enlightenment" become celibate. Nonetheless, these are relatively new developmental competencies, and the important point is that it is the motivations and competencies that normally enhanced fitness in earlier times that underpin our psychology (Buss, 1999).

2. Evolutionary theorists suggest the existence of fundamental organizing mechanisms in the brain that guide animals toward goals, such as for recognizing and seeking out mates, or avoiding threats, for biosocial goals and evolved strategies (Buss, 1999; Gilbert, 1989; McGuire &

Troisi, 1998). Strategies can be species specific (e.g., the breeding strategies of turtles differ from those of humans); can be age related and mature (e.g., sexual behavior comes on line with puberty); can be gender linked (e.g., men tend to take more risks and have different sexual strategies than women; see Leahy, this book); can be role linked (e.g., the way infants interact with parents is different from the way sexual partners interact, or the way subordinates defend against threats from conspecifics is different from that of dominants); and context linked (e.g., men tend to be more aggressive ("macho") and less affiliative when resources are short and the environment is hostile and/or competitive; Cohen, 2001). While we can, of course, debate and research the way strategies are modified by maturation and learning, and how they vary in terms of phenotypic expression (Barrett et al., 2002; Buss, 1999; McGuire & Troisi, 1998), it is important to note that strategies represent basic evolved dispositions to attend, process information, and take action. As we open up discussion on evolutionary approaches we will note the value of an evolved strategies approach and how it can inform ideas on the nature of priming and schema formation.

3. Dispositions and strategies evolved to serve fitness-enhancing goals but not necessarily to promote happiness or what we might regard as mental health (Buss, 2000). For example, for disorders such as anxiety, depression and paranoia, the mechanisms from which they emerge may be adaptations. Anxiety is related to various forms of defenses to threat (Marks, 1987); depression seems to be related to low positive affect and reduced exploration which might be useful for coping with attachment loss and defeat (Beck 1996, 1999a; Gilbert, 1992a, 2004); paranoia is often focused on threats from others of the same group/species (Gilbert, 2001a). Animals that lacked the mechanisms to appraise and regulate their behavior according to context would be at a serious disadvantage. However, this does not mean that these mechanisms for the control of affect and mood work adaptively in all contexts (as noted in points 4 and 8 below). Cognitive therapists suggest that schemas and assumptions interact with these mechanisms (Beck, 1999a).

4. The above being the case, we should note that all evolved mechanisms have a range over which they are adaptive and outside that range they may not be (Wakefield, 1999). Further, the range of adaptiveness includes triggers, frequency, duration, and intensity. Even obvious defense mechanisms for removing noxious substances from the body, such as diarrhea and vomiting, or high fever to fight infections, can

become real liabilities if they are too easily triggered, too frequent, too intense, or of too long duration (Nesse, 1999; Nesse & Williams, 1995). Cognitive therapy commonly addresses itself to the cognitive factors (as a subset of factors) involved in triggers, frequency, duration, and intensity of responses, and states of mind (Beck, Emery, & Greenberg, 1985). Genetic disposition and maturational stage are also factors.

5. Evolved design is not necessarily good design. For any strategy or disposition to evolve it simply has to out compete other designs and/or have some success in the gene pool. Moreover, a design in one area can compromise abilities in another (called a trade-off) (Gilbert, 1998a; Nesse & Williams, 1995). One can think here of the peacock's tail, which is great for attracting mates, but a handicap when trying to escape predators. Or one can think about the fact that our big brains, which give us our intelligence, come with the need for long periods of attachment and care. We are completely helpless at birth. This opens us to the risk of stress related damage to our maturing brains as a result of abuse by our caregivers (Schore, 2001), and by poorly organized attachment schemas (Liotti, this book).

6. Another reason evolution does not always come up with good designs is that evolution proceeds by changing and adapting preexisting designs; it cannot go back to the drawing board and start again. Thus, our brains did not appear *de novo,* but are the result of millions of years of evolution. This is reflected in their architecture (with sublimbic, limbic and cortical areas); our basic of menu of emotions, such as fear, anger, disgust, and joy; and various stress handling systems (Greenberg, this book; Panksepp, 1998). Not only can evolutionary design be at times poor design, it can come with serious handicaps. For example, our stress systems were designed to cope with relatively short-lived stressors such as predators or short fights and interchanges, but not chronic stress. There is now good evidence that a stress hormone called cortisol is useful for short-term defensive behavior but can actually damage the immune system and the brain if it is elevated for too long (Sapolsky, 1996, 2000).

7. New adaptations can run up against old ones and cause problems. For example, our capacity for imagination and metacognitions provides humans with considerable advances over other primates. It makes possible planning and forming internal models of actual and possible worlds, and gives rise to culture and science. However, it can also be a source of our most serious pathologies. By ruminating on the negative, for example, we can maintain maladaptive feedback between old,

limbic-based stress systems (e.g., cortisol production) and thoughts. Our imaginations can give rise to wonderful art but also the most hideous tortures. Our high-level thoughts and imaginations can play on primitive affect systems that evolved long before the capacities for imagination and metacognition. Cognitive therapists have long recognized this type of recursive process and Gilbert (1992a, 1992b, 2001a, 2001b) and Beck (1996; Beck et al., 1985) note how ruminations can play on and through older motivational and affect systems.

8. Many humanoid adaptations evolved to fit social and ecological contexts that existed thousands of years ago where there were high rates of birth and infant mortality; small, close-knit, isolated groups that may have been hostile to each other, where a person interacted with the same few people (maybe 100–150) throughout life; and where the lifestyle was primarily one of hunter-gatherer. Hence many of the typical ways we schematize relationships (e.g., as kin, friend, enemy) tend to reflect ways for organizing social information that fitted those lifestyles, a theme taken up by Bailey (this book). However, these hunter-gatherer social environments are increasingly things of the past, and our modern environments can compromise our functioning in a number of ways.

First, modern life may serve us well in many respects but it can also produce *contextual overload*. For example, modern lifestyles can overload physiological systems, for example, the cardiovascular system was not designed to cope with high-fat foods, low exercise, and smoking. Competitive behavior, social comparison, social anxiety, and fear of exclusion might function quite differently in small, close-knit, and stable groups than they do today in our large and constantly changing groups and megasocieties. Second, modern environments can produce contextual constraints, where new environments constrain adaptive behaviors. Modern marriages may constrain escape behavior from an abusive male; needing to keep up the payments on a house may prevent one from leaving a well-paid but highly stressful job (Leahy, 2000). Indeed such "entrapments" are very common in depression (Gilbert, 2001b; Gilbert & Allan, 1998). Third, environments can *frustrate evolved mechanisms* because they provide insufficient signals/inputs or the wrong kinds of input that is required for a mechanism to mature, and operate efficiently as designed. Indeed, it is very clear that mammals and humans have evolved in social contexts for many millions of years and now others (e.g., parents, siblings, and peers) *are part of the expected ecology*. Hence, our mental mechanisms are set up *expecting and needing* certain types of social input to mature and operate effectively (McGuire & Troisi, 1998). Unless we hear a language, we can't learn to speak; without early care we quickly die, and if we are abused as children, rather than loved, serious disturbances in the maturation of the brain can occur (Schore, 2001).

9. The interactions between evolved dispositions and culture show powerful connections that transcend the personal (see Cohen, 2001 for a fascinating discussion). For example, Gilmore (1990) and Overing (1989) found that in ecologies where men hunt in dangerous terrains that have many predators, or where there are other hostile groups or high intermale competitiveness, masculine identity tends to schematize around issues of bravery, traditional macho values, and clear gender differences. These social ecologies also impact on child-rearing practices (Barrett et al., 2002). Personal schemas of self and others cannot then be decontextualized from evolved dispositions/strategies on the one hand or cultural forms and personal histories on the other (Collins et al., 2000; Gilbert, 1995; Ridley, 2000).

Attachment Phenotypes and Social Strategies

Strategies are goal-seeking and guide organisms to behave in certain ways (Gilbert, 1989). Consider, for example, turtles that emerge on the beaches of Florida to breed at certain times of the year. Their goal is to breed in a specific way and they are guided to engage in these seasonal behaviors by intricate gene-neural codes that are sensitive to seasons and tides and help them return from journeys of thousands of miles to the same beaches on which they were born. Unlike turtles who may lay thousands of eggs of which only 1% to 2% may survive to adulthood to breed, mammals have evolved to have few offspring but to invest in and care for them (Barrett et al., 2002). This has given rise to mental mechanisms and strategies for care eliciting by the infant and care giving by the parent (Gilbert, 1989).

The interaction of these role enactments (care eliciting and care giving) between infant and parent (or other caregivers), gives rise to patterns of attachment (Bowlby, 1969, 1973). According to how this interaction goes, it will come to shape social-behavioral phenotypes in two fundamental ways. When parental investment is high, reliable, and affectionate it reflects and creates conditions for low threat and high safeness in the child's environment. However, when parental investment is low, unreliable, and/or hostile, the child is stressed and oriented to be attentive to threats. Over many years attachment theorists have illuminated some key interpersonal phenotypes, often called *attachment styles,* that result from these different rearing experiences. Collins and Feeney (2000) summarize these:

> Adult attachment researchers typically define four prototypic attachment styles derived from two underlying dimensions; *anxiety* and *avoidance*... The anxiety dimension refers to one's sense of self-worth and acceptance (vs. rejection) by others, and the avoidance dimension refers to the degree to which one approaches (vs. avoids) intimacy and interdependence with others. *Secure* adults are low in both attachment-related anxiety and avoidance; they are comfortable with intimacy, willing to rely on others for support, and confident that they are valued by others. *Preoccupied* (anxious-ambivalent) adults are high in anxiety and low in avoidance; they have an exaggerated desire for closeness and dependence, coupled with a heightened concern about being rejected. *Dismissing avoidant* individuals are low in attachment-related anxiety but high in avoidance; they view close relationships as relatively unimportant and they value independence and self-reliance. Finally, *fearful avoidant* adults are high in both attachment anxiety and avoidance; although they desire close relationships and the approval of others, they avoid intimacy because they fear being rejected. (p. 1054)

In a number of studies Mario Mikulincer (see Mikulincer, Birnbaum, Woddis & Nachmias, 2000), a prominent researcher on attachment relations, has found that securely attached people see others as relatively benevolent and can regulate stress by appropriate support seeking and self-management, while anxiously attached people show typical "protest" reactions to stress and become clingy and controlling. Avoidant attached people do not seek help for stress, nor see others as benevolent, use repression as a coping mechanism, and are overly self-reliant. Undoubtedly one could identify key self-other schemas associated with these styles, but before doing so it is useful to recognize the interaction between species-typical, biosocial, goal-seeking behavior (e.g., to elicit care from parents), and environmental contexts, which together give rise to basic, strategic orientations to self and others. Whereas people might be able to give voice to their schemas (e.g., to see the self as vulnerable to abandonment, or as mistrusting of others), they are unlikely to recognize these as phenotypic expressions of social-behavioral strategies shaped via attachment (and other) experiences.

Although we are oversimplifying, we can identify three basic strategic orientations to social life. First, a secure and safe early life is marked by relatively low threat and benign (resource-plenty) environments. Parents are available and responsive to the child and calming in times of stress. This sets a child on course to develop social phenotypes for *safe affiliation-exploration* (linked to a positive reward focus, affiliation, confident sociality, and positive affect). This strategy operates and matures when attention is relatively free from focusing on threat and linked to approach behavior (Gilbert, 1989, 1993). In humans it also utilizes competencies for empathy, compassion, and help giving, which aid in building affiliative relationships. In relatively safe environments the maturation of competencies to form alliances, help others and be helped by them is adaptive. Hence, for such people biosocial goals tend toward developing affiliative relationships, and their strategies will utilize competencies for empathy, care, and concern for themselves and others.

There are many reasons that all might not go so well, however. Environments might be harsh or resources scarce, meaning that a mother has to search for food, leaving offspring alone for long periods. There is now evidence in animals that foraging times (linked to resource availability) impact on infant development (e.g., Hofer, 1994). For humans there may be a host of stresses on the parents that make rearing their offspring difficult (e.g., war, poverty, domestic violence, and poor mental health; see Liotti, this book). Stresses that impact on the caregiver will affect his or her interaction and availability to the child. Moreover, stress on the mother (and the hormones associated with it) can impact on the developing fetus, thus becoming a very early influence on phenotypic expression. Other influences that can impact on the type and amount of investment a child receives can be related to parent-infant conflicts of interest, birth order, and sibling rivalry (for a fascinating and important discussion see Barrett et al., 2002).

Under such conditions the infant may have to work hard to elicit investments; safeness and resources (comfort and care) are not easily available. Even worse, the parents themselves may be abusive and a source of threat. Under these conditions social strategies must be modified to meet the challenges of the context in which the child is maturing. At least two alternative strategic orientations to those that flow from secure attachment (and remember, a secure attachment indicates a relatively benign environment) are possible. The first is what we might call the *social behavioral inhibition* strategies. People using these strategies may still have a key goal to seek stable attachments and elicit care, support, and love, but (perhaps) because of early disruptions in attachment are highly sensitive to rejections and failures in the investment of others. They usually see themselves in *subordinate positions*, feel inferior to others, and are easily triggered into using protective defensive behaviors typical of subordinates (Gilbert, 2004). These in turn are linked to punishment/loss avoidance and negative affect. In many ways they overlap with those identified as anxiously attached, noted above (Gilbert, 2004).

A second possible strategic orientation (especially if parents are abusive, environments are socially hostile, and especially for males) is to forgo trying to win others' investment from long-term affiliating and go for riskier but potentially higher, short-term payoff strategies. These people tend to develop more readily the strategies of *social exploitation,* characterized by low investment in relationships, multiple sexual partners, and a preparedness to threaten, defect from and exploit relationships. This strategy may actually be *handicapped* by the development of empathy and compassion. If this is the strategy a person selects and develops then he or she may well have schemas and rules to match (see Beck, 1996, 1999b), but these can grow out of strategic, nonconscious choices—they are phenotypes for social engagement (see Barrett et al., 2002, and Belsky, Steinberg, & Draper, 1990, for further discussion of this type of approach). It remains unclear how far the strategies themselves represent environmentally triggered gene-neural processes, given that we know that some genes can be turned on and off by environmental conditions (Ridley, 2000).

These strategies help coordinate various motivational systems. For example, in an excellent review of the literature and series of studies Elliott and Thrash (2002) offer an in-depth discussion of how approach-avoidance motivations underpin psychopathology and personality. Hence, although the implications for cognitive therapy of a strategies approach might be relatively novel, the idea of, and evidence for, basic strategic orientations such as approach-avoidance in people, are not. These strategic orientations have obvious flexibility, are not "all-or-nothing," show genotypic and phenotypic variability, can be context dependent, and, as Belsky and colleagues (1990) note, mother and father can affect their child's orientation to the social world (both their sexual and nonsexual strategies) in different ways. Note, too, how different strategies are linked to the coordination of different competencies (e.g., an affiliative strategy will go with the development of interest in, and competencies for, caring for others, while an exploitative strategy need not, and may in fact be handicapped by such). Moreover, note how a strategies and biosocial goal approach offers insight into how strategies, competencies, and biosocial goals become coassembled and interact (Gilbert, 1989). This has some similarities with Beck's (1996) concept of modes but also has differences (Gilbert, 1989, 2000a). These are important complexities to grapple with if we are to understand some of the origins of negative schemas identified by cognitive therapists (e.g., Young, Weinberger, & Beck, 2001).

Strategies Fit Niches

Although certain strategies can be significantly influenced by our genes (e.g., some infants are more behaviorally inhibited than others; Kagan, 1999), we also know that many of the people we regard as having personality disorders come from neglectful, demanding, or hostile/abusive backgrounds. There is now good evidence that growing up in these environments has a major impact on brain maturation (Schore, 2001; Teicher, 2002). Although one way to think about these effects is in terms of subtle brain damage, another way is to consider that their physiological maturation is fitting them to operate in a certain social niche—that of neglect, unpredictability, low affiliation, and hostility. In their niches these behaviors, manifested by increased anxiety and/or aggressiveness may be adaptations and *not disorders*. Even psychopaths may do very well reproductively. Indeed, Cohen (2001) has outlined how co-operative-affiliative behaviors versus exploitative behaviors and defections are linked to the relative payoffs of these behaviors in different social contexts. Thus, strategies are designed to fit niches (Barrett et al., 2002). And keep in mind that environments can affect strategies via gene-regulating effects (Ridley, 2000).

It is because there are implicit moral dimensions to our classification systems, and we often believe that mental health is synonymous with warmth or happiness, that we regard some people as disordered rather than following different strategies to fit different niches. So our language is often overmedicalized, about *mal*adaptive schemas, thinking *errors, breakdown* in self-control functions, *dysfunctional* attitudes or *failed* maturation, the need to be *more rational* or *realistic*—all potentially shaming. And as many social commentators have noted, as we confront problems of rising crime in some of the poorer sections of our societies, especially among young, antisocial males whom we shame and stigmatize, we might ask what socializing influences and social niches our societies have created to make their exploitative strategies so prominent.

Strategies and Schemas

Cognitive therapists have always recognized that automatic thoughts are exactly that—automatic; they are not the result, in the first instance, of careful reflective or conscious processing. There is now good evidence that some behaviors too are often automatic and are instigated without conscious control (Bargh & Chartland, 1999). A second level of processing may be that of metacognition, where one has conscious thoughts and feelings, and ruminations about one's thoughts and feelings; a good many difficulties can arise from this level of processing (Wells, 2000). However, one cannot evaluate an automatic thought until one has had one and has articulated it. Thus, over the long term, the ideal would be to root out the source of negative, automatic thoughts and emotions. In fact, cognitive therapists have long recognized that our automatic thoughts are generated by some process(es) that we might not (in the first instance) have conscious access to. In this regard, cognitive therapists have paid a lot of attention recently to the notions of rules (Beck, 1999b) and schema (Young et al., 2001). These are hypothetical, internal, information-organizing systems for self-other evaluations that come in various shapes and sizes. But like scientists searching for what happened before the "big bang" we should also inquire into where these schemas come from, and, more important, perhaps ask if they are the result of a more fundamental underlying organization of evolved mental mechanisms and strategies. For example, if individuals have abandonment or mistrust schemas this is telling us something important about how they detect and respond to threats and what creates safeness for them.

There is now increasing evidence that some of the processes that guide automatic thoughts may be the products of nonconscious strategic orientations that can underpin many forms of personality, social behavior, schemas and psychopathology (Barrett et al., 2002; Elliott & Thrash, 2002). For example, Leahy (this book) outlines the differences between optimistic and pessimistic strategies. Those studying self-esteem suggest that low self-esteem can be a (subordinate) damage limitation strategy (Baumeister, Tice, & Hutton, 1989), which helps to explain why low self-esteem can sometimes be difficult to change even in the context of success. Keltner and Harker (1989) have reviewed the evidence that the automatic shame response is a fast-acting defensive response, linked to submissive defenses, which people can find difficult to control. Below we will note how various cognitive distortions are related to "better safe than sorry" thinking (Gilbert, 1998b). There is much work showing that there are fundamental differences between people in approach and avoidance motivation, and that these differences may underpin personality differences and vulnerabilities to psychopathology (Elliott & Thrash, 2002).

Strategies not only underpin schemas and rules but values as well. For example, a person who follows affiliative strategies may find it relatively easy to develop rules and values to care about people and be helpful. For those following an exploitative strategy, however, such schemas, rules, and values may be far more difficult to learn and adopt. Hence the ease by which people acquire their schemas and rules is related to the strategies they are following.

Another implication of an evolved strategies and biosocial goal approach to psychopathology is that people may not be conscious of how some of their schemas are linked to basic strategies and defensive behaviors (Gilbert, 1989; McGuire & Troisi, 1998). Let me offer a clinical example to explore this idea. Sally was physically abused by her father. When she was in his presence her "inhibited and submissive defense" was often automatically activated. She would be anxious, quiet, and try to keep out of his way. This submissive strategy, forged over millions of years of animals living in dominance hierarchies, is linked to social inhibition strategies. It operates the algorithms/rules of: If in the presence of a hostile dominant, adopt submissive behavior, don't draw attention to self, and don't show social confidence that could be seen as a threat to the dominant. Even reptiles operate by this rule (MacLean, 1990).

For Sally, then, her submissive defenses were the best she could do to protect herself. Processes of sensitization and kindling of key neural, defensive circuitry may be a salient issue in such cases (Rosen & Schulkin, 1998). Indeed, Perry Pollard, Blakley, Baker, and Vigilante (1995) have outlined how repeated activation of threat-defenses can shift from being states to traits. Hence, this type of *priming* of defensive behaviors may be an underlying source for schema development. For example, with the maturation of self-awareness, Sally came to recognize her automatic tendencies to become submissive and inhibited if there were conflicts around or the chance of them. She then concluded she was a weak person (a metacognition).

So her negative self-schemas were built, at first, from the activation of adaptive defenses (triggered by another—her father), not the other way around. Sally did not consciously learn the rule to submit to a hostile dominant; rather it was an evolved strategy that was activated in her, run by an underlying psychobiological program and incorporated into her growing self-identity. Consciously articulated schemas of self came later and had to fit this strategy. To help Sally it was useful first to *clearly and positively* think about the value of her submissive response, not as a sign of weakness but as an adaptive defense—the best she could do. It was trying to protect her. This reduced the shame of her automatic fear-submissive response to conflict and metacognitions about it ("I'm weak"). Next we collaboratively thought about what she might need in order to develop new phenotypic alternatives. We focused less on her schema of "I am a weak person," although she could see how it increased feelings of depression and shame, but rather reframed this as part of a submissive way of thinking to protect the self. We thus worked on helping her explore dropping or moving on from this defense. We focused more on her pain of childhood and her later anger at being in that position. At first she was very frightened of anger (the affect linked to a more dominant attack strategy) with beliefs of "anger is bad, it hurts people; something bad will happen to me if I feel or express it." Because she had not learned skills to work with anger, and given what she was angry about, it often seemed to her that her anger could become too intense (rage) and overpowering. As she learned to experience and cope with anger and tolerate fearful feelings when she was assertive, the "weak" schema faded. You will not be surprised to know that Sally had problems, acting in many ways they might have been seen as dominant or assertive. So what we were working with was an instilled highly subordinate, defensive strategic orientation to social life, not just an affect inhibition problem or negative schema. Her schema of "weak" was part of her overall strategy to keep her out of trouble and in a low profile. Unfortunately, this strategy comes with increased risk of negative affect and depression because inhibition of positive, confident affect is one of its evolved subroutines (Gilbert, 1992a; Gilbert, 2004).

Sally was also a self-blamer. Now traditional cognitive therapists might focus on the evidence for and against self-blame, or link it to a consciously available schema of a bad self. However, it is well noted that abused people often blame themselves for the abuse. Are they just distorted in their thinking? Is this just because others have blamed them? Such might be so but the strategies approach suggests that these are important but secondary issues. Self-blame, in the context of abuse from which there is no escape, acts to inhibit people, keeps them in a low profile position, increases submissive behavior, stops expression of anger, and focuses on what they can do (e.g., avoid doing things that anger the dominant), all of which might be highly adaptive when one is confronted with a powerful, hostile dominant. Indeed, Sally could recall frequently trying to figure out what she might have done to anger her father. Interestingly, this style can sometimes also be seen when people see their God as powerful, dominant and potentially punitive, that is, they take a submissive, self-blaming ("I am a sinner") position. When self-blame is functioning in the service of nonconscious, submissive, defensive strategies, it may not easily change with reevaluation. Rather, the cognitive therapist would look at the thoughts related to the functions of self-blame and the fear of giving it up with clear discussion that this can be an understandable defense. Of course, some therapists do recognize the limitations of trying to challenge a negative self-schema head on (see Leahy, 2001). In general, the more abused people are, the more instilled, subordinate, and/or aggressive their defenses can be, and hence the more "safeness" they may need to change. Also note that in this type of approach some strategies and competencies can be underdeveloped and need to mature; if they start to come on line, they cannot be expected to arrive matured, integrated with skills, and rounded (see also Beck, Freeman, & Associates, 1990).

The therapeutic consequences are that whatever negative schemas people have, be they mistrust or abandonment (Young et al., 2001), these can be secondary to the activation of self-protective strategies that become incorporated into self-identities. Focusing on the early adaptive functions of these strategies, and recognizing that they are *designed* to be automatically triggered, can help "de-shame" people and give them new ways of thinking about cognitive biases. For example, one might explore who, how, or what this schema, or way of acting, is trying to protect.

Defense and Safeness

So far we have suggested that people can express different social strategies and phenotypes according to gene-environment interactions. We noted three possibilities: social behavioral inhibition, social affiliation, and social exploitation. As these strategies come on line and guide social behavior, the social environment will reward or punish people's efforts. Crucially, how they respond will be influenced by what strategy they are following. However, even at this level there may be many nonconscious decisions that automatically select a response from an evolved menu of options.

If animals are to survive and reproduce they must be capable of navigating their environment and meeting its challenges (threats and opportunities). This simple fact tells us much about how evolution has shaped brains and minds. Elsewhere, it has been suggested that animals evolved their brains around two central psychobiological organizing systems for information processing: *the defense and safeness systems* (Gilbert, 1989, 1993, 2001a), which in mammals loosely map on to punishment and behavioral inhibition systems and reward and behavioral approach systems (Elliott & Thrash, 2002). Many studies have indicated that the basic *types* of threat signals are those indicating punishments and nonrewards. Gray (1987) has outlined how both types of signals tell the animal that something is wrong (not as expected and not safe) and orients it to defensive action. If an animal actually encounters harm or an injury (a threat is realized), then its behavior will have to be oriented to adapt to the harm and avoid it in the future. Hence, humans, like other animals, have to make one essential judgment about nearly all situations, stimuli, and signals: the degree to which they indicate a threat or are safe (Gilbert, 1989, 2001a).

These decisions of risk are so basic to life that even the most simple organisms must have psychobiological control mechanisms that are able to recognize and respond to threats. Shellfish close up to a threat and expel noxious substances, octopuses squirt ink and take flight, and so forth. Aggression, escaping, hiding, and withdrawing are observable in many species as *basic patterns* of behavior for coping with threats (Dixon, 1998; Marks, 1987; Nesse, 1999).

Evolving some kind of fast threat detection-response system(s) or *defense system* is fundamental to all living organisms. Moreover, all other evolved motivations and strategies (be they for forming attachments or seeking out sexual partners) must be linked to the defense system, otherwise there would be no regulating of the behavior or ability to switch to rapid defense if needed (Gilbert, 1989, 1993). For example, if infants need attachments, then they also need to be alert and responsive to their loss. To put this another way, whatever strategies people are oriented to (e.g., affiliation or exploitation), they must be able to detect and respond to threats in order to accomplish the successful enactment of these strategies.

We will look at the input side of threat (i.e., appraisal) shortly but first note that humans have inherited, from our primate ancestors, a set of defensive responses (outputs) that are often available *for rapid use*. Table 1 offers a simple menu of these. These behaviors are seen commonly in therapy (e.g., a patient becomes aggressive, withdrawn or is submissive) and are indications to a therapist that the defense system is operative. They are often accompanied by certain automatic thoughts but this does not mean that the consciously offered automatic thought precedes the arousal of the defensive behavior (see Table 1.1).

Priming of Defenses

All these defensive strategies and behaviors are rooted in various underlying neuroarchitectures and physiology processes. For example, fight and flight are controlled by different aspects of the amygdala (LeDoux, 1998; Panksepp, 1998) and may be served by specialized and modularized systems (Ohman & Minka, 2001). Moreover, processing threat (in the first instance) can be via fast limbic-centered pathways and not reflective processing (Panksepp, 1998). Threats typically activate stress systems, such as the hypothalamic-pituitary-adrenal axis (HPA) and the autonomic nervous system (Toates, 1995). These systems can be primed in various ways: by previous learning and conditioning, and/or by physiological state, such as by high circulating cortisol or low serotonin levels (Perry et al., 1995). Priming can aid adaptation in various ways. First, if an animal has encountered a threat in the past, then the next time that threat exists it may spot it early and respond faster (Ohman & Mineka, 2001). Second, physiological priming may arise from genetic and personality differences that dispose to the selection of different strategies. Psychopaths (who use exploitation strategies), for example, might always select

TABLE 1.1. Some Common Defensive Behaviors

Specific Defense	Function
Defensive fight	Protection, deterrent
Escape/avoiding	To put distance between self and threat. Movement away reduces defensive arousal.
Help seeking	To elicit protection and support from another. Movement toward other acts as reassurance.
Submitting	To inhibit one's own threat-eliciting behavior (e.g., challenging others) and deactivate actual or possible aggression from another.
Hiding	Seeking cover to avoid being seen.
Camouflage	Concealing the self. Includes concealing inner feelings.
Cut off	Breaking contact with aversive arousal eliciting cues (e.g., covering one's eyes, turning away).
Demobilization (short term)	Freeze-faint to reduce activity in threatening environment.
Demobilization (long term)	Depressed mood, anhedonia, fatigue. Disengagement from and demobilization within high-threat and/or low-resource environments.

Note. From Gilbert, 2001a.

fight rather than fear or submission to social threats. Children with the temperament of behavioral inhibition, on the other hand, tend to select avoidance and withdrawal from novelty and threat (Kagan, 1999). In such cases the "selection" of responses or strategies for coping is not (in the first instance) under conscious or voluntary control. We also noted above how "priming of strategies" might begin very early in life and represent environmentally triggered gene effects (Ridley, 2000). And, of course, over time people will tend to select a defense that has appeared to work in the past and that they believe will be helpful. Third, priming can arise from state and social role effects and help the animal select the appropriate response. For example, primates who have high dominance tend to have higher levels of serotonin and dopamine and, if socially threatened, will counter-challenge/attack. The most subordinate, however, have lower levels of serotonin and dopamine, and if threatened will more quickly defend by flight or submission (Gilbert & McGuire, 1998). Fourth, priming can arise via mood-state effects. For example, as someone becomes depressed a whole set of defenses such as fight, flight and submission are more easily triggered, leading to angry and/or anxious presentations of the disorder. Although today, irritability and anxious self-focus may alienate potentially helpful others, in times past if an animal was depressed it had probably suffered a loss and was in a vulnerable position where having these defenses primed may have been adaptive.

One's Own Behavior as a Threat

The above pertains to signals picked up in the outside world but we should also note that threats can arise from *signals animals emit themselves*. For example, many mammalian infants who are separated from a caregiver will distress call. If the parent does not return they demobilize, become quiet, and stop emitting signals (show despair) because it is too dangerous to draw attention to themselves as unprotected juveniles (Bowlby, 1969). Subordinates do not stare at dominants, nor do they display confident assertive behavior, for to do so invites attacks, but dominants commonly use threat stares and displays toward subordinates. You will note that what is a threat and how an animal copes with it in a social context is mediated by the social role the animal experiences itself as being in (e.g., parent-offspring, dominant-subordinate). Of course, animals have no insight into what they are doing or why, nor do they need consciously available schemas of self and others. Rather they need to be able to detect signals in the environment and express automatic defensive or acquisitive routines (Gilbert, 1989, 2001a; Marks, 1987). As suggested elsewhere, evolved origins for some of the forms of interpersonal schemas probably evolved from these signal detection-response mechanisms.

Yet another reason our own automatic behaviors and action tendencies can become threats is that internal signals can also be conditioned; for example, people can learn that some of their thoughts and feelings invite attacks, like the parent who punishes displays of anger or distress (crying) in a child. For that child, elicitation of anger or distress becomes an internal stimulus for anxiety and affect inhibition (Ferster, 1973).

Manipulation of Defenses

For some strategies, and in some contexts, certain defensive behaviors must be inhibited. For example, in some hostile male environments (e.g., street gangs and prisons) one can be in serious trouble if one cries or expresses help-seeking behavior and does not aggressively retaliate to a threat to maintain one's reputation of toughness. On the other hand, in the context of close or affiliative relationships if one does not inhibit aggressive retaliation one can destroy the relationship. In the first context the aim is to show others one is "not safe" and should not be crossed, whereas in the second context one tries to show one is safe and (relatively) forgiving and caring. Empathy and compassion are useful in the second but not the first context.

For humans, however, both the expression and the inhibition of defensive behaviors can be skillfully and purposefully executed, based on theories about how others will react if they are expressed (derived from competencies for "theory of mind"), and for reasons of strategic self-presentation. We need to have some insight into how others are likely to appraise and respond to our behaviors. One might feign anger, distress, or submission to manipulate others. Or one might use *camouflage* to hide other defenses. If one is criticized at a meeting and feels anxious and angry one may try to appear relaxed and smile sweetly to show that one is in control of oneself and is not offended (Gilbert, 2001a). Failure to reveal difficult aspects of oneself, as in shame concealing, is, of course, a camouflage common to human social intercourse. In some pathologies people believe they are unable to use camouflage competently (people can know more about them than they would wish), or if one has a delusion one might believe others can read one's mind and thoughts. Thus, there is a perceived inability to consciously use some defenses. This may also point to a theory of mind difficulties.

Defensive processes, behaviors, and strategies are the bread and butter work of therapists (Gilbert, 1993), but are influenced by numerous complex processes; they can be triggered automatically, primed, conditioned, used consciously and strategically, and organized to fit the social context. Moreover, defensive behaviors can be accompanied by strong emotions such as fear, anger, or disgust, which themselves become a source of threat via metacognitions (e.g., one may become angry with one's own fear, or fearful of one's own anger). And, of course, emotions and defenses can be feigned.

It is also worth noting (although we cannot explore it in detail here) that some defenses and their emotions are "dissociated" at an automatic level. This serves the adaptive function of minimizing leakage in expression and the risk of acting on the emotions when to do so might be dangerous (see Ferster, 1973). To go to war and kill people requires us to dissociate feelings of compassion for the enemy and, at times, fear. Groups can collude in rituals and rehearsals of defilement of the enemy to ensure that this occurs. Who would drop bombs if they were really in touch with compassionate feelings about what their bombs were doing below?

Cognitive Processes

As noted above, the strategies and biosocial goals people are pursuing influence the detection and meaning of threats. Appraisal processes are involved at many stages of detecting a threat and selecting a response to it. Animals (including fish) never submit to predators, for example. As noted above, to a social threat some might automatically select fight while others select anxiety-escape. Attention mechanisms and arousal-control systems involved in threats are complex (Heinrichs & Hofmann, 2001; Hofmann, Moscovitch, & Heinrichs, this book). Although evaluations underpin judgments of threat and safeness, they can be made rapidly, automatically, and outside conscious control; this includes self-relevant evaluations (Greenberg, this book). People can feel threatened and start responding before they can consciously articulate what they feel threatened about (Koole, Dijksterhuis & van Knippenberg, 2001). In a number of fascinating experiments on cognitive priming, Baldwin and his colleagues found that if people are rapidly shown masked pictures of approving or disapproving faces (i.e., people did not know they had seen a face because it was presented too fast), these will still affect their self-evaluations. Being shown disapproving faces produced more negative self-evaluation than approving ones. Moreover, these effects are conditionable (see Baldwin & Fergusson, 2001 for a review). Another intriguing finding is that once an emotion is activated, it can influence subsequent processing. In other words, if one's immediate response to a threat is anger, then not only will the anger come with various action tendencies but also with dispositions for information processing that affects subsequent processing. Lerner and Keltner (2001) call this *appraisal tendency;* appraisals that are guided by the aroused affect. These findings fit the idea of basic defense and safeness processing systems that can organize response dispositions below the level of consciousness (see also McNally [2001] and Loewenstein, Weber, Hsee, & Welsch [2001] for fascinating discussions of such issues).

Cognitive Distortions. It is now recognized that in many domains people are not rational but use heuristics to make decisions quickly (Gilbert, 1998b; Leahy, this book; Tobena, Marks, & Dar, 1999). It is also clear that when one is in a state of stress the biological mediators of stress (e.g., cortisol) can bias information processing to increase the scanning for, and attention to, threat signals and ready behavior for action (Rosen & Schulkin, 1998). One reason for this is that evolution has, for some contexts, evolved the *better safe than sorry* strategy (Gilbert, 1998b). If an animal is eating lunch and hears a sound in the bushes it may be better to assume a danger and run than to wait for further information. One can overestimate danger and take action when one did not need to but one will survive. One only has to underestimate danger once (in this context) and one is dead. This implies that in some evolutionarily meaningful contexts there are built-in tendencies for cognitive distortions: to be better safe than sorry, or *overestimate* danger. These are highly susceptible to learning (e.g., "once bitten, twice shy") (Gilbert, 1998b). Different common fears/phobias (fear of animals, fear of the dark, social fears and paranoia) are related to evolutionarily meaningful situations (Gilbert, 2001a; Marks, 1987; Nesse, 1999). Indeed, there are in fact a variety of built-in negative biases to our information-processing systems (see Tobena et al., 1999), one of which may be variations in optimism and pessimism (Leahy, this book). Cognitive distortions then are not just schema driven but can reflect aspects of basic brain and strategic design, and can be primed.

Safeness

We have explored the nature of threats and response to threats. It is clear, however, that explorative behavior and resource seeking are related to the *balance* between safeness and threat such that risks can be taken to feel safe enough. We now know that risk taking is itself derived from complex processing systems, both conscious and nonconscious (Loewenstein et al., 2001). Here there are the classic issues of approach-avoidance conflict (Elliott & Thrash, 2002). As Bowlby

(1969, 1973) argued, one of the things a secure attachment (mother love) does is to create in the infant a climate of relative safeness that encourages play, exploration, and affiliative relationships. Indeed, there is good evidence that for many mammals early relationships are physiological regulators (Hofer, 1994). Schore (2001) has documented much evidence that affectionate, secure attachments (in comparison to insecure and/or abusive ones) psychobiologically regulate and educate the child's strategic orientation (social phenotypes) to the world (Collins & Feeney, 2000; Liotti, this book). In effect the child is learning that others are safe and helpful and the best way to get on in the world is to invest in and develop affiliative relationships.

Although some people may only feel safe if they can exercise aggressive control over others, it is also the case that when individuals feel safe because they see others as relatively affiliative and trustworthy, they are much more able to attend to certain types of information, are creative, trusting, and able to integrate information. There is increasing evidence, for example, that children and adults learn and function differently in contexts of threat than in contexts where the environment is nonthreatening (safe). Creativity, cooperative behavior, affiliative behavior, exploration, risk taking, and the integration of various psychological abilities and positive affect are enhanced in nonthreatening environments (Eisenberg & Mussen, 1989; Fogel, Melson, & Mistry, 1986). In socially threatening environments one finds less flexible, open, and explorative behavior; less prosocial behavior; more stereotyped, automatic defensive responses; and more negative and less positive affect.

Safeness Behaviors and Defensive Behaviors

Given the above, we need to clarify the distinction between safety behaviors (as defensive) and safeness behaviors (Gilbert, 1993). In recent years there has been great interest in what have been called safety behaviors. These are behaviors that are utilized to stop perceived catastrophic events (Clark, 2001; Clark & Wells, 1995). For example, social phobics with shaking hands may hide their hands in their pockets, panic patients avoid certain situations, shame-prone patients do not reveal their key feelings and experiences, while some use alcohol to control their anxiety. These behaviors are defensive and not safe(ness) behaviors, and can lead to more harm than good in some contexts. The key point is to help these patients see that in reality they may not create safeness but only the illusion of it. When people feel safe they do not need to rely on those defensive behaviors outlined in Table 1.1 (although knowing one could use them if needed also helps). Hence, when feeling safe they can be more explorative, develop more complex repertoires for thinking and behavior, and take risks.

Many of the behaviors used by patients are classic defenses well studied by behaviorists. For example, hiding one's hands in one's pockets is a form of camouflage; avoidance and escape are obvious defensive behaviors, but so, too, is aggression. Once we understand the difference between defensive behavior and genuine safeness-creating behavior, we can explore these differences with patients. Moreover, by locating theories of psychopathology in terms of the organization of strategies and their defensive behaviors we are able to see that a whole range of disorders are related to variations in the type and ease of triggering defensive behavior (Gilbert, 2001a). In this scheme aggressive (fight) defensive behaviors and emotions are just as much safety behaviors as those of fear and flight. Thus, one could argue that many forms of psychopathology are about how people code threat (develop rules and beliefs) according to the social strategies they are using and their defenses (Gilbert, 1993, 2001a).

For some, the threats are external (e.g., other people); for others they are internal and come from their own feelings, thoughts, or bodily processes. Because Clark and Wells's (1995) eloquent model for social anxiety illuminates the linkages between social contexts, cognitive processing, and activation of defensive behaviors that maintain key beliefs (and, I would add, basic strategies), it may turn out to be a highly appropriate and adaptable process model for a vast array of clinical problems (see also Dixon, 1998).

Human Warmth, Safeness, and Contentment

Nonetheless, whether social behavioral inhibition (e.g., submissiveness) and social exploitation are adaptive or not, problems in developing and sustaining affiliative relationships are hardly conducive to happiness, unless, perhaps, one can get into a dominant position and exert control over others. Indeed, there is good evidence that inhibition and exploitation are linked to negative affect (Elliott & Thrash,

2002). And, of course, aggressive, exploitative and mistrustful people can cause significant unhappiness for others (Beck, 1999b).

It turns out that apart from having the skills to control outcomes and ambitions evolution has made possible a different set of strategies that for humans, and indeed some other primates, are key to positive affect and health. There is now good evidence that from our earliest attachment relationships to those with our peers and sexual partners, relationships that are marked by positives, such as safeness, care, support, love, and affiliation, are positively linked to our immune systems, our neurotransmitters mediating moods, and our prosocial behaviors (Cacioppo, Berston, Sheridan, & McClintock, 2000; Field, 1998). Indeed, the desire to be valued and wanted by others, to be able to stimulate their positive emotions toward us is perhaps one of our most powerful motivations. If you think of all the people who are important to you, the chances are you would want them to associate with you because they value you (your skills and abilities) and care about you, not because they are frightened of you. The evolutionary history of why affiliative relationships are so important to humans, how they are so linked to positive affect, and how the skills to develop them may have fueled some of our intelligence, cannot be explored here (see Barkow, 1989; Gilbert, 2001c). Suffice to say that human warmth can be key to happiness.

However, as noted above, strategies and the phenotypes for strategies are designed to fit social niches. Affiliation, cooperation and sharing, and exchanges of human warmth are most likely in safe environments where others do not constitute major threats to the self (Gilbert, 1993). In threatening environments, affiliation, cooperation and sharing human warmth may be risky strategies that have poorer payoffs than fear based or exploitative ones (Cohen, 2001). The affiliative strategies need to mature in environments where others engage in mutually reciprocal affiliative roles (e.g., child-parent), such behavior is rewarded, has payoffs and is not taken advantage of, and provides role models (Eisenberg & Mussen, 1989). Affiliative strategies (and their phenotypes) that utilize capacities for empathy and care (Gilbert, 1989) need appropriate environments in which to mature and become incorporated into self-identities and our basic orientation to ourselves and the social world.

This has implications for therapy, of course. We not only want to help people think differently about themselves and behave more affiliatively, but we want to help them feel better about themselves and others. We recognize that for us to do this they need opportunities for certain emotional and relational experiences.

The secure or safe relationship is usually the one we try to re-create in therapy. Therapists try to help people feel *safe enough* to confront their fears and test out their beliefs. As Bailey notes (this book) this often calls on certain types of innate ways of classifying relationships. If the therapist is not able to convince the patient that it is safe enough to risk it, progress may be slow. The therapeutic relationship and trust in the therapist are key here. This may involve nonverbal communication (a therapist who always looks angry and flustered may not create much sense of safeness), therapist style, and personality. The well-known therapy factors of positive regard, empathy, and genuineness are helpful in part because they create a sense of safeness (Safran & Muran, 2000). Lately, work with very abused people has involved therapists being available via phone calls or other contacts (Linehan, 1993). In an evolutionary sense the therapist agrees to respond to distress calls, which can be the ontological first step to feeling safe.

As a rule, the more neglectful and abusive the patient's past, the more the therapeutic relationship comes into play. Not only does it offer a safe base for exploration and de-shaming, the therapist's warmth helps to activate potentially dormant affiliative strategies in the patient. However, activating these aspects of a person may take some time, for, as Beck and colleagues (1990) noted, they can literally have atrophied or be severely underdeveloped.

I suggest that we need to help patients activate the ability to feel warmth for the self—to recruit affects (e.g., altruism, empathy, and compassion) from the strategic options for social affiliation (Gilbert, 2000a). Because some people have never received much in the way of warmth and affiliation from others, they may be poorly equipped to use these abilities to help themselves when stressed; that is they cannot self-soothe.

Problem Focused Therapies:
The Role of Shame and Its Treatment

Different cognitive therapists have developed different types of interventions for different problems. Thus, treating a social phobia is different from treating OCD or psychosis. My own clinical work and research have been stimulated by working with the way shame operates in various disorders (Gilbert, 1998c). Shame can be seen partly as a form of submissive defense (Gilbert & McGuire, 1998; Keltner & Harker, 1998), associated with evaluations of being located in subordinate and inferior positions. Highly shame-prone people may see the outside world as rejecting of them because they are overweight, or don't have certain attributes to win approval, or are at risk of shameful exposure for (perceived) inadequacies. They can also be intensely self-critical and even self-hating—internally shaming of themselves. However you may wish to conceptualize self-attacking and self-denegration, there is good evidence that it is a major element of vulnerability to some psychopathologies. For example, Zuroff, Koestner, and Powers (1994) found that the degree of self-criticism in childhood is a predictor of later emotional problems. Hartlage, Arduino, and Alloy (1998) found that self-criticism may be a trait marker for depression. In a large study ($n = 489$) Murphy and colleagues (2002) found that self-disparagement, marked by feelings of personal inadequacy, is strongly associated with a lifelong risk of depression. Teasdale and Cox (2001) found that with a lowering of mood, recovered depressed people become more self-critical than never-depressed people. Importantly, Mongrain, Vettese, Shuster, and Kendal (1998) have found that self-criticism often goes with feelings of being subordinate and inferior and that self-critics have poorer affiliative relationships with others. Rector, Bagby, Segal, Joffe, and Levitt (2000) found that self-critics tended to have a poorer outcome with cognitive therapy than dependent people, but the extent to which they could modify self-criticism affected outcome. If one sees these problems as relating to highly internalized shame (and recent data from our department suggest that self-critics are very shame prone—indeed self-criticism is a form of internal shaming of the self), developing therapies for shame could be advantageous. So how might a strategies and evolutionary approach conceptualize shame difficulties and offer help? This is explored below.

One's Relationship With Oneself Is a Social One

While there is now general agreement that the mind is essentially designed for social relating, what is less well articulated in the literature is that the nature of internal "self-talk" is also inherently relational (Gilbert, 1989, 2000a; Hermans, 1996). My point is that the way we "talk to" and evaluate ourselves activates and coordinates certain patterns of our innate *social* strategies and mentalities (Gilbert,

1989). Highly shame-prone people tend to be *exploitative* and *aggressive* with themselves rather than affiliative, caring, and warm. To help them it is sometimes useful to try to develop more affiliation for the self and others.

The Internal Processes of Self-Attacking. Although the functions of self-attacking can be various (Driscoll, 1988), because our minds are designed for social relating, we can generate attacks on ourselves and then feel beaten down by them (submit). This is not a new view as such, for ever since Freud's conception of superego attacks on the ego, different therapists have conceptualized self-criticism in different ways, for example, as forms of self-punishment. However, it was Greenberg who first articulated clearly that it is not so much the criticism but the inability to defend oneself and to feel beaten down by it that is crucial to the affective response (Greenberg, 1979; Greenberg, Elliott, & Foerster, 1990). In evolutionary terms self-criticism is in essence hostile dominant-fearful submissive interchanges that take place internally (Gilbert, 2000a). In severe cases it is as if there is an inner war going on with "enemies" and hated parts of the self. In automatic thoughts self-attacks typically show up when people write such things about themselves as: "*You* failed at this. This is just another example of how useless *you* are. *You* are never going to succeed at anything. Why don't *you* just kill yourself."

We have explored this aspect of self-attacking in depression and schizophrenia and found that the more powerful and dominant/controlling a person feels his or her negative thoughts or voices to be, the more depressed and flight oriented the person is (Gilbert et al., 2001; see also Byrne, Trower, Birchwood, Meaden, & Nelson, this book). Thus internal self-attacking thoughts are exactly that—attacks—the very opposite of compassionate understanding and caregiving. Moreover, a person can feel harassed by them, not unlike the way a subordinate can feel harassed and beaten down by a dominant (Gilbert, 2004). This is certainly so for people who hear malevolent voices (Birchwood, Meaden, Trower, Gilbert, & Plaistow, 2000), but it is also the case for depressed people with self-critical thoughts (Gilbert et al., 2001).

It is often useful to use Socratic questions to explore the origins and functions of self-attacking: "When did it first occur, what was happening?" and "What did the attacking part hope to achieve by engaging in this controlling behavior?" Treating self-attacking as role related rather than just schema based offers different ways of working with these elements. Sometimes people think they self-attack for their own good, to force themselves to do things and improve themselves—the sergeant-major approach to life. At other times there is more contempt and a wish to destroy elements of the self, to root out the weak and undesirable. A number of cognitive therapists have recognized that rational, cognitive reevaluating of intense self-attacking thoughts may be limited. There are many reasons for this. One reason, as we have seen above, is that these are strategically informed ways of thinking, and like self-blame, they serve to keep the person in subordinate, defensive positions. Another reason is that if you ask people to imagine the self-critical part of themselves as if it were a person, they often say that this bullying part of them seems powerful, hostile, and dominant (Gilbert, 2000a). If you then ask, "How does this part of you rate your evidence that you are not the way this part of you makes out?" many patients quickly appreciate that this part of them may not be interested in evidence and sweep it aside. In other words, it behaves as most exploitative bullies do. Moreover, in severe forms of self-criticism and self-hatred there is much in the thinking style of these parts of the self that is just like the way enemies think about each other (Beck, 1999b). However, another reason that rational reevaluating may have limited impact is that some people are not able to do this with any warmth. Their challenges are cold and/or hostile ("Come on, stop thinking in black and white, stupid!") Hence, it can be helpful to create a new type of internal relationship to replace the dominant hostile, and the fearful, beaten-down, subordinate one: that is one based on affiliation to, and care for, the self and others with new affects (empathy and compassion). I have called this "developing the compassionate mind." It is not a new idea, and, as noted elsewhere (Gilbert, 2000a), a number of cognitive therapists have discussed the importance of developing compassion for the self, as have, of course, Buddhists for centuries. Greenberg (this book) also addresses this issue.

Although working with schemas of the self, exploring evidence for and against a negative self-view, and other basic cognitive techniques can be immensely helpful for some people (see Young et al., 2000), the approach outlined here adds a number of other elements (Gilbert, 2000a). First, schemas are seen as the result of, as much as the consequence of, the internal attacking relationship (just as we saw Sally's "weak self" schema emerging out of her submissive defenses). Second, we focus on possible functions of self-attacking, for example, to improve or cleanse and purify the self, the functions of these being to reduce the chances of being rejected by others or to be more dominant (e.g., "If you would only lose weight and look nicer, people might like you or respect you more"). Third, we note how internal self-talk can be like a relationship, and the self-attacking part can be conceptualized as using bullying tactics to exploit or coerce the person. We may use various "two-chair" techniques to give clarity to the thoughts and feelings of this part of the self. This often brings a lot more emotion into sessions than simply writing thoughts down (Greenberg, this book). This part may be named as "an internal bully" and space given to imagine what it may look like (e.g., size, facial expressions), as if it were an actual person. Both the two chairs and the imagination techniques can give insight into the feelings of power and dominance of this part of the self. People can then engage in dialogue back and forth between the chairs (Greenberg, this book). As noted above, because people may recognize that this bullying part of themselves is not interested in evidence against its views and judgments, such techniques and others can help them understand why reevaluations of their negative self-judgments can be so hard to believe or give up. They can help people discover that there may be identity issues centered on this type of internal relationship ("My self-attacking part has been with me for so long I don't know who I would be without it.") Fourth, we focus on the benefits and at times moral issues in developing care and compassion for the self. Fifth, we work on bringing compassionate feelings and thoughts into the process of change.

Compassionate Mind. Both the conceptualization of the power of self-attacking and the benefits of developing self-compassion are derived from cognitive-evolution and physiological theories (Gilbert, 2000a; Gilbert & Irons [in press]). At its simplest, this posits that negative and put-down, attacking signals, be they external or internal, generate stress, negative affect, and defensive responses. In contrast, just as externally provided warmth, care, and compassion are associated with safeness and certain physiological effects on immune and mood systems (see Cacioppo et al., 2000), so too, developing inner compassion (a different type of internal signal) may have physiological benefits and begin a possible shift to a warmer, self-soothing ability. Once one sees that internal relationships are working through mechanisms that evolved for external, social ones, then a host of options open up. For example, if the internal self-structure is such that one part sees another part as the enemy to be suppressed, controlled, or destroyed, then not only will this be mirrored in the thinking styles but also the way of working with enemies toward reconciliation (see Beck, 1999b) may be adaptable for hostile self-to-self relations.

Here we can only look at a few of the elements of compassionate mind development, the order of which depends on the person. One common element is that people may learn to be *empathic to their own distress* or situation. Some people bypass their sadness and focus on anger, or have thoughts like, "I am stupid/weak to let this upset me; I should be stronger. Feeling like this is pathetic. Why can't I pull myself together?" That is, they try to bully themselves out of it and feel ashamed of their distress (see Gilbert, 1992b, for a case example). Sometimes people will seek to challenge their negative thoughts in an effort to bypass real pain they feel unable to tolerate (e.g., for abuse or the early loss of a parent). Cognitive therapists should remain wary of being pulled into collusions of using cognitive techniques to avoid working with painful life experiences that patients, both consciously and nonconsciously, may use to maintain their negative beliefs and strategic orientations.

In fact, when one works on developing warmth to the self (e.g., being empathic to one's distress rather than trying to suppress it or reason it away), this can start a grieving process for some people (Gilbert & Irons (in press)). One needs to use caution here, as people can at first feel overwhelmed and threatened. One might look at the thoughts and fears of grieving and go step by step, helping the person to feel in control. Greenberg (this book) discusses how being able to process these emotions can advance integration of painful material and give it new meanings. (See also Kennedy-Moore & Watson, 1999, for an exploration of the complexities involved in accessing, expressing, and working with emotion).

Self-critics and those steeped in shame are often resistant/defensive (fearful and angry) to processing sad affect or grief. This is in major contrast to dependent types who have ready access to these emotions and can, in fact, have them too easily triggered. Not uncommonly, self-critics have been severely punished or shamed in the past for this kind of distress signaling (Gilbert, 1992b). They can struggle to be compassionate to others who are in distress, in part, perhaps, because their own defenses are being activated (Mongrain et al., 1998). This raises some rather difficult moral issues of how much one should shore up their efforts to be independent and cut off from social affiliation and warmth and how much one should be prepared to work through their resistance (Leahy, 2001), a theme well portrayed in the

film *Good Will Hunting*. Moreover, studies of grief suggest that grieving can sometimes be helpful and sometimes not, depending upon
the contexts, the supportive environment around the person, and the
type of relationship that has been lost (Bonanno & Kaltman, 1999).
In terms of the benefits of grieving for oneself and the painful events
in one's life there are no current data, only clinical anecdotes.

A second aspect of working this way is to bring feelings of warmth
and compassion into the reevaluation itself, perhaps using imagery
of a compassionate person and how he or she might look or sound.
Or one might prefer to ask people to create an image of a compassionate part of themselves, and then ask how this feels or what thoughts
this compassionate part of them has. In very damaged people the compassionate part of themselves may have thoughts similar to the self-
critical bully's. For example, one person whose mother had died when
she was young and whose father had taken to drink, leaving her to
care for her siblings, said, "Well, I can sort of feel compassion for what
I've been through, I suppose, but I still think that I should just pull
myself together and toughen up. This compassionate stuff feels weak
and wet." However, as she practiced some of the aspects noted here
she became less self-conscious and dismissive and more compassionate to herself, more in touch with unresolved grief over her
mother's death, and much gentler with herself in her coping efforts.

If we can help people develop even some feeling of warmth for the
self, we can then encourage them to go over their alternative coping thoughts in their minds, trying to generate as much compassion
and warmth as possible. The therapist may say, "Let's go through these
alternative thoughts you've written down again, but as you read them
try to imagine hearing them in your mind as if a compassionate part
of you were speaking them." Or the therapist might say, "I'd like
you to imagine the voice of someone who is very understanding of
the distress you feel. That person is speaking warmly and compassion-
ately to you to encourage and support you." The idea here is to get
a warm *emotional tone* in the alternative thoughts (Gilbert, 2000a, 2000b;
Gilbert & Irons [in press]). This can be practiced a number of
times in the therapy in order to directly undermine *the affect* of the
self-attacking. It is like trying to generate an alternative incompatible
affect to hostility, not unlike teaching people relaxation as a counter-
affect for anxiety. Warmth can be a counter to hostility, but it also
offers people the opportunity to experience and work with new affects
and meanings. This is discussed further by Greenberg (this book)

where he outlines how the activation of one emotion can help alleviate the effects of another. From an evolutionary point of view, we are trying to generate new internal signals that may stimulate those brain mechanisms that underpin the care and affiliative strategies.

Once we have stimulated the feelings of compassion by focusing on inner images of a compassionate part of the self or compassionate others, and exploring how they might look and sound, how they might feel and think, then we can help the patient begin to practice activating these images/thoughts in times of distress. One might use various chairs (e.g., have the compassionate mind chair) to enable people to practice the role of compassionate self-talk. Interestingly, for centuries, Buddhist meditation practices have focused on the issue of compassionate imagery (Mullen, 2001). Although the compassionate aspect of self can feel sad and empathize with the distress, it is important for the therapist to check that the person does not feel this part of him or her will become overwhelmed by the distress. For example, one patient said, "When I try to create a compassionate feeling in me it just feels very sad and powerless." The compassionate mind needs to be imbued with certain strengths—encouraging, empathizing, and supporting on the one hand, but also helping to reevaluate self-attacking thoughts on the other. In religious forms people imagine God or a Buddha that has greater power than the suffering part of the self does (Mullen, 2001). Eventually the compassionate self can interact with the bullying self and encourage the bullying self to better understand its own fears and motivations. This also can increase the perceived power and adult-like nature of the compassionate part of the self.

As in all forms of cognitive therapy, generating alternative thoughts and reevaluations are key to the process, but reevaluations need to be practiced with as much compassion and warm affect as possible. Some people find that spending a few moments creating an inner compassionate image helps them to decenter from their attacks and accept their reevaluations. There are many other aspects to compassionate mind work, such as developing forgiveness for self and others, practicing compassionate behavior, and perspective taking (Gilbert, 2000a; Gilbert & Irons (in press)). The key to the compassionate mind is not that we are teaching new skills as such, but rather trying to activate a perhaps dormant functional ability in the person.

The human capacity for compassion is one of the abilities that set us apart from other animals, and there is good evidence that care and affiliation, at least when coming from the outside, is calming and healing

(Cacioppo et al., 2000). Of course, we cannot give a person the memories of a loving mother or father, or a happy childhood if these never existed, but even small experiences of warmth may be helpful. So even if one has never really experienced them before it may be possible, with practice, to develop these abilities. They will also help one to tolerate rather than defend against painful feelings and memories.

Compassionate mind work is not an alternative to other cognitive techniques nor is it a means to bypass working with anger at others when it exists. Nor is it appropriate for all people. It has been developed for those who feel deep internal shame and for whom the inner and outer worlds have become cold. Careful research is needed to refine it and provide evidence for its effectiveness. How these evolutionarily derived elements of CBT might interface with other new and exciting approaches, such as mindfulness (Segal, Williams, & Teasdale, 2002), are for the future.

Conclusion

This chapter has outlined how humans have evolved with two basic psychobiological organizing systems (defense and safeness) that are linked to strategies for enacting social roles (Gilbert, 1989, 1993). I have argued that, either as a general orientation to life, and/or in specific social roles (such as caring, being cared for, sexual intimacy), people can approach life situations feeling relatively safe and able (optimistic), or enter them primed to a defensive, behaviorally inhibited strategic orientation (e.g., pessimistic, fearfully submissive; see Gilbert, 1989, pp. 26–27). Alternatively, they may engage social life using aggressive and exploitative strategies.

Strategies can be coded in gene-neural control systems of physiological state regulators. They can be difficult to detect directly and access consciously. Mostly, we are left becoming aware of their products (behaviors, thoughts, and feelings). We may not understand the underlying evolved functions of some of our negative thoughts and feelings, which are not necessarily there to make us happy or moral (Buss, 2000). Nor may we have much insight into how they may be the products of strategic orientations and decisions made in lower brain centers of primitive design. Of course, this does not mean that these strategies are adaptive to us today; often they are not (Gilbert, 2001b). Many of these strategies and the mechanisms controlling them evolved long ago. Also, strategic orientations and phenotypes developed in one phase of life might handicap another. For example, self-blame, mistrust, or social avoidance may be useful when young, and/or in a threatening environment, but may be a real handicap later in life if one's social environment becomes more benign. They can also handicap us because we have this extra level of ability for self-reflection and metacognition (Wells, 2000). The question is: How easy is it to change these phenotypes, and under what conditions do they change? And how easy is it to help people change if they cannot get away from hostile environments to more benign ones?

The relationship among personality, evolved strategies, phenotypes, mental modules, and cognitive schemas remains complex (Beck, 1996; Beck & Freeman, 1990) and much needs to be done (McGuire & Troisi, 1998; Perry et al., 1995). In regard to the concepts of schemas and rules, it has been suggested that although they can provide useful therapy heuristics, and can represent the type of strategies a person is using, they should not always be taken at face value for they may themselves be symptoms of primed strategic orientations associated with important neurophysiological mediators as, for example, data from studies of child abuse (Teicher, 2002). We also noted that certain strategies make some learning difficult. For example, psychopaths (exploiters) would find it easy to learn rules and develop beliefs that allow or justify killing and torture, but affiliative types would find this much more difficult. Psychopaths would find learning compassion for others much harder than do affiliative types.

Exploring a strategies approach with people can help to deshame them and focus on new challenges for change (e.g., maturational possibilities). Clearly, we are sailing at the edges of what scientific explorations of the mind have revealed to us. Nonetheless, increasingly sophisticated research in brain imaging and in priming, and information-processing research are beginning to illuminate the way strategies (e.g., for the fast detection of threats or opportunities) can influence processing and emotions before people are conscious of them.

In this context, cognitive therapy provides many opportunities for change, such as the classic cognitive-behavioral techniques of thought, feeling, and behavior monitoring; opportunities to learn to tolerate affect; opportunities to generate and practice alternative ways of thinking and behaving; running experiments; exposure to the feared or avoided; and providing corrective emotional experiences. Although corrective emotional experiences are often focused on the emotional interactions in therapy, such as working with the affects of the attachment system (Safran & Muran, 2000), other ways of offering them can focus directly on defensive behaviors as developed for social anxiety

(Clark, 2001), and now voice hearers (Byrne et al., this book). Other emerging ways of helping involve developing new (meditation-based) ways of processing our thoughts and feelings (Teasdale, 1999), helping people recruit and mature more positive and warm affects (Greenberg, this book), and, in particular, developing inner compassion (Gilbert, 2000a). These techniques try to create a more benign internal environment, in which a person is not continually harassed and stressed by his or her own self-condemnations. As we understand more about how our brains evolved and operate we will be presented with new challenges to develop ways to help people change. As Beck (1996) noted, to understand psychopathology and its treatment we must go "beyond belief."

References

Baldwin, M. W., & Fergusson, P. (2001) Relational schemas: The activation of interpersonal knowledge structures in social anxiety. In W. R. Crozier & L. E. Alden (Eds.), *International handbook of social anxiety: Concepts, research and interventions to the self and shyness* (pp. 235–257). Chichester, UK: Wiley.

Bargh, J. A., & Chartland, T. L. (1999). The unbearable automaticity of being. *American Psychologist, 54,* 462–479.

Barkow, J. H. (1989) *Darwin, sex and status: Biological approaches to mind and culture.* Toronto: University of Toronto Press.

Barrett, L., Dunbar, R., & Lycett, J. (2002). *Human evolutionary psychology.* London: Palgrave.

Baumeister, R. F., & Leary, M. R. (1995). The need to belong: Desire for interpersonal attachments as a fundamental human motivation. *Psychological Bulletin, 117,* 497–529.

Baumeister, R. F., Tice, D. M., & Hutton, D. G. (1989). Self-presentational motivation of differences in self-esteem. *Journal of Personality, 57,* 547–579.

Beck, A. T. (1987). Cognitive models of depression. *Journal of Cognitive Psychotherapy, 1,* 5–38.

Beck, A. T. (1996). Beyond belief: A theory of modes, personality and psychopathology. In P. Salkovskis (Ed.), *Frontiers of cognitive therapy* (pp. 1–25). New York: Oxford University Press.

Beck, A. T. (1999a). Cognitive aspects of personality disorders and their relation to syndromal disorders: A psycho-evolutionary approach. In C. R. Cloninger (Ed.), *Personality and psychopathology* (pp. 411–430). Washington, DC: American Psychiatric Association.

Beck, A. T. (1999b). *Prisoners of hate: The cognitive basis of anger, hostility and violence.* New York: HarperCollins.

Beck, A. T., Emery, G., & Greenberg, R. L. (1985). *Anxiety disorders and phobias: A cognitive approach.* New York: Basic Books.

Beck, A. T., Freeman, A., & Associates. (1990). *Cognitive therapy of personality disorders.* New York: Guilford.

Belsky, J., Steinberg, L., & Draper, P. (1990). Childhood experiences, interpersonal development, and reproductive strategy: An evolutionary theory of socialization. *Child Development, 62,* 647–670.

Birchwood, M., Meaden, A., Trower, P., Gilbert, P., & Plaistow, J. (2000). The power and omnipotence of voices: Subordination and entrapment by voices and significant others. *Psychological Medicine, 30,* 337–344.

Bonanno, G., & Kaltman, S. (1999). Toward an integrative perspective on bereavement. *Psychological Bulletin, 125,* 760–776.

Bowlby, J. (1969). *Attachment and loss: Attachment* (Vol. 1). London: Hogarth.

Bowlby, J. (1973). *Attachment and loss: Separation, anxiety and anger* (Vol. 2). London: Hogarth.

Bowlby, J. (1980). *Attachment and loss: Sadness and depression* (Vol. 3). London: Hogarth.

Buss, D. M. (1999). *Evolutionary psychology: The new science of mind.* Boston, MA: Allyn & Bacon.

Buss, D. M. (2000). The evolution of happiness. *American Psychologist, 55,* 15–23.

Cacioppo, J. T., Berston, G. G., Sheridan, J. F., & McClintock, M. K. (2000). Multilevel integrative analysis of human behavior: Social neuroscience and the complementing nature of social and biological approaches. *Psychological Bulletin, 126,* 829–843.

Clark D. M. (2001). A cognitive perspective on social phobia. In W. R. Crozier & L. E. Alden (Eds.), *International handbook of social anxiety: Concepts, research and interventions to the self and shyness* (pp. 405–430). Chichester, UK: Wiley.

Clark, D. M., & Wells, A. (1995). A cognitive model of social phobia. In R. G. Heimberg, M. R. Liebowitz., D. A. Hope, & R. R. Schneier (Eds.), *Social phobia: Diagnosis, assessment and treatment* (pp. 69–93). New York: Guilford.

Cohen, D. (2001). Cultural variation: Considerations and implications. *Psychological Bulletin, 127,* 451–471.

Collins, N. L., & Feeney, B. C. (2000). A safe haven: An attachment theory perspective on support seeking and care giving in intimate relationships. *Journal of Personality and Social Psychology, 78,* 1053–1073.

Collins, W. A., Maccoby, E. E., Steinberg, L., Heatherington, E. M., & Bornstein, M. H. (2000). Contemporary research on parenting: The case for nature and nurture. *American Psychologist, 55,* 218–232.

Dixon, A. K. (1998). Ethological strategies for defence in animals and humans: Their role in some psychiatric disorders. *British Journal of Medical Psychology, 71,* 417–445.

Driscoll, R. (1988). Self-condemnation: A conceptual framework for assessment and treatment. *Psychotherapy, 26,* 104–111.

Eisenberg, N., & Mussen, P. N. (1989). *The roots of prosocial behavior in children.* New York: Cambridge University Press.

Elliott, A. J., & Thrash, T. (2002). Approach-avoidance motivation in personality: Approach and avoidance temperament and goals. *Journal of Personality and Social Psychology, 82,* 804–818.

Ferster, C. B. (1973). A functional analysis of depression. *American Psychologist, 28,* 857–870.

Field, T. M. (1998). Touch therapy effects on development. *International Journal of Behavioral Development, 22,* 779–797.

Fogel, A., Melson, G. F., & Mistry, J. (1986). Conceptualising the determinants of nurturance: A reassessment of sex differences. In A. Fogel & G. F. Melson (Eds.), *Origins of nurturance: Developmental, biological and cultural perspectives on caregiving* (pp. 53–68). Hillsdale, NJ: Erlbaum.

Gilbert, P. (1989). *Human nature and suffering.* London: Erlbaum.

Gilbert, P. (1992a). *Depression: The evolution of powerlessness.* Hove, Sussex: Erlbaum; New York: Guilford.

Gilbert, P. (1992b). *Counselling for depression.* London: Sage.

Gilbert, P. (1993). Defence and safety: Their function in social behaviour and psychopathology. *British Journal of Clinical Psychology. 32,* 131–153.

Gilbert, P. (1995). Biopsychosocial approaches and evolutionary theory as aids to integration in clinical psychology and psychotherapy. *Clinical Psychology and Psychotherapy, 2,* 135–156.

Gilbert, P. (1998a). Evolutionary psychopathology: Why isn't the mind better designed than it is? *British Journal of Medical Psychology, 71,* 353–373.

Gilbert, P. (1998b). The evolved basis and adaptive functions of cognitive distortions. *British Journal of Medical Psychology, 71,* 447–463.

Gilbert, P. (1998c). What is shame? Some core issues and controversies. In P. Gilbert & B. Andrews (Eds.), *Shame: Interpersonal behavior, psychopathology and culture* (pp. 3–38). New York: Oxford University Press.

Gilbert, P. (2000a). Social mentalities: Internal "social" conflicts and the role of inner warmth and compassion in cognitive therapy. In P. Gilbert & K. G. Bailey (Eds.), *Genes on the couch: Explorations in evolutionary psychotherapy* (pp. 118–150). Hove: Psychology Press.

Gilbert, P. (2000b). *Overcoming depression: A self-guide using cognitive behavioural techniques* (Rev. ed.). London: Robinsons; New York: Oxford University Press.

Gilbert, P. (2001a). Evolutionary approaches to psychopathology: The role of natural defences. *Australian and New Zealand Journal of Psychiatry, 35,* 17–27.

Gilbert, P. (2001b). Depression and stress: A biopsychosocial exploration of evolved functions and mechanisms stress. *The International Journal of the Biology of Stress, 4,* 121–135.

Gilbert, P. (2001c). Evolution and social anxiety: The role of social competition and social hierarchies. In F. Schneider (Ed.), *Social anxiety: Psychiatric clinics of North America, 24* (pp. 723–751). Philadelphia: W. B. Saunders.

Gilbert, P. (2004). Depression: A biopsychosocial, integrative and evolutionary approach. In M. Power (Ed.), *Mood disorders: A handbook for scientists and practitioners* (99–142). Chichester, UK: Wiley.

Gilbert, P., & Allan, S. (1998). The role of defeat and entrapment (arrested flight) in depression: An exploration of an evolutionary view. *Psychological Medicine, 28,* 584–597.

Gilbert, P., & Bailey, K. (Eds.). (2000). *Genes on the couch: Explorations in evolutionary psychotherapy.* Hove, London: Routledge.

Gilbert, P., Birchwood, M., Gilbert, J., Trower, P., Hay, J., Murray, B., Meaden, A., Olsen, K., & Miles, J. N. V. (2001). An exploration of evolved mental mechanisms for dominant and subordinate behaviour in relation to auditory hallucinations in schizophrenia and critical thoughts in depression. *Psychological Medicine, 31,* 1117–1127.

Gilbert, P., & Irons, C. (in press). Focused therapies and compassionate mind training for shame and self-attacking. In P. Gilbert (ed), *Compassion: Conceptialisations, research and use in psychotherapy.* London: Brunner-Routledge.

Gilbert, P., & McGuire, M. (1998). Shame, social roles and status: The psychobiological continuum from monkey to human. In P. Gilbert & B. Andrews (Eds.), *Shame: Interpersonal behavior, psychopathology and culture* (pp. 99–125). New York: Oxford University Press.

Gilmore, D. D. (1990). *Manhood in the making: Cultural concepts of masculinity.* New Haven, CT: Yale University Press.

Gray, J. A. (1987). *The psychology of fear and stress* (2nd ed.). Cambridge, UK: Cambridge University Press.

Greenberg, L. S. (1979). Resolving splits: Use of the two-chair technique. *Psychotherapy: Theory, Research and Practice, 16,* 316–324.

Greenberg, L. S., Elliott, R. K., & Foerster, F. S. (1990). Experiential processes in the psychotherapeutic treatment of depression. In C. D. McCann & N. S. Endler (Eds.), *Depression: New directions in theory, research and practice* (pp. 157–185). Toronto: Wall & Emerson.

Hamilton, W. D. (1964). The genetical evolution of social behavior, Parts 1 & 2. *Journal of Theoretical Biology, 7,* 1–52.

Hartledge, S., Arduino, K., & Alloy, L. B. (1998). Depressive personality characteristics: State dependent concomitants of depressive disorders and traits independent of current depression. *Journal of Abnormal Psychology, 107,* 349–354.

Heinrichs, N., & Hofmann, S. G. (2001). Information processing in social phobia: A critical review. *Clinical Psychology Review, 21,* 751–770.

Hermans, H. J. (1996). Voicing the self: From information processing to dialogical interchange. *Psychological Bulletin, 119,* 31–50.

Hofer, M. A. (1994). Early relationships as regulators of infant physiology and behavior. *Acta Paediatrica, 397*(Suppl.), 9–18.

Kagan, J. (1999). The concept of behavioural inhibition. In L. A. Schmidt & J. Schulkin (Eds.), *Extreme fear, shyness, and social phobia* (pp. 3–13). New York: Oxford University Press.

Keltner, D., & Harker, L. A. (1998). The forms and functions of the nonverbal signal of shame. In P. Gilbert & B. Andrews (Eds.), *Shame: Interpersonal behavior, psychopathology and culture* (pp. 78–98). New York: Oxford University Press.

Kennedy-Moore, E., & Watson, J. C. (1999). *Expressing emotion: Myths, realities, and therapeutic strategies.* New York: Guilford.

Koole, S. L., Dijksterhuis, A., & van Knipperberg, A. (2001). What's in a name: Implicit self-esteem and the automatic self. *Journal of Personality and Social Psychology, 80,* 669–685.

Leahy, R. L. (2000). Sunk costs and resistance to change. *Journal of Cognitive Psychotherapy, 14,* 355–371.

Leahy, R. L. (2001). *Overcoming resistance in cognitive therapy.* New York: Guilford.

LeDoux, J. (1998) *The emotional brain.* London: Weidenfeld and Nicolson.

Lerner, J. S., & Keltner, D. (2001). Fear, anger and risk. *Journal of Personality and Social Psychology, 81,* 146–159.

Linehan, M. (1993). *Cognitive-behavioral therapy for borderline personality disorder.* New York: Guilford Press.

Loewenstein, G. F., Weber, E. U., Hsee, C. K., & Welsch, N. (2001). Risk as feelings. *Psychological Bulletin, 127,* 267–286.

Marks, I. M. (1987). *Fears, phobias, and rituals: Panic, anxiety and their disorders.* Oxford, UK: Oxford University Press.

MacLean, P. (1990). *The triune brain in evolution.* New York: Plenum Press.

McGuire, M. T., & Troisi, A. (1998). *Darwinian psychiatry.* New York: Oxford University Press.

McNally, R. J. (2001). On the scientific status of cognitive appraisal models of anxiety disorders. *Behaviour Research and Therapy, 39,* 513–521.

Mikulinces, M., Birnbaum, G., Wodis, D., & Nachmias, O. (2000). Stress and accessibility of proximity-related thought: Exploring the normative and intra individual component of attachment theory. *Journal of Personality and Social Psychology, 18,* 509–523.

Mongrain, M., Vettese L. C., Shuster, B., & Kendel, N. (1998). Perceptual biases, affect, and behavior in relationship of dependents and self-critics. *Journal of Personality and Social Psychology, 75,* 230–241.

Mullen, K. (2001). Pleasing to behold: Healing and the visualized body. *Mental Health Religion and Culture, 4,* 119–132.

Murphy, J. M., Nierenberg, A. A., Monson, R. R., Laird, N. M., Sobol, A. M., & Leighton, A. H. (2001). Self disparagement as a feature and forerunner of depression: Findings from the Stirling County study. *Comprehensive Psychiatry, 43,* 13–21.

Nesse, R. M. (1998). Emotional disorders in evolutionary perspective. *British Journal of Medical Psychology, 71,* 397–416.

Nesse, R. M. (1999). Proximate and evolutionary studies of anxiety, stress and depression. *Neuroscience and Behavioral Reviews, 23,* 895–903.

Nesse, R. M., & Williams, G. C. (1995). *Evolution and healing.* London: Weidenfeld and Nicolson.

Ohman, A., & Mineka, S. (2001). Fears, phobias, and preparedness: Toward an evolved module of fear and fear learning. *Psychological Bulletin, 108,* 483–522.

Overing, J. (1989). Styles of manhood: An Amazonian contrast in tranquillity and violence. In S. Howell & R. Wills (Eds.), *Societies at peace: Anthropological perspectives.* London: Routledge.

Panksepp, J. (1998). *Affective neuroscience.* New York: Oxford University Press.

Perry, B. D., Pollard, R. A., Blakley, T. L., Baker, W. L., & Vigilante, D. (1995). Childhood trauma, the neurobiology of adaptation and "use-dependent" development of the brain: How "states" become "traits." *Infant Mental Health Journal, 16,* 271–291.

Rector, N. A., Bagby, R. B., Segal, Z. V., Joffe, R. T., & Levitt, A. (2000). Self-criticism and dependency in depressed patients treated with cognitive therapy or pharmacotherapy. *Cognitive Therapy and Research, 24,* 571–584.

Ridley, M. (2000). *Genome: The autobiography of a species.* London: Fourth Estate.

Safran, J. D., & Muran, J. C. (2000). *Negotiating the therapeutic alliance: A relational treatment guide.* New York: Guilford.

Rosen, J. B., & Schulkin, J. (1998). From normal fear to pathological anxiety. *Psychological Bulletin, 105,* 325–350.

Sapolsky, R. M. (1996). Why stress is bad for your brain. *Science, 273,* 749–750.

Sapolsky, R. M. (2000). Glucocorticoids and hippocampus atrophy in neuropsychiatric disorders. *Archives of General Psychiatry, 57,* 925–935.

Schore, A. (2001). The effects of early relational trauma on right brain development, affect regulation, and infant mental health. *Infant Mental Health Journal, 22,* 201–269.

Segal, Z. V., Williams, J. G., & Teasdale, J. D. (2002). *Mindfulness-based cognitive therapy for depression.* New York: Guilford.

Teasdale, J. D. (1999). Emotional processing: Three modes of mind and the prevention of relapse in depression. *Behaviour Research and Therapy, 37,* 29–52.

Teasdale, J. D., & Cox, S. G. (2001). Dysphoria: Self-evaluative and affective components in recovered depressed patients and never depressed controls. *Psychological Medicine, 31,* 1311–1316.

Teicher, M. H. (2002). Scars that won't heal: The neurobiology of the abused child. *Scientific American, 286*(3), 54–61.

Toates, F. (1995). *Stress: Conceptual and biological aspects.* Chichester, UK: Wiley.

Tobena, A., Marks, I., & Dar, R. (1999). Advantages of bias and prejudice: An exploration of their neurocognitive templates. *Neuroscience and Behavioral Reviews, 23,* 1047–1058.

Wakefield, J. C. (1999). Evolutionary versus prototype analyses of the concept of disorder. *Journal of Abnormal Psychology, 108,* 400–411.

Wells, A. (2000). *Emotional disorders and metacognition.* Chichester, UK: Wiley.

Young, J. E., Weinberger, A. D., & Beck, A. T. (2001). Cognitive therapy for depression. In D. Barlow (Ed.), *Clinical handbook of psychological disorders* (3rd ed., pp. 264–308). New York: Guilford.

Zuroff, D. C., Koestner, R., & Powers, T. A. (1994). Self-criticism at age 12: A longitudinal study of adjustment. *Cognitive Therapy & Research, 18,* 367–385.

Acknowledgment. I would like to thank Professors Michael McGuire and Kent Bailey, Bob Leahy and Stefan Hofmann for the helpful comments on earlier versions of this chapter.

Chapter 2

Recognizing, Assessing, and Classifying Others: Cognitive Bases of Evolutionary Kinship Therapy

Kent G. Bailey

The need to belong is a fundamental and powerful human motivation (Baumeister & Leary, 1995) that emanates from the mammalian, primate, and hominid/human ancestry of modern human beings (Mellen, 1981). Ancestral hominid and early human species lived in small, intimate, and often inbred groups typically numbering in the 25–50 range (Lewin, 1993; Service, 1962) but may have numbered up to 70–80 individuals by *Homo habilis* (Dunbar, 1992). Groups might reach 150–200 in later phases of ancestral history and 500 or more in tribal groupings of *Homo sapiens* (see Aiello & Dunbar, 1993); however, even then extended in-group relations were intensely intimate, relative to out-group relations. Whether in band or tribe, members moved together as a group; engaged in communication about mating, parenting, grooming, food-seeking and food consumption; and, in general, acted out species scripts in an intricate social ecosystem (Caporael & Baron, 1997)

Over evolutionary time, social togetherness within the group became central to the physical and emotional well-being of the individual (Panksepp, Nelson, & Bekkedal, 1997). Real or threatened disruptions of this natural sociality were stressful, aversive, and likely to carry costs in personal and inclusive fitness in ancestral contexts. In today's world, signals that indicate disruptions and threats to group acceptance remain highly aversive and stressful (Baumeister & Tice, 1990; Hazan & Shaver, 1994; Weiss, 1979). Moreover, such losses or disruptions put one at risk for various forms of both physical and psychological pathology (Baumeister & Leary, 1995; DeLongis, Folkman, & Lazarus, 1988; Goodwin, Hunt, Key, & Samet, 1987; Henderson, 1982; House, Landis, & Umberson, 1988; Lynch, 1979).

Not surprisingly, many forms of relationship have evolved into powerful psychobiological regulators. For example, insecure attachment with early parenting figures can be detrimental to one's physiological functioning (see Carter, Lederhendler, & Kirkpatrick, 1997, and Liotto, this book), subsequent child rearing practices (see Hazan & Zeifman, 1994), sense of self and self-regulation (Bowlby, 1988; see also Swann & Brown, 1990), internal working models and system of meanings (Simpson & Rholes, 1998), and overall psychological health in adulthood (see Atkinson & Zucker, 1997). It may also be a precursor to family incest (Erickson, 1993, 2000), adult sexual deviance (Stroufe & Fleeson, 1986), sexual promiscuity (Brennan, Shaver, & Tobey, 1991), and conflicted dating and mating relationships (Zeifman & Hazan, 1997).

In ancestral environments, loss of support in specific dyadic relationships (e.g., parent-child relations or mateships), loss of membership in the genetic family aggregation, or, worse still, banishment from the band, were catastrophic events. Ancestral life was often brutal and short under the best of circumstances, and death could strike any time through disease, famine, accidents, natural catastrophes, predation, or hostile invasion (see Nesse & Williams, 1995). Caporael and Baron (1997) point out that "humans are an obligately interdependent species, unable to survive and reproduce outside a group context" (p. 328). However, with the security provided by family support and band membership the individual could pursue species goals (e.g., mating, reproduction, and parenting) even under unfavorable conditions.

The Kinship Model

The concept of kinship is a central organizing construct in social science and one of the fundamental concerns of anthropology. Kinship goes to the heart of being human: patterns of attachment to significant others; patterns of recognition, naming, and social classification; patterns of marriage, parenting, and family organization; patterns of time, space, and resource sharing; and patterns of shared language, beliefs, rituals, and symbols. Kinship is about how people relate to each other in their everyday affairs (Parsons, 1966) and "solidarity of the kinship unit" is a defining feature (Parsons, 1964). As Wilson (1993) says, "The lives of most people are centered around the enduring facts of human existence—coping with family, establishing relationships, and raising children" (p. 5). We recall here the oft-quoted words of Edmond Leach (1966): "Human beings, wherever we meet them, display an almost obsessional interest in matters of sex and kinship" (p. 41).

Kinship Formation

There is a powerful natural tendency to form kinships, but they do not spring from the forehead of Zeus fully formed. Two individuals may be genetically related or biologically linked (mother and infant, brother and sister, father and daughter, etc.), but they cannot form a *kinship relationship* until each is aware of the other's existence, each develops reliable criteria for recognizing the other, and each is willing to classify the other as kin (see Bailey, 2000, and also Hirschfeld, 1986). For example, neither of two siblings separated at birth might know of the other (no kinship), one might know of the other but not care (no kinship), one might know of the other and readily *classify* him or her as kin pending a meeting (one-way kinship but no *relationship* until the other reciprocates), or both may immediately and unreservedly classify the other as kin (two-way kinship relationship). Any given social dyad may involve no kinship, one-way kinship, or two-way reciprocal kinship.

The category of no kinship characterizes virtually all of the possible dyadic combinations of the world's 6 billion people, whereas two-way reciprocal kinships are extremely rare by comparison. Based on samples of Canadian college students, Salmon and Daly (1996) found that in brother-sister pairs with identical kindreds sisters recalled more relatives ($M = 31.9$) than did brothers ($M = 27.5$). Our research indicates that American college students list only five or so biological kin and five or so psychological kin that can be depended on in time of need (Nava, 1994). Thus, we may surmise that only 30 or so kinship objects occupy the cognitive fields of most people, and the number is far less for those likely to provide reliable social support. The numbers are further restricted in terms of those who are considered "closest kin." Bailey and Nava (1989) found that the mother was considered the closest kin for nearly one-half of their college-age respondents (54% for females and 42% for males), whereas fathers were chosen far less frequently (8% for females and 25% for males). Brothers and sisters differed little in choosing a sibling as closest kin (M = 14% for males and females combined). In a later study, Nava (1994) asked college students (N = 200) to identity their closest parent and 83% of the females and 73% of the males chose the mother.

Whereas the Nava data focused on closest biological kin, Salmon and Daly (1996) asked their Canadian college students (N = 300; 150 females and 150 males) slightly different questions. First, students were asked to list 10 different statements in response to the question, "Who are you?"; 53% of the females and 51% of the males mentioned a family category (mother, father, sibling, etc.), a family name, or both in defining themselves. Females were more likely to mention family roles (e.g., "I am a daughter"), whereas males were more likely to mention their surname (e.g., "I am a Smith"). In fact, 44% of the females characterized themselves as a daughter, but only 12.5% of the males mentioned being a son. Second, students were asked to name the one person (whether family member or not) that he or she felt closest to. Males and females responded similarly across the categories of relatives, mates, and unrelated friends (that is, between biological and psychological kin), with mothers being chosen by 25.7% of males and females combined, mates by 25.7%, unrelated friend by 27.7%, and fathers by only 7%. Clearly, for these young, mostly freshman, college students away from home, psychological kin in the form of unrelated friends and mates were a major part of their cognitive field of relationships.

Cognitive Mechanisms in Kinship Formation

Kinship is a natural cognitive category that is central to many forms of social behavior (see Hirschfeld, 1986). The fundamental mechanisms of kinship (e.g., recognition, assessment of relative value and closeness, classification into meaningful categories, and processes of naming) revolve around attributions, thoughts, and decisions about oneself in relation to others. Non-kinship and two-way kinship relations are fairly straightforward cognitively, but one-way or non-relational kinship is a complex category. One-way kinship falls under the heading of *imbalanced kinships* (Bailey, 2000) where one member of a social dyad contributes far more than the other. In fact, the passive member of the one-way kinship dyad might know little or nothing of the individual who views him or her as kin or a loved one, and, for all practical purposes, the active member is a nonentity. Examples might include the obsessive infatuation of an adopted child with the unknown birth mother, the agonizing longing for a deceased loved one, the delusional attribution of kinship in psychotics ("I am the sister of the Virgin Mary"), or the malattribution of kinship in erotomania where the object of affection files charges rather than reciprocating in kind.

Once one member of a dyad firmly classifies the other as kin or a loved one there is a tendency to project or attribute reciprocal classification to that person. That is, a person who heavily invests in another often presumes that the kinship object reciprocates in kind despite little or no supporting evidence. Such stretching of reality and downright distortion is especially common where sexual love is involved. As one elderly client said of a wife who had reluctantly stayed in a loveless marriage for 60 years, "She loves me dearly and our marriage has been a perfect one. There has never been an unkind word between us in all these years." Even more dramatic are the projections that sperm-donor offspring often have about their almost mythical natural fathers. In California donors agree in writing to allow offspring to contact them upon reaching age eighteen, and one such daughter said she hoped her natural father would be "a 1950s, all-American type of dad" (Wronge & Scheinin, 2002, p. A7).

Clearly, kinship formation is a complex process involving a sequence of psychological operations. Figure 2.1 outlines the process of one-way kinship formation for the kinship subject or classifier. First, there must be a *kinship object* to start the process in motion. Typically the kinship object is a real person in the subject's social world; this was no doubt the usual case in ancestral environments. In modern society, however, individuals are exposed to numerous possible kinship objects through chance encounters, identification with entertainment, athletic, and political figures, creation of objects in fantasy, and so on.

Once an object has been identified or created, he or she possesses or is attributed certain defining characteristics that allow a person to *recognize* him or her in a reliable way. There is a large literature on kinship recognition in animals and human beings (Hepper, 1991; Holmes & Sherman, 1982; Pfennig & Sherman, 1995), and Erickson (2000) states that "to behave adaptively organisms must in some, presumably

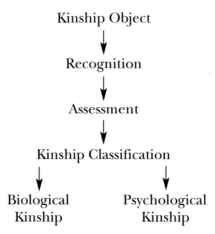

Figure 2.1. The process of kinship formation.

unconscious way, 'recognize' their kin" (p. 216). Technically, kin recognition refers to "the differential treatment of conspecifics as a function of their genetic relatedness" (Holmes & Sherman, 1982). For present purposes, kin recognition is defined as establishing and implementing reliable methods for identifying a kinship object. If an object cannot be reliably identified, then kinship cannot be formed initially or effectively maintained thereafter. If a college student cannot recognize mom after a long absence due to changes in appearance or behavior, or if the student's capacity for recognition is compromised in some way (e.g., alcohol inebriation), the kinship *relationship* is momentarily suspended. They are still technically kin but the relationship cannot operate when one or both parties cannot recognize the other.

In theory, we must perpetually *re-recognize* loved ones of long-standing each time we encounter them or think of them in memory. Kinship recognition is so subtle and automatic that we take it for granted. However, without an internal image of the person (mom's "picture" in the mind's eye), the necessary *who* of the kinship is lost. One of the most devastating losses of function in advanced Alzheimer's disease is the ability to recognize even the closest loved ones. The disease "gradually robs a patient first of recent memory, then of more remote memory, and finally of the abilities to recognize family members and to function independently" (Kolb & Whisaw, 1990, pp. 830–831).

The next stage in kinship formation is *assessment*. To quote Daly and Wilson (1988), "Our hypothesis is that natural selection has shaped psychological mechanisms of interpersonal 'valuation' such that Ego will ordinarily tend to value other individuals in rough proportion to their expected contribution to Ego's inclusive fitness" (p. 32). The probable first step in assessing possible kin objects is to clarify their in-group versus out-group status (Bailey, 1994, 2000). Krebs and Denton (1997) tell us that "Research in social psychology has revealed that when we encounter other people, we immediately and automatically classify them as in-group or out-group, and this categorization structures our subsequent perceptions of them" (p. 21). I suggest that the individual first clarifies *species status* ("Is this a member of my species?"), next, "Is the object safe or a threat?" (see Gilbert, this book). Only then does the evaluation process address *kinship status* ("Is this person a member of my family, clan, or tribe, and, if so, how close?").

Next, the crucial matter of *kinship value* is assessed (see Daly, Salmon, & Wilson, 1997). An individual might be a member of one's own species and kin aggregation, but nevertheless be essentially worthless to one's inclusive fitness. The individual might be severely handicapped physically or mentally, reared by a rival group (and now group loyalty is questionable), or too genetically and socially distant to add much to one's inclusive fitness. In the last analysis, assessment processes were designed by natural selection to evaluate possible or current kin objects in terms of their likely contribution to the evaluator's inclusive fitness system. The goal is not merely to have kin, but "good and useful kin."

After successfully passing through the recognition and assessment filtering systems, the object is *classified* into appropriate *kinship categories*. The most fundamental distinction at this point is between *biological kinship* (genetic relationship plus classification as kin) and *psychological kinship* (classification as kin without genetic relationship). Both of these categories are considered to be true kin and have been discussed at length elsewhere (Bailey, 1987, 1988, 2000). Both kinship terms are "sincerely employed," to use Hirschfeld's (1986) criterion. Whether or not a person and potential kin-object share family genes, *true kinship* occurs when a person *makes the cognitive decision to classify the object as either biological or psychological kin*. True kin stands in contrast to categories such as nominal kin (e.g., this is a "family restaurant"), kin-like relations (warm relations in the absence of classification), or acquaintanceships and friendships in the absence of classification (Bailey, 2000). In the kinship model, there can be no kinship without classification as either biological or psychological kin.

Kinship formation is then an essentially cognitive phenomenon erected upon an implicit *decision* to incorporate someone into one's own preexisting inclusive fitness system. This does not mean that we rationally evaluate others as if buying a car or choosing a stockbroker; much to the contrary, the process is ancient, wired into the brain, more or less automatic, and probably more unconscious than conscious (see Gilbert this book, and Smith, 1999). The evolved human mind consists of numerous psychological mechanisms and adaptations (Cory, 2000) with their own structures, functions, and algorithms. Many of these were designed to assess, evaluate, structure, or otherwise solve problems in interpersonal and individual-group relationships. Gilbert (2000), for example, argues that various evolved *social mentalities* (e.g., information-processing strategies and algorithms for care eliciting/seeking, care giving/providing, mate selection, alliance formation, and ranking behavior) are the foundation stones for the concept of self, systems of internal meaning, role-taking behavior, social signaling, self and other evaluation processes, and a host of other crucial functions. The kinship assessment mechanism appears to be one of the most basic and universal of these social mentalities.

Kinship Relationships

We have seen that one can engage in a one-way kinship with an object who may be unaware of one's existence or who may be nothing more than a wishful projection. Typically, however, people engage in *kinship relationships* involving mutual recognition, assessment, and classification. This does not mean that the kinship relationship is necessarily enjoyable, personally enhancing, or psychologically healthy for the parties involved. A kinship relationship merely requires that both parties classify each other as either biological or psychological kin; beyond that the relationship may go in a multitude of directions. Moreover, no human relationship is perfectly balanced in terms of resource sharing, costs versus benefits, or precise equity in expressed love and affection. Even the best of human kin relations involve competition, occasional conflict, and control issues.

In today's world, kinship relations operate within a larger context of family, clan, tribal, ethnic, religious, and nationalistic presses and role expectations. In most cultures, individuals are not completely free to relate to others as they might choose in the abstract. In fact, observance of prevailing kinship rules, including whom one can have sex with, marry, or associate with, is generally reinforced by strong sanctions. Transgressions carry the risk of being disowned or even killed (e.g., honor killing of an adulterous wife). Moreover, many different forms of kin-related social behavior are illegal and punishable by law: child abuse or exploitation, spouse abuse, incest, failure to pay child support, bigamy, spousal or child abandonment, and so on. Clearly, there are numerous familial and extrafamilial presses ranging from home to nation that limit, modulate, and otherwise affect our social relationships including kinship.

Human beings expect and need various kinds of social input to develop, mature, and operate effectively (McGuire & Troisi, 1998), and indeed, human beings evolved to seek out certain social roles and to pursue various social goals (Gilbert, this book). For example, each of the following kinship roles is a complex amalgamation of human needs on the one hand and cultural presses on the other: mother, father, offspring, brother, sister, grandparent, cousin, uncle or aunt, husband or wife, or in-law. Daly, Salmon, and Wilson (1997) and Wilson and Daly (1997) argue for a relationship-specific kinship psychology in which specialized motivational and information-processing devices cope with the particular demands of particular kinship categories. Clearly, once a kinship object is classified and included within a person's inclusive fitness system he or she may be pushed/pulled toward a pre-existing role configuration (e.g., "mother" if she has produced offspring), or simply accepted as a generic family member pending more specific categorization.

Inclusion into a preexisting kinship system is a serious matter. The new kin not only assumes new role expectations but a host of responsibilities and possible liabilities as well. In the worst case scenario, the object may find him- or herself confined in a "golden cage" of kinship (Maryanski & Turner, 1992) or a tangled "web of obligation" (Bailey & Wood, 1998). Indeed, kinship relations may be adaptive biologically even when fraught with tension and conflict (as when healthy offspring are reared in an unhappy marriage). Moreover, kinship relations are structured more around obligations, responsibilities, and role expectations than by warm feelings, mutual enjoyment, or receipt of material resources (Bailey, 2000; Bailey & Wood, 1998). Nevertheless, most kin relations do involve warm feelings and hedonic outcomes, and these appear to yield the most beneficial physical and psychological outcomes (Bailey, 2000).

Figure 2.2 outlines the dynamics of dyadic kin relations in terms of hedonic (warm/pleasurable) and agonic (conflictual/unpleasurable) outcomes (see Chance, 1988; Gilbert, 1989, 1992). In both higher primates and humans, social relations tend to be either hedonic, agonic, or some mixture of the two (Price, 1988), and these two mental modes extend into every nook and cranny of human experience.

Hedonic and agonic outcomes are strongly influenced by the degree of *balance* in existing relationships (see Baumeister & Leary, 1995, on mutuality and reciprocity in relationships, and Bloch & Sperber, in press, on institutionalized imbalances in kinship systems). Each member of the biological or psychological kinship dyad implicitly takes on various obligations and role assignments, and each derives some degree of emotional and/or material benefit from the relationship. Any kinship relationship automatically pulls its members into a complex arena of give and take; each member constantly monitors and *assesses* current levels of balanced or mutual giving. This cost:benefit assessment is different from that in kinship formation, where the focus is on the person and whether and how he or she fits into the kinship array (Bailey, 2000).

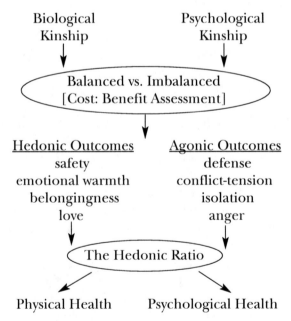

Figure 2.2. Kinship relations.

Cost:benefit assessment characterizes all relationships where potential or actual social exchanges are involved, and its function is to detect imbalances, deception, exploitation, and unfairness in a relationship patterns of giving and receiving (Bailey, 2000). Such assessment addresses valued resources that include provision of love, sex, emotional support, advice and decision-making, and a host of fiduciary and material goods. Assessment is most active in the early phases of kinship where roles are being defined, and it may be more or less suspended in happy and stable relationships of long-standing. Extremely close intimates may, in fact, be turned off by demands for precise reciprocity (Shackelford & Buss, 1996), and many close kin are no doubt resigned to obligate giving without balanced reciprocation. However, introduction of significant change, stress, or additional imbalance into a relationship will immediately reactivate the assessment mechanism, and failure to resolve the problem may lead to agonic outcomes.

When a member of the kinship dyad views the relationship as reasonably balanced, then the *hedonic-agonic ratio* (Figure 2.2) favors hedonic outcomes (e.g., feelings/perceptions/thoughts of safety, warmth, belonging, and love). The opposite occurs when a personally unfavorable imbalance is detected. When biological and psychological kinships are both balanced and strong (e.g., firm and reliable classification as kin), they are most conducive to good physical and psychological health in modern human beings (see Bailey, 2000, for references). By contrast, grievously imbalanced relationships with a high agonic-hedonic ratio may have dysphoric and even deadly consequences.

Bailey (2000) discussed a case in which a client precipitated a marital crisis by telling his wife about a brief affair that had occurred over twenty years ago. The crisis was greatly aggravated by the preexisting relationship imbalance that had characterized their twenty-seven years of marriage. Although the wife was the more intelligent and resourceful partner in their highly successful family business, the husband was very protective of his role as the titular head of the company. As the wife operated behind the scenes as the heart and soul of the company while simultaneously raising two children, great resentment was building that spilled over after the infidelity was revealed. The husband was immediately reclassified in psychological kinship terms and became the hated outsider and an enemy. The wife had not given up on him entirely, however, and she put him through several months of rather brutal guilt inducement, fits of screaming and recrimination, and actual physical beatings several times. His guilt was monumental and he was willing to make any concession, but she was unable to forgive or reestablish the psychological kinship. In the fall of 2001, he suffered a stroke and died at age 61.

The Cognitive Bases of Kinship

Kinship is a major tributary in the cognitive flow of information that defines culture (Bloch & Sperber, 2002), and it is particularly attractive as a lexical/conceptual domain (Hirschfeld, 1986). Following recent developments in cognitive science, including parallel distributed process models and neural network models, anthropologists have turned their attention to the collective representations that underlie shared cultural knowledge. In 1996, the American Anthropological Association hosted a session on *distributed cognition* that focused on the roles that shared expectations and meanings play in linguistic and nonlinguistic communication, cooperative behavior and mutual understanding, and culture in general. In his paper on kinship and cultural phenomena, Dwight Read (1996) pointed out that culture is located in the minds of individuals, and, moreover, that kinship is a powerful exemplar of the social flow of information. From the concrete use of kinship names to the most abstract kinship meanings, *processes of cognition* are always a part of the picture (see Hirschfeld, 1986).

All psychological adaptations in humans have motivational, emotional, behavioral, and cognitive components, and this is true of kinship. For example, we are motivated to attach, bond, and socialize with valued others; we experience feelings of warmth and affection toward the valued other; we seek out, interact with, and sacrifice for valued others; and we share beliefs and symbols with them. In my approach to kinship psychology, cognition is the defining component given the fundamental importance of first classification as kin, and then second, the assignment of selected kin into conceptually rich and psychologically meaningful social role domains (mother, father, daughter, brother-in-law, and so forth). Processes of recognition, cost:benefit assessment, warmth, altruism, shared values, and a host of other variables contribute to kinship experience, but the initial willingness to classify the other as "family" and as a genuine relative (biological or psychological) is the essence of kinship.

This line of reasoning leads to the *cognitive rule of kinship,* that is, kinship formation and kinship relations are predicated first on an initial classification of the object as kin; the object is implicitly and isomorphically reclassified as kin each time he or she enters one's field of conscious perception or memory. Isomorphic reclassification assumes that any and all assessment mechanisms have been more or less deactivated during the time that the object is out of the person's cognitive field of kinship relations. Activation of assessment mechanisms immediately places classification under threat and in the worst-case scenario can lead to seriously diminished kinship value or even *declassification,* where the kinship object loses kinship status. That is exactly what happened in the earlier example involving the unfaithful husband and the unforgiving wife. Much of the misery in human relations can be attributed to the threat of diminished reclassification or actual loss of kin status. In the final analysis, stable and satisfying kinship relations are erected upon secure classification as kin with little or no threat of declassification (strong kinships) and fair and equitable relations between members of the kinship dyad (balanced kinships).

Implications for Evolutionary Kinship Therapy

The implications of kinship theory and kinship psychology for the practice of psychotherapy have been discussed elsewhere (Bailey, 1988; Bailey, 2000; Bailey & Wood, 1998; Bailey, Wood, & Nava, 1992). However, a fundamentally important therapy issue will be briefly addressed here: the underlying kinship dynamics of the client-therapist relationship.

Kinship and the Client-Therapist Relationship

There is agreement among modern psychotherapists that the client-therapist bond (Orlinsky & Howard, 1986), helping attachment (Orlinsky, 1989), friendship (Schofield, 1964), working alliance (Bordin, 1979), or personal relationship (Derlega, Hendrick, Winstead, & Berg, 1991) is fundamental to the treatment process. Its many functions include serving as a safe and open environment for exploring painful issues (i.e., a secure base); offering a confiding partnership for mutually exploring treatment options (Arkowitz, 1992); providing a setting for "regressively renegotiating" transference issues in evolutionary psychoanalysis (Slavin & Kriegman, 1992); serving as an empowering "band of two" in the treatment process (Glantz & Pearce, 1989) and a powerful agent of client insight, change, and growth (Kriegman, 2000); and exerting a physiological and psychological regulating effect on the client's emotional, behavioral, and cognitive systems (Troisi & McGuire, 2000). The therapeutic relationship is also a strong empirical predictor of positive therapy outcomes (Orlinsky, 1989).

Cognitive therapists, like other therapists, know that the client-therapist relationship is important—and sometimes crucial—in terms of both process and outcome. They often refer to the relationship as "collaborative" (e.g., Beck, Rush, Shaw, & Emory, 1979) but fail to recognize that collaboration is often an *outcome* as well as a *cause* of positive relating. Moreover, client-therapist collaboration is a highly complex process of social interaction that is likely to activate various kinship mechanisms in both parties. Recognition and assessment mechanisms are necessarily activated in all stable and meaningful relationships (i.e., "collaboration"), but problems may arise when one or both parties progress into the realm of kinship classification. The cognitive therapist is in a particularly good position to discern when the therapist or the client is moving into the dangerous waters of kinship attribution and classification.

Despite its many salubrious aspects, the client-therapist relationship raises a serious conundrum from the evolutionary standpoint. If human beings are evolutionarily prepared to pursue self-interest and the interests of those they classify as kin (i.e., inclusive fitness), and, given that clients and therapists represent separate and implicitly competitive inclusive fitness systems, then how does the client-therapist relationship work at all, much less have psychological benefits? How does this disquieting fact intersect with issues of therapist professionalism and neutrality versus client trust and emotional neediness, therapist power and client compliance, therapist and client differences in levels of personal involvement in therapy, and therapist versus client biosocial goal-seeking efforts within the therapy context (see Bailey & Gilbert, 2000)? Moreover, given that highly stressed clients are often inclined to view the therapist as a kinship object potentially advantageous to their inclusive fitness systems (see Bailey, Wood, & Nava, 1992), what is the therapist to do when "real" relationship issues surface in treatment?

Slavin and Kriegman (1992) address these questions in their book on evolutionary psychoanalysis. While acknowledging the fundamental benefits of the client-therapist relationship, they, nevertheless, see it as an unnatural phenomenon that requires the client to reveal deeply personal matters to an unrelated other (the therapist) in a context where both participants actively pursue goals of inclusive self-interest. Moreover, strategies of deception and self-deception characterize both parties in the process, and failure of the therapist to acknowledge this fact is problematic. The evolutionary approach puts a whole new face on the issue of countertransference, and places a heavy burden on the therapist to truly "know thyself" when it comes to biosocial goal-seeking in the therapy context.

The kinship model sees the client-therapist relationship as a quasi-kinship or kin-like phenomenon (Bailey & Wood, 1998; Erickson, 2000; O'Connor, 2000; Wood, 1997) where natural kinship forming and maintenance mechanisms are constrained and modulated in both parties to fit the professional context of treatment. However, this does not mean that such mechanisms and their associated cognitive meanings are completely nullified or neutralized, especially where the kinship-deprived client is concerned (Bailey, Wood, & Nava, 1992). The typical client-therapist dyad falls under the category of imbalanced relationships where the therapist gives relatively little in terms of social intimacy (Slavin & Kriegman, 1992), but where the stressed and often lonely client is highly motivated to form one-way and unreciprocated kin or kin-like relations with the therapist. The relationship essentially ends for the therapist with the end of the session, but the client may nurse hurt feelings until the next session, obsess about "how does the therapist *really* feel about me"?, engage in fantasies about rescuing or being rescued by the therapist, engage in sexual fantasies involving the therapist, or simply dream of "being family" with the therapist (see the case of Jennie in Bailey, 2000, regarding the latter issue). Especially needy clients often yearn for the therapist to fill long-lost parental roles much in the way that the sperm donor children mentioned earlier long for their "mythical" biological fathers. Slavin and Kriegman (1992) quote a revealing request by a desperate patient to her therapist (cited in Eigen, 1991): "What I need is simple . . . it is simply what you'd give a child of your own. The simplest thing in the world." So simple and profound, yet so impossible in the context of professional psychotherapy.

How can the *central dilemma of the client-therapist relationship*, that is, the collision of independent inclusive fitness systems and the inherent imbalances in emotional neediness and giving, be resolved? Rarely, if ever, can it be resolved by allowing a full-fledged two-way balanced kinship to develop. Such kinships have been the natural staple of human relationships throughout human evolution, but we must concede at the outset that the client-therapist relationship will be of a lesser order. Moreover, it is not appropriate to allow a serious, one-way, nonreciprocal kinship to develop that is based on sexual attraction, the need to classify the therapist as family, or some combination of the two. I believe that these issues account for much of what is called transference in therapy. *Kinship transference* projects a system of unrealistic meanings on the therapist and, like traditional forms, it requires subtle exploration of a patient's thoughts and images, mutual understanding, and compassionate resolution. If the therapist cannot be a parental object (biological kin) or a non-genetic relative in the form of a spouse, in-law, or close friend (psychological kin), then what options are left for a real relationship?

In broader terms, we are asking, "How may genetic strangers interact with one another in a way that preserves some of the good of family consanguinity while at the same time maintaining necessary boundaries and independent fitness systems?" Disciplinary issues, professional ethics, personal theories, and proprietary matters place even more restrictions on the client-therapist relationship than the usual stranger-to-stranger interaction. The kinship model proposes that the central dilemma of client-therapist relationship is partially resolved when we cast the relationship in *kin-like terms* (Wood, 1997). That is, client and therapist may activate recognition and assessment processes (with primary emphasis on reciprocal exchange) but short of any hint of *classifying the other as psychological kin.* Both client and therapist act as if the other could have been "true kin" under other circumstances, and fair and balanced exchanges of emotional warmth, respect, and concern are allowed. Moreover, this approach tends to negate the *kinship double standard* or kinship favoritism that naturally comes into play when genetic strangers barter, negotiate, and engage in reciprocal exchanges (Bailey & Wood, 1998). However, both parties must be clear that the relationship cannot be allowed to progress to true kinship because of the inherent professional and ethical constraints on the practice of psychotherapy.

Conclusion

Kinship is a powerful organizer of thoughts, attributions, and desires in social contexts. In contrast to attachment theory, it addresses a wide range of relationships over the life span and provides a comprehensive system of classifying and categorizing all significant others in a person's social life space. In therapy, many patients will have streams of automatic thoughts about their therapist (e.g., to parent or be parented; to be supported by a strong, reliable friend/ally; or to impose roles of sibling, lover, or "good old uncle" onto the therapist). These streams of thoughts will, as a minimum, activate kinship recognition and assessment mechanisms, and are likely to bring kinship attribution/classification into play. Patients who have disturbed early kinship relationships or fractured current ones, may actively look for someone to assume a central kinship role in their lives. Other similarly deprived patients may be so emotionally damaged, lonely, and socially alienated that they are hostile to others, withdrawn, and resigned to being outsiders. Clearly, each of our patients exhibits a different and unique pattern of kinship needs, kinship support, and kinship cognitions. Thus, it behooves cognitive therapists to be aware of and to tune into kinship thoughts and images, to recognize that some of these thoughts are related to evolved kinship-seeking mechanisms, and (as in most evolutionary approaches to psychotherapy) to share these ideas with their patients. The meaning of these issues for the wider work of therapy can be explored with patients with a special focus on automatic thoughts about kinship in their social relationships.

References

Aiello, L. C., & Dunbar, R. I. M. (1993). Neocortex size, group size, and the evolution of language. *Current Anthropology, 34,* 184–193.

Arkowitz, H. (1992). A common factors theory of depression. In J. C. Norcross & M. R. Goldfried (Eds.), *Handbook of psychotherapy integration* (pp. 402–432). New York: Basic Books.

Atkinson, L., & Zucker, K. J. (Eds.). (1997). *Attachment and psychopathology.* New York: Guilford.

Bailey, K. G. (1987). *Human paleopsychology: Applications to aggression and pathological processes.* Hillsdale, NJ: Erlbaum.

Bailey, K. G. (1988). Psychological kinship: Implications for the helping professions. *Psychotherapy, 25,* 132–142.

Bailey, K. G. (1994). Our kind-their kind: Response to Gardner's we-they distinction. *ASCAP Newsletter, 7,* 5–8.

Bailey, K. G. (1997, June). *Evolutionary kinship therapy: Merging integrative psychotherapy with the new kinship psychology.* Paper presented at the annual meeting of the ASCAP Society, Tucson, AZ.

Bailey, K. G. (2000). Evolution, kinship, and psychotherapy: Promoting psychological health through human relationships. In P. Gilbert & K. Bailey (Eds.), *Genes on the couch: Explorations in evolutionary psychotherapy* (pp. 42–68). Philadelphia: Taylor & Francis.

Bailey, K. G., & Gilbert, P. (2000). Evolutionary psychotherapy: Where to from here? In P. Gilbert & K. Bailey (Eds.), *Genes on the couch: Explorations in evolutionary psychotherapy* (pp. 333–348). Philadelphia: Taylor & Francis.

Bailey, K. G., & Nava, G. (1989). Psychological kinship, love, and liking: Preliminary validity data. *Journal of Clinical Psychology, 45,* 587–594.

Bailey, K. G., & Wood, H. E. (1998). Evolutionary kinship therapy: Basic principles and treatment applications. *British Journal of Medical Psychology, 71,* 509–523.

Bailey, K. G., Wood, H. E., & Nava, G. R. (1992). What do clients want? Role of psychological kinship in professional helping. *Journal of Psychotherapy Integration, 2,* 125–147.

Baumeister, R. F., & Leary, M. R. (1995). The need to belong: Desire for interpersonal attachments as a fundamental human motivation. *Psychological Bulletin, 117,* 497–529.

Baumeister, R. F., & Tice, D. M. (1990). Anxiety and social exclusion. *Journal of Social and Clinical Psychology, 9,* 165–195.

Beck, A. T., Rush, A. J., Shaw, B. F., & Emory, G. (1979). *Cognitive therapy of depression.* New York: Guilford.

Bloch, M., & Sperber, D. (2002). Kinship and evolved dispositions: The mother's brother controversy reconsidered. *Current Anthropology, 43,* 723–748.

Bordin, D. (1979). The generalizability of the psychoanalytic concept of the working alliance. *Psychotherapy: Theory, Research, and Practice, 16,* 252–260.

Bowlby, J. (1988) *A secure base: Parent-child attachment and healthy human development.* New York: Basic Books.

Brennan, K. A., Shaver, P. R., & Tobey, A. E. (1991). Attachment styles, gender, and parental problem drinking. *Journal of Personal and Social Relationships, 8,* 451–466.

Caporael, L. R., & Baron, R. M. (1997). Groups as the mind's natural environment. In J. A. Simpson & D. T. Kendrick (Eds.), *Evolutionary social psychology* (pp. 317–344). Mahwah, NJ: Erlbaum.

Carter, C. S., Lederhendler, I., & Kirkpatrick, B. (Eds.). (1997). *The integrative neurobiology of affiliation.* New York: New York Academy of Sciences.

Chance, M. R. A. (Ed.). (1988). *Social fabrics of the mind.* London, UK: Erlbaum.

Cory, G. A., Jr. (2000). *Toward consilience: The bioneurological basis of behavior, thought, experience, and language.* New York: Kluwer Academic/Plenum.

Daly, M., Salmon, C., & Wilson, M. (1997). Kinship: The conceptual hole in psychological studies of social cognition and close relationships. In J. A. Simpson & D. T. Kendrick (Eds.), *Evolutionary social psychology* (pp. 265–296). Mahwah, NJ: Erlbaum.

Daly, M., & Wilson, M. (1988). *Homicide.* New York: Aldine De Gruyter.

DeLongis, A., Folkman, S., & Lazarus, R. S. (1988). The impact of daily stress on health and mood: Psychological and social resources as mediators. *Journal of Personality and Social Psychology, 54,* 486–495.

Derlega, V. J., Hendrick, S. S., Winstead, B. A., & Berg, J. H. (1991). *Psychotherapy as a personal relationship.* New York: Guilford.

Dunbar, R. I. M. (1992). Neocortex size as a constraint on group size in primates. *Journal of Human Evolution, 22,* 469–493.

Eigen, M. (1991). Boa and flowers. *Psychoanalytic Dialogues, 1*(1), 106–118.

Erickson, M. T. (1993). Rethinking Oedipus: An evolutionary perspective on incest avoidance. *American Journal of Psychiatry, 150*(3), 411–416.

Erickson, M. T. (2000). The evolution of incest avoidance: Oedipus and the psychopathologies of kinship. In P. Gilbert and K. Bailey (Eds.), *Genes on the couch: Explorations in evolutionary psychotherapy* (pp. 211–231). Philadelphia: Taylor & Francis.

Gilbert, P. (1989). *Human nature and suffering.* Hillsdale, NJ: Erlbaum.

Gilbert, P. (1992). *Depression: The evolution of powerlessness.* New York: Guilford.

Gilbert, P. (1997). The biopsychology of meaning. In M. Power & C. R. Brewin (Eds.), *The transformation of meaning: Reconciliation theory and therapy in cognitive, behaviour and related therapies* (pp. 33–56). New York: Wiley.

Gilbert, P. (2000). Social mentalities: Inner "social" conflict and the role of inner warmth and compassion in cognitive therapy. In P. Gilbert and K. Bailey (Eds.), *Genes on the couch: Explorations in evolutionary psychotherapy* (pp. 118–150). Philadelphia: Taylor & Francis.

Glantz, K., & Pearce, J. K. (1989). *Exiles from Eden.* New York: Norton.

Goodwin, J. S., Hunt, W. C., Key, C. R., & Samet, J. M. (1987). The effect of marital status on stage, treatment, and survival of cancer patients. *Journal of the American Medical Association, 258,* 3125–3130.

Hazan, C., & Shaver, P. R. (1994). Deeper into attachment theory. *Psychological Inquiry, 5,* 68–79.

Hazan, C., & Zeifman, D. (1994). Sex and the psychological tether. *Advances in Personal Relationships, 5,* 151–177.

Henderson, S. (1982). The significance of social relationships in the etiology of neurosis. In C. Parks & J. Stevenson-Hinde (Eds.), *The place of attachment in human behavior* (pp. 205–231). New York: Basic Books.

Hepper, P. G. (1991). Recognizing kin: Ontogeny and classification. In P. G. Hepper (Ed.), *Kin recognition* (pp. 259–288). Cambridge, UK: Cambridge University Press.

Hirschfeld, L. A. (1986). Kinship and cognition: Genealogy and the meaning of kinship terms. *Current Anthropology, 27,* 217–242.

Holmes, W. G., & Sherman, P. W. (1982). "Kin recognition in animals." *American Scientist, 71,* 46–55.

House, J. S., Landis, K. R., & Umberson, D. (1988). Social relationships and health. *Science, 241,* 540–544.

Kolb, B., & Whisaw, I. Q. (1990). *Fundamentals of human neuropsychology.* New York: Freeman.

Krebs, D. L., & Denton, K. (1997). Social illusions and self-deception: The evolution of biases in person perception. In J. A. Simpson & D. T. Kendrick (Eds.), *Evolutionary social psychology* (pp. 21–48). Mahwah, NJ: Erlbaum.

Kriegman, D. (2000). Evolutionary psychoanalysis: Toward an adaptive, biological perspective on the clinical process in psychoanalytic psychotherapy. In P. Gilbert & K. Bailey (Eds.), *Genes on the couch: Explorations in evolutionary psychotherapy* (pp. 71–92). Philadelphia: Taylor & Francis.

Leach, E. (1966). *Virgin birth* (pp. 39–49). Proceedings of the Royal Anthropological Institute of Great Britain and Ireland, London, England.

Lewin, R. (1993). *Human evolution: An illustrated introduction.* Oxford, UK: Blackwell Scientific.

Lynch, J. J. (1979). *The broken heart: The medical consequences of loneliness.* New York: Basic Books.

Maryanski, A., & Turner, J. H. (1992). *The social cage: Human nature and the evolution of society.* Stanford, CA: Stanford University Press.

McGuire, M., & Troisi, A. (1998). *Darwinian psychiatry.* New York: Oxford University Press.

Mellen, S. L. W. (1981). *The evolution of love.* San Francisco: Freeman.

Nava, G. R. (1994). *Actual and perceived social support, love, liking, and family love as predictors of perceived obligation/entitlement and depression.* Unpublished doctoral dissertation, Virginia Commonwealth University, Richmond, Virginia.

Nesse, R. M., & Williams, G. C. (1995). *Why we get sick.* New York: Random House.

O'Connor, L. E. (2000). Pathogenic beliefs and guilt in human evolution: Implications for psychotherapy. In P. Gilbert & K. Bailey (Eds.), *Genes on the couch: Explorations in evolutionary psychotherapy* (pp. 276–303). Philadelphia: Taylor & Francis.

Orlinsky, D. E. (1989). Researchers' images of psychotherapy: Their origins and influence on research. *Clinical Psychology Review, 9,* 413–441.

Orlinsky, D. E., & Howard, K. I. (1986). The psychological interior of psychotherapy: Explorations with the therapy session reports. In L. S. Greenberg & W. M. Pinsof (Eds.), *Psychotherapeutic process: A research handbook* (pp. 477–501), New York: Guilford.

Panksepp, J., Nelson, E., & Bekkedal, M. (1997). Brain systems for the mediation of social separation-distress and social-reward. Evolutionary antecedents and neuropeptide intermediaries. In C. S. Carter, I. Lederhendler, & B. Kirkpatrick (Eds.), *The integrative neurobiology of affiliation* (pp. 78–100). New York: New York Academy of Sciences.

Parsons, T. (1964). *Essays in sociological theory.* New York: Free Press of Glencoe.

Parsons, T. (1966). *Societies: Evolutionary and comparative perspectives.* Englewood Cliffs, NJ: Prentice Hall.

Pfennig, D. W., & Sherman, P. W. (1995, June). Kin recognition. *Scientific American,* 98–103.

Price, J. S. (1988). Alternative channels for negotiating asymmetry in social relationships. In M. R. A. Chance (Ed.), *Social fabrics of the mind* (pp. 157–195). Hove: Erlbaum.

Price, J. S. (1992). The agonic and hedonic modes: Definition, usage, and the promotion of mental health. *World Futures, 35,* 87–113.

Read, D. W. (1996). *Cultural phenomena as seen through the lens of kinship.* Paper presented at the annual meeting of the American Anthropological Association held San Francisco, CA.

Salmon, C. A., & Daly, M. (1996). On the importance of kin relations to Canadian men and women. *Ethology and Sociobiology, 17,* 289–298.

Schofield, W. (1964). *Psychotherapy: The purchase of friendship.* Englewood Cliffs, NJ: Prentice Hall.

Service, E. R. (1962). *Primitive social organization: An evolutionary perspective.* New York: Random House.

Shackelford, T. K., & Buss, D. M. (1996). Betrayal in friendships, mateships, and coalitions. *Personality and Social Psychology Bulletin, 22,* 1151–1164.

Simpson, J. A., & Rholes, W. S. (Eds.). (1998). *Attachment theory and close relationships.* New York: Guilford.

Slavin, M. O., & Kriegman, D. (1992). *The adaptive design of the human psyche.* New York: Guilford.

Smith, D. L. (1999). Maintaining boundaries in psychotherapy: A view from evolutionary psychoanalysis. In C. Feltham (Ed.), *Controversies in psychotherapy and counseling* (pp. 132–141). London: Sage.

Sroufe, A., & Fleeson, J. (1986). Attachment and the construction of relationships. In W. Hartup & Z. Rubin (Eds.), *Relationships and development* (pp. 51–71). Hillsdale, NJ: Erlbaum.

Swann, W. B., Jr., & Brown, J. D. (1990). From self to health: Self-verification and identity disruption. In B. R. Sarason, I. G. Sarason, & G. R. Pierce (Eds.), *Social support: An interactional view* (pp. 150–172). New York: Wiley.

Troisi, A., & McGuire, M. T. (2000). Psychotherapy in the context of Darwinian psychiatry. In P. Gilbert and K. Bailey (Eds.), *Genes on the couch: Explorations in evolutionary psychotherapy* (pp. 28–41). Philadelphia: Taylor & Francis.

Weiss, R. S. (1979). The emotional impact of marital separation. In G. Levinger & O. C. Moles (Eds.), *Divorce and separation: Context, causes, and consequences* (pp. 201–210). New York: Basic Books.

Wilson, J. Q. (1993). *The moral sense.* New York: The Free Press.

Wilson, M., & Daly, M. (1997). Relationship-specific social psychological adaptations. In G. Bock & G. Cardew (Eds.), *CIBA Foundation symposium on characterizing psychological adaptations* (pp. 253–268). Chichester, UK: Wiley.

Wood, H. E. (1997, June). *Staying in the therapy zone: Kinship and the art of therapeutic process.* Paper presented at the meeting of the ASCAP society, Tucson, AZ.

Wronge, Y. S., & Scheinin, R. (2002, February). Years later, here's Dad. *Richmond Times-Dispatch,* p. A7.

Zeifman, D., & Hazan, C. (1997). Attachment: The bond in pair-bonds. In J. A. Simpson & D. T. Kendrick (Eds.), *Evolutionary social psychology* (pp. 237–263). Mahwah, NJ: Erlbaum.

Chapter 3

Evolutionary Perspectives on Emotion: Making Sense of What We Feel

Leslie S. Greenberg

O ver the last decades the tide has clearly shifted away from viewing emotion as disruptive, and it has become clear that emotions are an evolutionary-based adaptive resource. Emotions involve an evolutionary-based meaning system that informs people of the significance of events to their well-being and organizes them for rapid adaptive action (Frijda, 1986; Izard, 1991; Tomkins, 1963). From birth on, emotion is a primary signaling system that communicates intentions and regulates interaction (Sroufe, 1996). Affect thus provides both information to self and other and action tendencies to organize adaptive action. Emotion thereby regulates self and other, and gives life much of its meaning.

Arguments that support the biological origins of emotion are based both on observations of the phylogenetic continuity of emotional expression and on evolutionary arguments on how selective forces have shaped emotions. Most emotion theorists now agree that an evolutionary foundation is important in understanding emotion (Plutchik, 1980). The key evolutionary argument is that specific situations proposed adaptive challenges, and that individuals with a genetic tendency to adjust to the demands of the situation had an increased ability to cope. This gave them increased reproductive success. Emotion has multiple functions and has been argued to give advantages in a number of domains: communication, motivation, physiology, and cognition. It essentially involves a biologically based meaning system that informs people of the significance of events to their well-being and organizes them for adaptive action (Frijda, 1986). Emotion gives people feedback about what is important and meaningful, about what is good or bad for them, and provides action tendencies to attain affective goals. It is both a primary means of meaning construction at the basis of adaptive viability and a primary signaling system at the basis of attachment. The meaning construction function is seen clearly in how emotion influences cognition, as when anger leads to the attribution of blame. The attachment function is seen clearly in the other-regulating qualities of the infant's cry of distress.

Emotional Experience

According to a number of emotion theories, an important (although not the only) source of emotion production at the psychological level is the tacit appraisal of a situation in terms of one's goals, concerns, or needs (Frijda, 1986; Oatley & Jenkins, 1992). Emotions inform us that an important need, value, or goal may be advanced or harmed in a situation (Frijda, 1986), and they tell us how individuals appraise themselves and their worlds (Greenberg & Korman, 1993; Lazarus, 1991). Emotions are involved in setting goal priorities (Oatley & Jenkins, 1992). They also produce biologically based relational action tendencies that result from the appraisal of the situation based on these goals/needs/concerns (Frijda, 1986; Greenberg & Korman, 1993; Greenberg & Safran, 1986, 1987; Oatley & Jenkins, 1992; Safran & Greenberg, 1991). Action tendencies have been defined as the readiness to act in a particular way so as to establish, maintain, or alter the relationship with one's environment (Arnold, 1960; Frijda, 1986). Different action tendencies correspond to different emotions. For example, fear is associated with the mobilization for flight, while anger involves the urge to attack, repel, or break free.

Research in the bioevolutionary domain suggests that there are a number of innate primary emotions, each with a characteristic action tendency and facial expression (Ekman & Friesen, 1975; Izard, 1991, 1984; Plutchik, 2000). Examples of primary emotions are fear, joy, and anger. With their attendant action tendencies, primary emotions are thus hardwired expressive-motor responses that mobilize the individual for adaptive action and convey pertinent information to others. Primary emotions focus attention, interrupt other behavioral and cognitive activities, and prepare the organism for the execution of adaptive behavior. Other, more complex emotions, like pride and jealousy, are less obviously associated with concrete or particular action tendencies or with facial expressions. Instead, a given social context or a developed script more fully defines these emotions. But more complex emotions still appear to be based on appraisals of the relevance of a situation to a need/goal/concern, are motivational in nature, and inform people of the significance of events to them.

In order to aid survival, evolution has blessed humanity with more negative basic emotions than positive ones. Negative emotions such as anxiety, anger, sorrow, and regret are useful or they would not exist. Unpleasant feelings draw people's attention to matters important to their well-being. Healthy adaptation thus necessitates learning to be aware of, to tolerate, and to regulate negative emotionality (Frijda 1986; Tomkins, 1962), as well as to enjoy positive emotionality for the benefits it endows (Fredrickson, 1998). Dysfunction in the ability to access and process emotional information, both positive and negative, thus disconnects people from one of their most adaptive orientation and meaning production systems (Frijda, 1986; Izard, 1991).

Although it is important to recognize the adaptive function of emotions it is clear that emotions can at times be maladaptive, either through misapplication or through learning. Evolutionary adaptive emotions do not always work adaptively, especially in modern environments. Many of our emotions were designed to work in simpler and smaller ancestral social environments. Retaliatory rage is one thing in monkeys but quite different if one has a gun or access to nuclear weapons. The desire to be special and approved of in a small, stable hunter/gatherer group might look very different in modern-day large groups and competitive lifestyles and in societies with huge variations in resources. Social anxiety might function quite differently when one is unlikely to meet many strangers. In other words, it is difficult to talk simply about the adaptiveness of emotion outside of the contexts for which they were adapted (see Gilbert, this book). In addition, since evolution creates variations within species, the affect repertoires of humans show individual differences, such that some people are more easily triggered into anxiety, rage, or joy than others. The focus in this chapter on the general processes of adaptive affective meaning making and affect regulation should therefore not be taken as a denial of the importance of within-group variation, that is, of individual differences as a source of difficulty, or of the existence of maladaptiveness in the emotional domain.

Emotional Expression

The expression of emotion also has an important evolutionary basis. For millions of years, long before verbal language evolved as a communication device, affect and affect expressions (e.g., facial and postural displays) functioned as the main form of social communication, signaling intent and desire. The innate internal mechanisms needed to send and decode social displays are therefore deeply encoded in the human brain. Without them we would struggle to make sense of even the most basic of displays such as a smile or grimace. Indeed, the production of facial expressions has been found in nonhuman primates, the infants, the deaf and blind, and across cultures (Ekman, 1973), suggesting, as Darwin (1872) first noted, that facial expressions have a biological basis and a long phylogenetic history.

An ethological, adaptionist view of facial expressions suggests that facial displays, like many other types of ritualized signals, reliably indicate what behavior is to follow (Fridlund 1994). An organism that displays its intentions can modify the behavior of others in the social group without actually having to perform the entire, energetically costly behavior pattern. The form of the message created by the sender generally evolves in concert with the ability of the recipient to understand the message in an energetic cost-effective way. Facial expressions evolved as a cost-effective way to communicate intentions, which are easily monitored.

Dangerous situations require fast responses for survival, making the perception and recognition of danger especially important. One of the most common and persistent sources of danger to social organisms is aggression from other members of the social group. In the case of aggression, baring of the teeth could warn another of impending attack, giving the recipient the opportunity to change its behavior. By this means, a dangerous attack can be avoided and the survivability of both parties is enhanced by the production and subsequent perception of a display (Fridlund, 1994). Many ethologists consider anger to be the emotional correlate to attack or aggression, a contention supported by the fact that humans and other animals, especially primates, display many of the same facial characteristics during anger and attack. Therefore, angry faces are processed with the same priority and efficiency as are other dangerous environmental stimuli.

Cognition, Emotion, and Motivation

The preceding view on emotional experience and expression implicates both cognition and motivation in emotion. The cognitive processes involve automatic appraisals of situations in relation to one's well-being. These appraisals are essentially implicit, nonlinguistic evaluations regarding what is good or bad for the self; have high survival value; and often are processed with reference to one's perceived ability to cope (Lazarus, 1991). The appraisals are made in reference to underlying goals, needs, and concerns, the motivational components of emotions. Motivation has been defined as the disposition to desire the occurrence or nonoccurrence of a situation (Frijda, 1986). Thus, needs, goals, and concerns are represented internally as standards against which situations are evaluated. If the appraisal of the situation and the need or concern are sufficiently undermatched or mismatched, emotion follows in the form of an action tendency. The action tendency organizes the individual to act in a way conducive to attaining or safeguarding a goal or need.

While this view of emotion includes important roles for cognitive and motivational processes, affect cannot be reduced to these individual components. Affect is instead a neuropsychologically independent means of informing the individual and others, through visceral sensations, action tendencies, and expressive displays, of its nonlinguistic evaluative responses with regard to self and world. That is, emotion provides people with feedback about what is important and meaningful to them and communicates it to others. Thus, people ignore their own and others' emotions at a cost. Dysfunction in peoples' ability to access emotional information means that they have become "disconnected" from one of their most adaptive orienting systems while the inability to read others' emotions leaves them at a social disadvantage. The emotion system is thus a crucial focus of therapeutic attention in individual and couples therapy and an important target of therapeutic change (Greenberg & Johnson, 1988; Greenberg & Safran,

1987). Emotion needs to be attended to for its adaptive information, to be evoked and restructured when maladaptive. When appropriate unexpressed attachment-enhancing emotions need to be expressed and accepted in intimate relationships.

Emotion and its motivational components need to be given a role alongside of cognition in treating disorder. All influence meaning. Emotions too long have been viewed as targets or dependent variables rather than as potential independent variables that can be changed and systematically evoked to motivate constructive thought and action. There has, however, long been a line of argument that has posited a bidirectional link between the cognitive and affective elements of disorder (Greenberg, 2002; Greenberg & Paivio, 1997; Greenberg & Safran, 1987; Izard, 1991; Tomkins, 1963). Cognition and memory clearly are mood dependent (Blaney, 1986; Forgas, 2000; Palfia & Salovey, 1993). Teasdale (1997) states "cognitions may be so powerfully influenced by affective states that cognitions appear to be a consequence of emotional state" (p. 67). Forgas (2000), in his Affect Infusion model, shows that the infusion of affect into cognition depends on the type of processing that is occurring. It is when processing is substantive in ambiguous, open situations, like most interpersonal experiences, that affect is most likely to influence the construction of beliefs. By contrast, more controlled processing in explicit problem-solving situations is most impervious to affect infusion effects. The key question now is not whether affect influences cognition but rather when does emotion influence cognition and when does the reverse occur? It is thus important to understand the independent contribution of both emotion and cognition in the production of human distress, and possibly even more important to understand their complex interaction.

Damasio (1999) attributes the emergence of consciousness itself to emotional awareness. According to Damasio, emotion first and foremost provides information about the status of the body-self in the environment, and knowing springs to life in the story of changes in this status. In this view, feeling is the awareness of the emotional impact of the physical environment on the body and it is this that gives rise to consciousness. The first narrative thus involves the brain linking a nonverbal account of the self in the process of being modified to its cause. Feeling is the conscious result of this account. Consciousness thus comes into being in the creation of this account and is manifest as the feeling of knowing. It is only later that self-reflective consciousness and linguistic representation emerge. The brain thus can be seen to possess two important meaning systems: one based on a symbolic-conceptual language and the other based on a sensory-motor language. Body talk, then, is intelligent brain talk and people need to pay attention to "feeling knowledge" and make sense of it with their linguistic conceptual abilities in order to be able to benefit consciously from its evolutionarily adaptive offerings.

The feeling dimension of emotion is thus the earliest form of consciousness. It is most free of cognitive or intentional processes and is what happens to us. The complexity of emotion, however, resides in the fact that emotion includes more than feelings that simply arise and are not directed toward anything. Emotion also involves the more intentional components of cognition, evaluation, and motivation, (all of which are intentional, that is, related to objects). The cognitive component consists of information about situations; the evaluative component assesses the personal significance of the information. The motivational component addresses needs, wishes, goals, and readiness to act in the situation. Typical emotional states involve both the feeling and the intentional components. These are not separate entities but different aspects of a larger whole. Rather than focusing on the causal relation between the components we need to see them as complementing each other. What can be discriminated, however, are automatic and deliberatively produced affect.

When is Affect Primary? Recent developments in neuroscience on the analysis of fear suggest that the emotional processing of simple sensory features occurs extremely early in the processing sequence. The initial emotional processing of simple sensory features occurs subcortically out of awareness, as inputs from the thalamus are received in the amygdala (LeDoux, 1990, 1996). This processing occurs prior to the synthesis of objects and events from simple sensory perceptions. Learned fear responses do not appear to depend on a complex analysis of the cue stimulus (appraisal), as the implicated circuits run through the primitive thalamus and function even in the absence of an intact sensory cortex (Lang, 1994).

Recent functional brain imaging studies have provided evidence consistent with LeDoux's view that the amygdala can perform its role in the processing of emotional stimuli nonconsciously. Employing functional magnetic resonance imaging (fMRI), Whalen and colleagues (1998) have demonstrated amygdala activation in response to emotional stimuli (facial expressions) even when conscious awareness of the stimuli is prevented by backward masking. In addition, autonomic physiological and motoric aspects of emotion have been shown to occur in response to an emotional stimulus that is not consciously recognized (e.g., in studies employing backward masking of visual emotional stimuli) or outside of attentional focus (Öhman & Soares, 1994). It should be noted that in these studies backward masking prevents conscious awareness of the emotionally salient stimulus itself, but does not necessarily prevent the person from being aware of emotional experience in response to the nonconsciously-processed stimulus. More recently, Whalen, Shin, McInerney, Hakan, Wright, & Rauch (2001) have shown that the amygdala reacts more strongly to faces of fear than to other faces.

As well as being activated automatically, the amygdala receives input from the cortex, allowing for conscious processing to affect emotionality, but this occurs only after information is first received from the thalamus. This suggests the operation of a second level of emotional processing, involving complex perceptions and concepts received from the cortex, occuring only after a more immediate intuitive appraisal by the emotional brain from the initial input. LeDoux (1996) suggests that there are two different paths for producing emotion: what he terms the "low" road, when the amygdala senses danger and broadcasts an emergency distress signal to brain and body, and the slower "high" road, in which the same information is carried through the thalamus to the neocortex. Because the shorter amygdala pathway transmits signals more than twice as fast as the neocortex route, the thinking brain often can't intervene in time to stop emotional responses. Thus the automatic emotional response has already occurred before one can stop it, be it jumping back from a snake, snapping at an inconsiderate spouse, or yelling at a disobedient child. As LeDoux has emphasized, fundamentally, the initial precognitive, perceptual, emotional processing of the "low" road is highly adaptive because it allows people to respond quickly to important events before complex and time-consuming processing has taken place. However, emotion can also be produced without activation of the amygdala (Teasdale et al., 1999). These are the emotions that are more meaning-dependent but they are often still dependent on more implicit meanings that need to be brought to awareness.

Essentially, as well as producing emotion, this form of dual functioning of the human brain appears to result in other forms of dual processing. Two kinds of learning, one a more conceptual, logical form, the other a more perceptual, associationistic one (Pascual-Leone, 1987, 1990a, 1990b), and two types of memory, one factual, the other emotional (van der Kolk, 1995), are also apparent. The cortex produces more conscious conceptual forms of learning and memory that involve facts and reasoning, while the emotional brain aids in producing more automatic associative forms of learning and memory that involve immediate experience and perception. Two levels of processing result: a conscious, conceptual processing system and a tacit, experiential one. These two systems allow for "knowledge by description" (conceptual knowing), and "knowledge by acquaintance" (experiential knowing). Emotional experience can thus be produced by automatic, schematic processing or by more conscious, deliberative processes. These two levels of processing have been noted by a number of authors to be important in understanding both human functioning and therapeutic change, and this suggests that both biology and culture are important codeterminers of human emotionality (Bohart & Wugalter, 1991; Buck, 1988; Epstein, 1994; Greenberg, Rice, & Elliot, 1993).

Making Sense of Emotional Experience: From Biology and the Brain to Culture and Social Meaning

In addition to a bioevolutionary approach to emotion, a view of the creation of personal meaning that takes personal learning and culture into account is necessary to fully comprehend the role of emotion in human functioning. Emotion is a primary meaning system that is fundamentally adaptive in nature, helping the organism to process complex situational information rapidly and automatically in order to produce action, expression, and meaning appropriate for meeting important organismic needs (e.g., self-protection, support). However, in addition to possessing a biologically based in-wired meaning and expressive system the individual is an active agent constantly constructing meaning. Personal meaning, as we have seen, is constructed by synthesizing information from two information processing systems that yield qualitatively distinct subjective experiences: the biologically based experiential or schematic system and the more culturally derived conceptual or reflexive system. The former is an implicit level of emotional processing responsible for the elicitation of hot emotional feelings while the latter is a conscious and controlled level of emotional processing that generates cooler processing of emotional information. The activation of the schematic system generates stronger emotional feelings than does the activation of the reflexive system, which explains and forms narratives of experience. The client is thus seen as an active constructor of meaning. In this view, in order to change, clients' need to experience what they talk about in therapy, they have to develop new narratives that assimilate experience into existing cognitive structures and generate new ones. Understanding an emotion always involves putting it in narrative form. As witnessed in literature and in therapy, all significant emotions occur in the context of an important story, and all important stories involve key emotions.

The discrete emotions, such as anger and fear, result in biologically based expression and goal-directed action tendencies, such as anger displays or flight. These emotions are innate and organized and depend on the lower brain. Nevertheless, the experience of these emotions involves awareness of them, and, therefore, they are always to some degree synthesized with other levels of processing. Feeling an emotion involves experiencing body changes in relation to and integrated with the evoking object or situation and one's past emotional learning. Emotions and feelings refer to the synthesis in constructive consciousness of a variety of levels of information processing. Feeling emotion also allows for the formation of emotion networks or schemas, because consciously feeling something involves higher levels of the brain and entails a synthesis of emotion-cognition-motivation and action into internal organizations. With development, rather than being governed simply by biologically and evolutionarily based affect motor programs, emotional experience is produced by highly differentiated structures that have been refined through experience, and bound by culture into schemas or organized units in memory.

Much emotional experience is initially generated by automatic processes that produce primary responses following simple perceptual appraisals (Greenberg & Korman, 1993; Scherer, 1984). Automatic processes, however, are followed immediately by more complex activity in which sensory, memorial, and ideational information is integrated, yielding a higher-level sense of our self and of the world. Neuroscientists like Damasio (1994) have argued that the formation of systematic connections between categories of objects and situations on the one hand, and primitive, preorganized emotions on the other, leads the maturing human to be capable of a second, higher-order type of emotional experience. Much adult emotional experience is of this higher order, generated by learned, idiosyncratic schemas that serve to help the individual to anticipate future outcomes. This higher-level synthesis of a variety of levels of processing has been referred to as an emotion scheme (Oatley, 1992; Pascual-Leone, 1991) and has been identified as a principal target of intervention and therapeutic change (Greenberg & Paivio, 1997; Greenberg, Rice, & Elliott, 1993). Once formed, emotion schemas produce more complex bodily felt feelings. These feelings are generally no longer a result of purely innate responses to specific cues, but of acquired responses based on one's lived emotional experience. Thus, for example, over time the innate response of joy at a human facial configuration becomes differentiated into feelings of pleasure with a specific caregiver and contributes to the development of basic trust.

An example of this second, higher-level emotion would be the pit in one's stomach that one might experience upon unexpectedly encountering an ex-spouse. Regardless of whether the experience can subsequently be fully articulated (i.e., exactly what one feels and why one feels that way) the experience is tacitly generated. Perhaps most important, these representations serve as memory-based schemas associated with emotional experiences that guide appraisals and serve as blueprints for physiological arousal and action.

Emotion schemas are implicit, idiosyncratic, affective/cognitive, organizational structures that when activated serve as the basis for human experience and self-organization (Greenberg 2002, Greenberg & Paivio, 1997; Greenberg et al., 1993). They can be adaptive, or, through learning and experience, maladaptive. An example of the development of a maladaptive emotion schema is seen in a child whose initiatives for closeness are met with unpredictable responses of either love or abusive rejection from parents. As a consequence, the child is likely to develop schemas in which intimacy and fear are associated and are connected with beliefs or expectancies that others will harm. Later in life, when the individual gets close to others, these schemas may be activated, and patterns of physiological arousal associated with the original abuse, plus associated negative beliefs or expectations formed by experience, will be evoked. The person may feel afraid, physically shrink away from closeness, and tacitly appraise intimacy as threatening, even though the individual knows consciously that this reaction may be unfounded in a current relationship.

Change in experience of this type is brought about first by activating the maladaptive experience and then by accessing adaptive feelings of sadness at what is missed, the yearning for closeness, and even anger at the abuse. These adaptive emotions are attended to and validated, are used to challenge maladaptive beliefs, and are integrated with the existing negative experience and views. This process of accessing the adaptive and bringing it into contact with the maladaptive helps transform or replace the maladaptive schemes (Greenberg, 2002; Greenberg & Paivio, 1997).

A Dialectical-Constructivist View: Integrating Biology and Culture

In a dialectical-constructivist view (Greenberg & Pascual-Leone, 1995; Greenberg et al., 1993; Guidano, 1991; Mahoney, 1991; Neimeyer & Mahoney, 1995; Pascual-Leone, 1987, 1990a, 1990b, 1991) personal meaning involves the self-organization and explication of one's own emotional experience. This involves an integration of reason and emotion, a combining of head and heart, in which people are constantly engaged in a circular process of making sense of their experience and thereby constructing new experience.

In this view, symbol and bodily felt referent are viewed as interacting to carry meaning forward, and newly symbolized experience is organized in different ways to construct new views. Attending to, and discovering of, preconceptual elements of experience influence the process of meaning construction. New experiential elements can come from many sources—from within, and sometimes from without—to influence constructions. People are then viewed as constantly striving toward making sense of their preconceptual experience by symbolizing it, explaining it, and putting it into narrative form. Preconceptual tacit meaning carries implications and acts to constrain but does not fully determine meaning. Rather, it is synthesized with conceptual, explicit meaning to form explanations constrained by experiencing (Greenberg & Pascual-Leone, 1995, 2001).

Classic cognitive theories of emotions suggest that emotion is elicited by the activation of a unique type of knowledge in the form of associative networks (Bower 1981). This postulate raises several problems, however, such as the difficulty of accounting for the distinction between hot embodied emotion and cold emotion knowledge. Rather than emotion knowledge networks, we postulate the existence of two emotional information processing systems that yield qualitatively distinct subjective experiences: the schematic system, which is an implicit level of emotional processing responsible for the elicitation of hot emotional feelings—experiential knowledge of acquaintance—and the reflexive system, which is a conscious and controlled level of emotional processing that generates cold processing of emotional information—conceptual knowledge by description. The activation of the schematic system generates stronger emotional feelings than does the activation of the reflexive system. Research by Schaefer & Philipott (2001) and by van Reekum & Scherer (in press) has demonstrated that the activation of schematic emotion yields stronger self-report and skin conductance levels of emotional intensity and quicker response times than does the reflexive processing of emotion.

Therapists need to recognize the importance of both systems and must constantly work back and forth between clients' emotional schematic experience and their reflexive narratization in order to help them make sense of their emotional experiences in consciousness. As discussed, converging evidence in experimental and social psychology and in neurophysiology suggests that much of the processing involved in the generation of emotional experience occurs independently of, and prior to, conscious, deliberate, cognitive operations. Therefore, working at the purely conceptual level to effect emotional change may not produce enduring change. Instead, therapeutic interventions are more likely to succeed if they target the schematic processes that automatically generate the emotional experience that underlies clients' felt senses of themselves. I am suggesting that these schemas are complex affective structures based on an integration of biology, experience and culture. There is a growing body of evidence that emotional arousal and increased depth of experience in therapy predicts outcome in different approaches (Greenberg 2002; Greenberg, Korman & Paivio 2001, Greenberg & Malcolm, 2002).

Emotion-Focused Change Principles

Given the importance of the evolutionary-based emotion system in the change process, it is important to specify principles of emotional change. First we need to distinguish between the following different types of emotions (Greenberg, 2002): *Primary adaptive emotions* are the very first automatic emotional responses people have on reacting to a stimulus. These are core emotional experiences, such as sadness at loss and fear at threat. *Secondary emotions* are reactions to prior emotions, thoughts, or beliefs, such as anger in response to hurt, fear of fear, or anxiety from catastrophizing. These are more superficial or reactive emotions. *Adaptive emotions,* such as anger at violation and sadness at loss, are those whose adaptive values are clear. *Maladaptive emotions,* such as shame at being defective and fear-based inadequacy, are those that lead to dysfunction.

Three principles of emotional change in the affective domain emerge from a dialectical-constructivist view of evolutionary-based emotionality (Greenberg, 2001, 2002). These principles prompt therapists to work with their clients toward: (1) increased awareness of emotion, (2) enhancing emotion regulation, and (3) changing emotion with emotion.

Increased *emotional awareness* enhances functioning in a variety of ways. Becoming aware of and symbolizing primary emotional experience in words provides access to both the adaptive information and the adaptive action tendency in the emotion, helps people make sense of their experience, and promotes assimilation of experience into their ongoing self-narrative. Symbolizing traumatic emotion memories in words helps promote their assimilation into a person's ongoing self-narrative (van der Kolk, 1995). This principle includes exposure to emotion and its symbolization in awareness.

The second principle of change addresses *emotion regulation,* which is accomplished by promoting the client's ability to receive, to attain a working distance from, and to soothe emerging painful emotional experience. Here amygdala-based emotional arousal needs to be approached, allowed, and accepted, rather than avoided or controlled. In this process people need to use their higher brain centers, not to control emotion, but to consciously recognize the alarm messages being sent from the amygdala and then to act to calm the activation. People need to act in terms that will help them down-regulate the affective alarm signal within. This is achieved by learning skills of acceptance of emotion, by self-empathy, and by the provision of cognitive, affective, and physiological soothing. The soothing of emotion can be provided by individuals themselves by self-soothing methods such as diaphragmatic breathing, relaxation, compassion, and calming self-talk. Soothing also can be obtained interpersonally. In the form of the other's empathic attunement to affect, and through validation by another person. This principle of working with emotion involves the person's acknowledging emotion and receiving its message. It is the recognition and soothing of the emergency signal, rather than its control, that helps turn off the alarm signal. Clients in underregulated states (e.g., rage) are encouraged to access a more soothing, comforting state in order to help regulate the internal distress. This can be done through the use of metaphors or images, such as taking care of the wounded part inside, finding an inner voice of strength, or finding an imagined safe place to go to when feeling overwhelmed. The use of meditative techniques to adopt an observer's stance toward underregulated emotion, and the learning of distress tolerance and emotion regulation skills are important means of dealing with affect that is too overwhelming (Linehan, 1993). Internalizing the protectiveness of the therapist is also helpful. For example, having clients imagine taking the therapist back with them into the abusive scene as a protection against the abuse or threat combines clients' learning how to self-soothe with internalizing the soothing function of the therapist.

The third and probably most important change principle involves the changing of emotion with emotion. This suggests that a primary maladaptive emotion state is transformed best by changing it with another, more adaptive, emotion. Greenberg and Paivio (1997), for example, suggest that a key means of transforming maladaptive emotions, such as the shame of feeling worthless and the basic anxiety of feeling unlovable, is by accessing alternate healthy adaptive emotions to act as resources in the personality. In this view the new alternate feelings may have been present in the original situation, but were not accessed or expressed, or may be new, currently available responses to the past situation. Reason is seldom sufficient to change automatic, emergency-based (amygdala) emotional responses; One needs to transform one emotion with another (Greenberg, 2002). Thus maladaptive anger can be changed by accessing adaptive sadness, maladaptive fear, by accessing more boundary-establishing emotions of adaptive anger or of disgust, or by evoking the softer feelings of compassion. Maladaptive shame can be replaced by accessing self-comforting feelings and by accessing pride and self-worth. Withdrawal emotions from one side of the brain are replaced with approach emotions from another part of the brain or vice versa. Once the alternate emotion has been accessed it is used to transform the original state.

This principle shares some features with the notion of reciprocal inhibition that was key to early behavior therapy in which desensitization was used to teach a relaxation response to anxiety. This behavioral view of eliciting and working with anxiety affects has, to some degree, been lost in CBT. Although desensitization focused predominantly on anxiety, there were also examples of applying this principle more broadly to changing other types of emotion, as is proposed here. In addition, numerous responses, other than relaxation responses and incompatible with anxiety, have been used in behavior therapy. Most common were assertiveness, sexual responses, and motor responses (Wolpe, 1969). Lazarus and Abramovitz (1962) used emotive imagery such as pride, mirth, and excitement of adventure to change anxiety, whereas Goldstein, Serber, and Piaget (1970) found induced anger to be effective in modifying fear. The use of emotion to change emotion was especially effective when classical conditioning of affects was seen as the operating mechanism.

It is important to note that the principle proposed here goes beyond both ideas of reciprocal inhibition and those of exposure and habituation. In the view proposed here, maladaptive feeling does not simply attenuate by the person's feeling it and essentially getting used to it. Rather, another feeling is used to transform or undo it. For example, a key means of transforming the shame of feeling worthless and the aroused core anxiety of feeling unlovable is by accessing alternate healthy adaptive emotions such as pride, anger, joy, or even humor. Rather than exposure to the bad feeling leading to its attenuation, another emotion is accessed to undo the first one. The newly accessed, alternate feelings are resources in the personality that help change the maladaptive state. Maladaptive shame can be transformed by accessing anger at violation and self-comforting feelings, and by accessing pride and feelings of self-worth. In this process the tendency to shrink into the ground in shame is transformed by the thrusting forward tendency in newly accessed anger at violation. Withdrawal emotions from one side of the brain are transformed by approach emotions from another part of the brain or vice-versa (Davidson, 2000). Once the alternate emotion has been accessed it either transforms, undoes, or replaces the original state. The new alternate feelings may have been present in the original situation, but were not accessed or expressed, or they may be new, currently available responses to the past situation.

The transformation process also is not one of counterconditioning or reciprocal inhibition, as suggested in desensitization, but rather a dialectical synthesis of a new response from the prior ones by a process of integration of elements. Change occurs when opposing emotions are coactivated, and new, higher-level schemas are formed by synthesizing compatible elements from the coactivated schemas. Just as schemas for standing and falling, in a toddler, can be dynamically synthesized into a higher-level schema for walking, by a dialectical process (Greenberg & Pascual-Leone, 1995; Pascual-Leone, 1991) so too can schemas of different emotional states be synthesized to form new integrative structures. This synthesis is brought about both by the automatic processes of the combination of compatible response elements and by more deliberative, reflexive processes in which new structures are formed by the creation of new meanings that integrate old views into higher-level ones. For example, fear from abuse can be transformed by anger to form a more assertive sense of self. This occurs by synthesis at different levels and across levels. First fear's tendency to run is combined with anger's tendency to thrust forward, and then these are synthesized with cognitive changes such as holding the other accountable for wrongdoing and seeing oneself as deserving. A new emotion schema is formed by an integration of compatible aspects of evoked response tendencies with new views to form a truly novel response of feeling empowered and being able to stand one's ground (Greenberg & Pascual-Leone, 1995; Pascual-Leone, 1987). Similarly, shyness can be transformed by love into a new form of sensitive contact. In this process the tendencies to eagerly approach (associated with the desire for closeness) and to fearfully withdraw (associated with the fear of rejection) can be integrated into sensitive contact with the help of deliberate reflection on the cost of inaction. If a novel response such as a sensitive checking out of the interest of the desired other is to be eventually synthesized, the fear and the love need to be evoked together, attended to with increased attentional capacity, and reflected on. This type of activation of emotions and reflection on them is much more likely to be facilitated in the safety of therapy.

Empirical evidence is mounting to support the importance of the process of changing emotion with emotion. Muscular action and facial expression have been shown to change emotional states (Berkowitz, 1999; Flack, Laird, & Cavallaro, 1999). Frederickson (2001) has reported on how positive emotions undo lingering negative emotions. The basic observation is that key components of positive emotions are incompatible with negative emotions. She suggests that by broadening a person's momentary thought-action repertoire a positive emotion may loosen the hold that a negative emotion has on that person's mind. The experiences of joy and contentment were found to produce faster cardiovascular recovery from negative emotions than a neutral experience. Such results suggest that positive emotions fuel psychological resilience. These studies indicate that emotion can be used to change emotion, and in the above case, more specifically, that positive affect does regulate negative feelings. There is also growing evidence that positive affect enhances flexibility, problem solving, and sociability (Isen, 2000). Frederickson (1998) demonstrated how positive emotions such as joy, interest, pride, and love broaden peoples' momentary thought-action repertoires, which in turn serve to build their enduring resources to cope with life.

Conclusion

The dialectical constructivist view presented attempts to do justice to both the evolutionary base of emotion and its socially and culturally constructed elements. The reality of immediate, subjective, emotionally based experience and the active, constructive, cognitive processes by which people create meaning from immediate experience are also recognized. Becoming aware is neither a purely passive process of simply perceiving sense experience nor a purely constructive one of radically forming reality by imposing predetermined distinctions or categories on experience to create meaning. Rather, experience is simultaneously discovered and created (Greenberg & Safran, 1987; Greenberg et al., 1993) in a dialectical manner in which the dialectic is between the immediately sensed and the conceptually mediated, between peoples' emerging experience and their previously constructed views. Thought and emotions both play a role in experience, and experience and behavior are ultimately generated out of the dialectical interplay between two streams of consciousness, one a conceptual, reasoning system, the other the rapid, adaptive action, emotion system.

References

Arnold, M. B. (1960). *Emotion and personality*. New York: Columbia University Press.

Beck, A. T., Rush, A. J., Shaw, B. F., & Emery, G. (1979). *Cognitive therapy of depression*. New York: Guilford.

Berkowitz, L. (1999). Anger. In T. Daglesh & I. M. Power (Eds.), *Handbook of cognition and emotion* (pp. 411–428). London: Wiley.

Blaney, R. H. (1986). Affect and memory: A review. *Psychological Bulletin, 99*(2), 229–246.

Bohart, A., & Wugalter, S. (1991). Changes in experiential knowing as a common dimension in psychotherapy. *Journal of Integrative and Eclectic Psychotherapy, 10*, 14–37.

Bower, G. H. (1981). Mood and memory. *American Psychologist, 36*, 129–148.

Buck, R. (1988). *Human motivation and emotion*. New York: Wiley.

Damasio, A. (1994). *Descartes' error: Emotion, reason, and the human brain*. New York: Putnam.

Damasio, A. (1999). *The feeling of what happens*. New York: Harcourt-Brace.

Darwin, C. (1897). *The expression of emotions in man and animals*. New York Philosophical Library. (Original work published 1872)

Davidson, R. (2000). Affective style, mood and anxiety disorders: An affective neuroscience approach. In R. Davidson (Ed.), *Anxiety, depression and emotion*. Oxford, UK: Oxford University Press.

Ekman, P., & Friesen, W. (1975). *Unmasking the face*. Englewood Cliffs, NJ: Prentice Hall.

Epstein, S. (1994). Integration of the cognitive and psychodynamic unconscious. *American Psychologist, 49*(8), 709–724.

Flack, W., Laird, J. D., & Cavallaro, J. (1999). Emotional expression and feeling in schizophrenia: Effects of specific expressive behaviors on emotional experiences. *Journal of Clinical Psychology, 55*, 1–20.

Forgas, J. (2000). Mood and judgements: The Affect Infusion Model (AIM). *Psychological Bulletin, 117*(1), 39–66.

Fredrickson, B. L. (1998). What good are positive emotions? *Review of General Psychology: New Directions in Research on Emotion, 2*, 300–319.

Frederickson, B. (2001). The role of positive emotions in positive psychology: The broaden-and-build theory of positive emotions. *American Psychologist, 56*(3), 218–226.

Fridlund, A. (1994). *Human facial expression*. San Diego, CA: Academic Press.

Frijda, N. H. (1986). *The emotions*. Cambridge, UK: Cambridge University Press.

Goldstein, A. J., Serber, M., & Piaget, G. (1970). Induced anger as a reciprocal inhibitor of fear. *Journal of Behavioural Therapy & Experiential Psychiatry, 1*, 67–70.

Greenberg, L. (2002). *Emotion-focused therapy: Coaching clients to work through feelings*. Washington, DC: American Psychological Association.

Greenberg, L., & Johnson, S. (1988). *Emotionally focused couples therapy*. New York: Guilford.

Greenberg, L., & Korman, L. (1993). Integrating emotion into psychotherapy integration. *Journal of Psychotherapy Integration, 3*, 249–266.

Greenberg, L., Korman, L., & Paivio, S. (2001). Emotion in humanistic therapy. In D. Cain & J. Seeman (Eds.), *Humanistic psychotherapies: Handbook of research and practice* (pp. 499–530). Washington DC: American Psychological Association.

Greenberg, L., & Malcolm, W. (2002). Resolving unfinished business: Relating process to outcome. *Journal of Consulting & Clinical Psychology, 70,* 406–416.

Greenberg, L., & Pascual-Leone, J. (2001). A dialectical constructivist view of the creation of personal meaning. *Journal of Constructivist Psychology, 14*(3), 165–186.

Greenberg, L. S., & Bolger, L. (2001). An emotion focussed approach to the over-regulation of emotion and emotional pain. *In-Session, 57* (2), 197–212.

Greenberg, L. S., & Paivio, S. C. (1997). *Working with the emotions in psychotherapy.* New York: Guilford.

Greenberg, L. S., & Pascual-Leone, J. (1995). A dialectical constructivist approach to experiential change. In R. A. Neimeyer & M. J. Mahoney (Eds.), *Constructivism in psychotherapy* (pp. 169–191). Washington, DC: American Psychological Association.

Greenberg, L. S., Rice, L. N., & Elliott, R. (1993). *Facilitating emotional change: The moment by moment process.* New York: Guilford.

Greenberg, L. S., & Safran, J. D. (1987). *Emotion in psychotherapy: Affect, cognition, and the process of change.* New York: Guilford.

Greenberg, L. S., & Safran, J. D. (1989). Emotion in psychotherapy. *American Psychologist, 44,* 19–29.

Guidano, V. F. (1991). *The self in process.* New York: Guilford.

Hermans, H. J. M., Kempen, H. J. G., & Van Loon, R. J. P. (1992). The dialogical self: Beyond individualism and rationalism. *American Psychologist, 47,* 23–33.

Isen, A. (1999). Positive affect. In T. Dagleish & M. Power (Eds.), *Handbook of cognition and emotion* (pp. 521–539). London: Wiley.

Izard, C. E. (1984). Emotion cognition relationships and human development. In C. E. Izard, J. Kogen, & R. B. Yojone (Eds.), *Emotion, cognition and behavior* (pp. 17–37). New York: Cambridge University Press.

Izard, C. E. (1991). *The psychology of emotions.* New York: Plenum.

Lang, P. J. (1994). The varieties of emotional experience: A meditation on James-Lange theory. *Psychological Review, 101*(2), 211–221.

Lazarus, R. (1991). *Emotions and adaptation.* New York: Oxford University Press.

Lazarus, A., & Abramovitz, A. (1962). The use of "emotive imagery" in the treatment of children's phobias. *Journal of Mental Science, 108,* 109–195.

LeDoux, J. E. (1996). *The emotional brain: The mysterious underpinnings of emotional life.* New York: Simon & Schuster.

LeDoux, J. E. (1990). Information flow from sensation to emotion plasticity in the neural computation of stimulus value. In M. Gabriel & J. Moore (Eds.), *Learning and computational neuroscience: Foundations of adaptive networks* (pp. 3–52). Cambridge, MA: Bradford Books/MIT Press.

Linehan, M. M. (1993). *Cognitive-behavioral treatment of borderline personality disorder.* New York: Guilford.

Mahoney, M. (1991). *Human change processes.* New York: Basic Books.

Neimeyer, R., & Mahoney, M. (1995). *Constructivism in psychotherapy.* Washington, DC: American Psychological Association.

Oatley, K. (1992). *Best laid schemes.* Cambridge, UK: Cambridge University Press.

Oatley, K., & Jenkins, J. (1992). Human emotions: Function and dysfunction. *Annual Review of Psychology, 43,* 55–85.

Öhman, A., & Soares, J. J. F. (1994). Unconscious anxiety: Phobic responses to masked stimuli. *Journal of Abnormal Psychology, 103,* 231–240.

Palfia, T. P., & Salovey, P. (1993). The influence of depressed and elated mood on deductive and inductive reasoning. *Imagination, Cognition, and Personality, 13,* 57–71.

Panksepp, J. (2001). The neuro-evolutionary cusp between emotions and cognitions. *Consciousness and Emotion, 1*(1), 15–54.

Pascual-Leone, J. (1987). Organismic processes for neo-Piagetian theories: A dialectical causal account of cognitive development. *International Journal of Psychology, 22,* 531–570.

Pascual-Leone, J. (1990a). An essay on wisdom: Toward organismic processes that make it possible. In R. J. Sternberg (Ed.), *Wisdom: Its nature, origins, and development* (pp. 244–278). New York: Cambridge University Press.

Pascual-Leone, J. (1990b). Reflections on life-span intelligence, consciousness and ego development. In C. Alexander & E. Langer (Eds.), *Higher stages of human development: Perspectives on adult growth* (pp. 258–285). New York: Oxford University Press.

Pascual-Leone, J. (1991). Emotions, development and psychotherapy: A dialectical constructivist perspective. In J. Safran & L. Greenberg (Eds.), *Emotion, psychotherapy and change* (pp. 302–335). New York: Guilford.

Plutchik, R. (1980). *Emotion: A psychoevolutionary synthesis.* New York: Harper & Row.

Plutchik, R. (2000). *Emotion in psychotherapy.* Washington, DC: American Psychological Association.

Safran, J., & Greenberg, L. (Eds.). (1991). *Emotion, psychotherapy and change.* New York: Guilford.

Schaefer, A., & Philipott, P. (2001). Emotion and memory. In T. J. Mayne & G. A. Bananno (Eds.), *Emotions: Current issues and future directions* (pp. 82–122). New York: Guilford.

Scherer, K. R. (1984). Emotion as a multicomponent process: A model and some cross-cultural data. In P. Shaver (Ed.), *Review of personality and social psychology* (Vol. 5, pp. 36–63). Beverly Hills, CA: Sage.

Sroufe, L. A. (1996). *Emotional development: The organization of emotional life in the early years.* New York: Cambridge University Press.

Teasdale, J. D. (1997). The relationship between cognition and emotion: The mind-in-place in mood disorders. In D. M. Clark & C. G. Fairburn (Eds.), *Science and practice of cognitive behaviour therapy* (pp. 67–93). Oxford, UK: Oxford University Press.

Teasdale, J. D. (1999). Emotional processing, three modes of mind and the prevention of relapse in depression. *Behaviour Research and Therapy, 37,* 53–57.

Teasdale, J., Howard, R., Cox, S., Ha, Y., Brammer, M., Williams, S., & Checkley, S. (1999). Functional MRI study of the cognitive generation of affect. *American Journal of Psychiatry, 156,* 209–215.

Teasdale, J. D., Taylor, M. J., Cooper, Z., Hyhurst, H., & Paykel, E. S. (1995). Depressive thinking: Shifts in construct accessibility or in schematic mental models? *Journal of Abnormal Psychology, 104,* 500–507.

Thompson, R. F. (1986). The neurobiology of learning and memory. *Science, 233,* 941–947.

Tomkins, S. (1963). *Affect, imagery and consciousness: The negative affects* (Vol. 1). New York: Springer.

Tomkins, S. (1983). Affect theory. In P. Ekman (Ed.), *Emotion in the human face* (pp. 163–194). New York: Cambridge University Press.

Tugade, M., & Frederickson, B. (2000, August). *Resilient individuals use positive emotions to bounce back from negative emotional arousal.* Paper presented at the International Society for Research in Emotion, Quebec City.

van der Kolk, B. A. (1995). The body keeps the score: Memory and the evolving psychobiology of posttraumatic stress. *Harvard Review of Psychiatry, 1,* 253–265.

van Reekum, C. M., & Scherer, K. R. (in press). *Testing multilevel processing of appraisal: Evidence from computer game generated emotions.* Proceedings of the XIth conference of the International Society for Research on Emotions, Quebec City.

van Reekum, C. M., & Scherer, K. R. (1998). Levels of processing in appraisal: Evidence from computer-game generated emotions. In A. Fischer (Ed.), *Proceedings of the Xth conference of the International Society for Research on Emotions* (pp. 180–186). Amsterdam: International Society for Research on Emotions.

Whalen, P. J., Rausch, S. L., Etcoff, N. L., McInerny, S., Lee, M. B., & Jenike, M. A. (1998). Masked presentations of emotional facial expressions modulate amygdala activity without explicit knowledge. *Journal of Neuroscience, 18,* 411–418.

Whalen, P. J., Shin, I., McInerney, S., Hakan, F., Wright, C., & Raunch, S. (2001). A functional MRI study of human amygdala responses to facial expression of fear versus anger. *Emotion, 1*(1), 70–83.

Wolpe, J. (1969). *The practice of behavior therapy.* Oxford, UK: Pergamon.

Part Two

Specific Disorders

Chapter 4

Pessimism and the Evolution of Negativity

Robert L. Leahy

U nlike Jean Jacques Rousseau, who looked at the world and saw a vast population in chains, I look at the world and see a majority of people beset with anxiety, depression, phobias, substance abuse, and difficulty maintaining monogamous attachments. Is it the repressive nature of culture or is it the preadapted inclinations toward certain forms of thinking, feeling, and behavior that account for this apparently sorry state? The argument presented in this chapter is that much of our psychopathology can be understood as evolved, context-triggered predispositions toward pessimism, phobia, and anxiety that were useful in the evolutionary expected or relevant environment. The environment in which much of our evolution took place may have disappeared before the literate historical record, but its impact on thinking persists because the hardwiring in the brain is not so easily modified by experience or current environments (Gilbert, this book).

If we examine the distribution of fears in the general population, we notice a number of important facts. First, the most common fears are those related to natural danger, such as snakes and bugs (22%), heights (18%), water (12%), and thunder (9%) (Chapman, 1997; Marks, 1987). Second, these fears are commonly found irrespective of culture; the distribution is nonrandom and universal (Poulton &

Menzies, 2002). Third, one can argue that we are born with dispositions for certain fears and need to learn to become unafraid through
exposure. Thus, in the Dunedin study, fear of heights was less for those
who had actually suffered a serious fall (Poulton, Davies, Menzies,
Langley, & Silva, 1998). In another study, 77% of mothers described
their children as afraid of water the very first time the children were
confronted with water in a pool or lake (Graham & Gaffan, 1997).
These data support the view that fears may not be based on associative learning but rather are predisposed tendencies that are later
"unlearned."

Evidence for the high frequency of depression and anxiety in all
cultures suggests that humans are not born free and everywhere they
run the risk of the chains of dysphoria and anxiety (Meyer & Deitsch,
1996; Weissman, Bland, Joyce, & Newman, 1993). The universal nature
of these problems suggests that "psychopathology" is, in fact, part of
human nature, rather than an aberration to be eliminated through better social engineering (Nesse, 2000; Price, 2002). What accounts for
this universal tendency toward fear, pessimism, and self-criticism?

Information Processors or Reproductive Systems?

During the 1970s, there was an increasing emphasis on human cognition as an information-processing system, much akin to new models of artificial intelligence. Thus, models of cognition would evaluate the importance of recency versus primacy effects, categorization,
and other memorial processes (Schacter, 1996). These models assumed
that intelligence was similar to a collector and categorizer of information. In contrast to this "artificial intelligence" model, evolutionary
models have emphasized the modularity of intelligence (Cosmides &
Tooby, 2002). This approach stresses the importance of different kinds
of cognitive processes that are preadapted to information with evolutionary significance. Thus, modularity would propose that preadapted
categories and processes would differ for intelligence (and information) related to searching for food sources and sexual partners, procreation, protection of offspring, social domination, submission, and
detection of predators. The difference between the information processing and the modularity models is the difference between cognitive systems that are analogized to computers and those grounded in
evolutionary challenges related to survival.

Consider the following: Jurassic Jack is our primitive man from the Stone Age. His cognitive processes must solve problems of great urgency—namely, those related to his own survival and the progeneration of his genes. Assume that correct and incorrect answers to these questions constitute wagers, with consideration of probabilities and the valence and extremity of outcomes. Moreover, he plays this game against others who wager their resources against their perceived chances within this environment. There are winners and losers and Jack prefers to win. Now, in some cases, the wager may be trivial, more for the fun of the game. In other cases, he may be asked to ante up and place all his chips in the pot. Jack asks the evolutionary existential question, "When to hold and when to fold?"

Jack is focused on the following: How likely is it that he is wrong? How bad will the outcome be if he makes the wrong guess? His cognitive and perceptual systems are oriented toward asking the following questions:

- Will this kill me?
- Can I eat this without dying?
- Will this person dominate me?
- Will I be able to copulate?

One might consider Jurassic Jack as lacking humor, although some have argued that humor and creativity might increase the probability of copulating, since these abilities would be attractive to members of the opposite sex and potential allies, possibly as a sign of his intelligence and ability to provide food. Jurassic Jack searches for answers to questions that, in his case, always seem to have critical importance. For him, information is related to the problems that he needs to solve.

Compare our primitive friend, Jack, with the computer in front of me. The nature of its intelligence is constrained by the engineers who have designed the hardware and the genius who created the software. The questions that this computer asks are binary "yes" and "no" as to which direction to turn in firing an electrical charge. It must distinguish between "yes" and "no" in its various permutations embedded within a language that appears arbitrary. But, what if I were to design a computer whose sole purpose was to detect if someone was to pull the plug or remove the motherboard? What kind of intelligence would work then? It might develop a surveillance system with landmines around the outlet on the wall. It might prohibit humans and small mammals from coming close. It would essentially be a threat-sensitive, paranoid computer. This would be the beginning of computer modularity intelligence and would lead to the evolution of increasingly paranoid computers based on early detection systems of invasion by plug-pullers.

Evolutionary cognition is based on modularity—that is separate systems of thought and perception that are addressed to solving problems of survival of the individual and his or her genes. It is irrelevant to Jurassic Jack what the population is of the nearby settlement—unless this information is related to the chance of being killed or of securing sexual partners, in which case, it is *very* relevant. For the computer model of information processing, it is irrelevant whether I am writing about the dismal performance of my favorite team or a strategic plan against my neighbor. Indeed, for the computer, information processing is processing hedonically irrelevant information. In contrast, for the modular mind, information is related first and only to egocentric issues.

Psychopathology Solves Problems

Feeding Sources, Protection Against Predators, Conspecifics, and Procreation

Human cognition in the environment of evolutionary adaptedness (EEA) is needed to solve three problems: (a) access and utilization of feeding sources, (b) protection against predators and conspecifics, and (c) procreation and survival of offspring. Individuals who engaged in behavior that increased the likelihood of their genes surviving into later generations would increase the likelihood that these behavioral tendencies would persist in future generations. Thus, individuals who sacrificed their own interests to increase the likelihood that their children would survive would increase the probability that these parental and protective behaviors would be manifested in future generations. The model of *inclusive fitness* proposes that since individuals share more genes in common with more closely related relatives (e.g., siblings), they will direct more of these caretaking behaviors toward genetically more similar individuals (Hamilton, 1963). Inclusive fitness assumes that *kinship selection* is a means by which genetically similar individuals represent the genetic investment of single individuals (see Bailey, this book). Thus, according to inclusive fitness theory, one individual may sacrifice his life or immediate interests to protect the genes that he has in common with other members of the group. This helps account for apparently altruistic behavior in groups—such as parental nurturance, childbearing, shared defense, and warning signals (Hamilton, 1963; Ridley, 1996; Wilson, 1975).

Individuals in a primitive environment faced the challenges of finding access to feeding sources, protection against predators, and procreation of offspring. Although an immediate assumption would be that optimism and activity would be the best strategies to utilize, the argument presented here is that pessimism, avoidance, and retreat are often preferred. Feeding sources vary in terms of density, predictability, and seasonal appearance. Exploration of these potential sources involved some risk of exposure to predators, distance from one's own group, and exertion of energy (Shettleworth, 1998). Given that much of evolutionary history was lived close to the edge of survival, miscalculations could prove fatal. For example, exerting considerable energy to explore food sources that are sparse would lead, in the long run, to a negative return on caloric energy, resulting in death. Thus, the primitive mind would need to consider the trade-off of searching in one area versus another or, in the alternative, opt for staying home. During the lean months of winter, this problem could be solved through vegetative depression or hibernation, with hoarding behavior preceding hibernation.

In the current period, vegetative symptoms of depression characteristic of seasonal affective disorder (SADS) and atypical depression parallel such an adaptation to seasonal variation in food sources. Atypical depression may reflect activation of mechanisms and strategies for the preadaptation to long winters: the symptom pattern consists of significant weight gain, hypersomnia, a leaden feeling in arms and legs, rejection sensitivity (which leads to withdrawal), and a preference for sweets and carbohydrates. I shall argue that these vegetative symptoms are "investment strategies" reflecting a perception that future resources and opportunities will be scarce and that the present time is not only a time to hold, but also a time to collect—in this case, calories. The reduced metabolic rate, resulting in lower calorie burn-off, is indicative of a reduced consumption of resources by the body itself: thus, more high-calorie food is consumed, but less is burned off, reflecting a strategy of conservation of caloric resources.

Importance of Binge Eating and Hoarding

In our high-calorie, high-fat North American culture of labor-saving devices, we are often perplexed by the increase of obesity. Why are so many people obese? The answer may have less to do with psychopathology than with availability and natural metabolism. Matching individuals on calorie intake, we find that the predictor of obesity is metabolic rate, a factor that is largely inherited (Price, 2002). Is this the cruel intent of nature to plague us with genes predisposing toward adipose tissue? Or, more likely, were our slowly metabolizing ancestors more capable of storing calories in fat cells to make it to the long-distant and unpredictable next meal? Is obesity an adaptation to a world of starvation and limited resources that, in the current fast-food environment, has outlived its utility?

Similarly, the same can be said of binge eating. Is this a consequence of low self-esteem and regression to the oral phase, or is binge eating a recrescence of natural inclinations in a starvation environment to eat high-fat, sweet, high-calorie foods as quickly as possible, lest one be overtaken by a competing predator, higher on the food chain, looking for a tasty meal? Binge eating may be part of the modular mind adapted to an eat-and-run mentality of prehistoric dining.

We can view binge eating as a reflection of a caloric hoarding and consumption strategy: "Get as many calories and fat as quickly as possible." For many binge eaters, the binge is followed by somnolence, further conserving the energy recently consumed. Once again, this strategy represents a "savings" of calories, unlike an exploration for sexual partners, where the latter strategy might require utilization of calories, reduced opportunities for feeding, and the risk of exposure to predators. It is as if the modular mind is saying, "Now is the time to consume calories, reduce activity, and forego sexual union," thus, the binge, torpor, somnolence, and rejection sensitivity. We should note, however, that although we can identify possible strategies such as these, which play a powerful role in the coordination of affect and behavior, we have much to learn about how and why they become triggered in modern contexts. Second, people can develop negative schema of self because of the strategy that then forms complex feedback loops. Although binge eating is often linked to self-esteem and may even be seen as a cause, binge eaters who do not put on weight may be less likely to suffer low self-esteem or feel bad about their bingeing than those who become fat and are shamed in their social contexts.

Low self-esteem comes from carrying stigmatizable traits, not the other way around. Thus in cultures where fatness is valued, bingeing is not associated with low self-esteem (e.g., Sumo wrestlers).

Spontaneous Remission of Depression and Emerging Mania

Investment strategies may account for the spontaneous remission of most depressions, especially those with a seasonal pattern. Environmental opportunities change. "There is a time for everything under Heaven," as Ecclesiastes observed. Hoarding, conserving, and withdrawing may increase survival during the lean months, but in times of abundant resources, such as the warmer months, the individual might be rewarded by the expenditure of calories in searching for food and sexual partners. The seasonal pattern, or spontaneous remission, may reflect the sequential balancing of survival against starvation versus procreation of offspring.

What would be the adaptive value of spontaneous remission of depression? Perhaps the answer lies in the fact that environments change: new food sources appear, making exploration and procreation more successful. This is especially true with seasonal fluctuation in food sources. In (temperate) climates, such as New England, winters are barren, providing a few nuts and wild game, but the spring and summer provide harvests of significant quantity. Perhaps for this reason SADS is usually marked by hypomanic or euthymic mood during the warmer months and depressed mood at the onset of winter. SADS may be an expression of the modular and strategically orientated mind that prepares for the worst through a pattern of hibernation: decreased motor activity, increased somnolence, decreased metabolic rate, and the elimination of sexual and exploratory activity. Similarly, hoarding behavior may also be an expression of the mind that collects resources against the privation of a long winter of discontent.

Rejection sensitivity may be adaptive if there is little food to support the individual and his partners, but sociability and hypomania may be adaptive if there are abundant resources, but that will last only a few months. The sociable or hypomanic individual operates with the investment model that there is a limited *window of opportunity* to get what you can while it is available. Thus, mania is often driven by the fear of overlooking opportunities, while depression is often motivated by a desire to protect the nest and avoid further loss (Leahy, 1997b, 2001a).

Why would hypomania and extreme optimism have a limited window of opportunity? Why is it that few people maintain a prolonged optimistic and hypersexual pattern today, given that we have, in the West at least, all but removed seasonal variation of resource availability? One might imagine that the exhilarated Don Juan of the primitive world would sire many hypomanic offspring and that progress would march on with little feet toward a better and more abundant world. The reason that life is not always perceived in such happy terms is that primitive humans struggled within a Malthusian balancing act of procreating many offspring who would likely die from starvation, cold, and predation. Overzealous happy Don Juans would sire many offspring who would compete with one another for scarce resources. Better, then, to have Don Juan balance his optimism against the pessimism of the Sorrows of Young Werther. Optimism is, by "nature," self-limiting, since too much optimism carries the seeds (literally and figuratively) of its own destruction.

The Value of Variation and the Modular Mind

Variation is of significance to cognitive processes because variation implies the chance of obtaining needed resources. Darwin's (1871) evolutionary model of the "fittest" is not that the "fittest" individual is stronger and smarter, but rather that "fitness" is determined through natural selection. Natural selection refers to environmental factors that are ever changing. Thus, a trait that may be "fit" in one environment may confer large costs in another. Fitness is always understood in terms of environmental demands, change, and survival. Indeed, this model of natural selection applies to the concept of intelligence and evolution, such that we can define intelligence as the ability to adapt to different environments (see Godfrey-Smith, 2002; Sternberg, 2002). Since there are many independent tasks for the individual to solve, such as finding food, procreating, and protecting against predators, evolutionary psychologists propose that different systematic programs have evolved to solve these independent problems. Thus, there may not be one intelligence or general factor, but rather separate sets of abilities and plans, known collectively as the "modular mind" (Tooby & Cosmides, 1992).

One aspect of the modular mind is its ability to respond to tasks under conditions that may vary considerably. For example, responding to feeding sources is different from responding to procreation demands. Different information, strategies, and behaviors are required. The individual must respond to variation in the environment for both tasks—scarcity and threat will affect the strategies employed. These strategies and the various modularity components will ultimately be determined by *inclusive fitness*—that is, how likely is it that one's genes will survive?

I argue that a central component of the evolution of depressive, manic, and worrisome thought is the need to respond to variation. Food sources may vary as to their density (high-low), distribution (predictable-patchy), and temporal appearance (e.g., seasonality) (Shettleworth, 1998). Thus, evolutionary cognition would be wise to establish some tendency to respond with variation of effort, searching, and consumption. Pessimism is one strategy that allows consideration of this variation.

Consider a mind that notices that a patch of resources appears satisfying. Why not continue to remain within that patch forever, since it continues to be rewarding? Research on grazing behavior indicates that animals will prefer the rewarding patch, but will spontaneously fluctuate a response to sample other areas for food (Krebs, Kacelnik, & Taylor, 1978). The value of this alternating strategy of investment is that it allows occasional searching for better payoffs, which is a strategy that may have low cost for short exploration and may carry a potential for high payoff in the event that the previously preferred patch is depleted. This suggests that investment strategies need to be open to new information by intentionally seeking variation in the environment even at times of plenty. Information is a resource to be constantly pursued. For example, what is the adaptive value of habituation? The answer is quite simple: You will look at something different. Familiarity breeds boredom. A similar pattern of exploring alternatives is reflected in the Coolidge Effect—the increased drive for novel sexual partners (Buss, 1994).

Both worry and mania reflect such a searching for new information. In the case of worry, the search is for potential problems and in the case of mania the search is for better payoffs. Individuals who worry often describe themselves as attempting to anticipate problems, find solutions, and motivate themselves to do better (Borkovec, Ray, & Stoeber, 1998; Wells, 2000). Worry, in a sense, is an essential component of an evolving culture, since it allows one to anticipate threats to the status quo that are not immediately apparent. Moreover, there is a low cost to worry in a procreative sense, since worriers do not often reduce their options for partners or food.

Mania may be viewed as a search strategy for more fulfilling alternatives. The manic individual will engage in increased motor activity, travel, sexual activity, and socializing, all behaviors that, in the right circumstances, will increase the likelihood of discovering food sources and sexual partners.

Varieties of Pessimism

Adaptive Pessimism

Perhaps the cognitive model has given pessimism a bad name. After all, pessimism is often associated with depression, sadness, hopelessness, and suicide—all traits that psychologists attempt to eliminate, but that nature, through genetic transmission, seems to provide recurring challenges for us to consider. The view taken here is that pessimism is sometimes quite *adaptive*. Indeed, pessimism can be life saving, life enhancing, and socially responsible. I make the case for the "dark side" of the mind, because—in a metaphorical and economic way—the dark side is the shadow made necessary by the bright side of optimism.

Just as Einstein might contend that God does not play dice with the universe, I would suggest that evolutionary pressures toward survival would not produce widespread traits that are generally maladaptive. Pessimism is such a trait. Pessimism involves a negative view of the past, present, and future; energizes itself through self-criticism, negative filters, and discounting the positive; rejects advice that seems to others quite plausible; and—in its darkest form— forsakes all hope and chooses suicide. Indeed, suicide, for some, is the termination of pessimism, its logical conclusion: "Pessimism shall live no more."

We shall examine the varieties of pessimism and how they can prove useful, given certain environments. We must keep in mind that the optimistic, progress-obsessed psychotherapist may be contending with a much more powerful force of the modular mind adapted to a world of scarcity, predation, and unpredictability. Telling the pessimist to move forward to a social gathering may be experienced by the listener as an invitation to a beheading. For the pessimist, progress may contrast with protection, preservation, and preparation for the worst.

Dimensions of Pessimism

Consider two dimensions of pessimism. The first refers to whether pessimism is focused on the past or future. The second dimension suggests that pessimism leads to inhibiting or facilitating certain behaviors. Reflective (or past-oriented) pessimism focuses the individual on losses, threats, or mistakes of the past. This ability to utilize information about past negatives can lead either to regret or self-correction. The depressed individual ruminates on his regrets of the past, often criticizing himself for his mistakes or losses. The adaptive value of this is that self-criticism—and withdrawal—will allow the individual time to think about how he went wrong in order to avoid further mistakes (Beck, 1987; Stevens & Price, 2000). If individuals did not reflect and regret, they might be less likely to learn from their losses, thereby reducing their eventual fitness.

Along with this tendency to reflect on past mistakes is the tendency to inhibit behavior in the face of a loss. Depressed individuals rely on a behavioral inhibition system (BIS). BIS is a system that responds to loss, deprivation, and failure by inhibiting further action (Gray, 1981). The hardwiring of the BIS is similar to a "stop-loss" process in the brain that minimizes the possibility of repeating a loss or a poor payoff of behaviors.

Anticipatory pessimism takes the form of worry and hopelessness. The individual either predicts that bad things may happen, in which case, he may worry until he finds a solution (Dugas, Buhr, & Ladouceur, 2004), or he may predict that nothing will work out and, therefore, reduce his behavior (Alloy, Abramson, Metalsky, & Hartledge, 1988). The adaptive value of anticipatory pessimism is that potential solutions may be found and future problems may be avoided. In the case of hopelessness and depression (or pessimism), the payoff may come by reducing the likelihood of throwing good money after bad.

Pessimism may also differ as to whether the negative event is close or distant in time or space and whether the event is approaching or receding at various degrees of velocity. For example, Riskind's (Riskind, Long, Williams, & White, 2000; Riskind & Williams, 1999) looming vulnerability model suggests that negative events that are viewed as approaching rapidly and that are getting nearer the target of the self are also viewed as more threatening, requiring activation of behavior or cognitions to avoid impact. The "duck" or "dodge" response to threat (Beck, 1987; Beck, Emery, & Greenberg, 1985;

Riskind et al., 2000; Riskind & Williams, 1999) allows the individual to cope with the movement through space and time of negative events. Individuals who utilize rapid responses to escape and avoid might be more adaptive in environments with rapidly appearing or approaching threats. Pessimistic activation of responses that can detect and respond to imminent threat would provide advantages that a more reflective (slower) program would fail to provide. Because of the need of adaptive pessimistic strategies to respond quickly, these strategies would have to rely on the immediacy and intense discomfort of emotions (Greenberg, 2001 and this book; LeDoux, 1996). Emotions are immediate, require no reflection, and mobilize the individual to engage in action to produce immediate change. Individuals who rely on *emotional reasoning, catastrophizing, personalizing, or selective filters* to discern, evaluate, or respond to a threat would have the advantage of detecting and avoiding negative impact with threat. This is consistent with the concept of *automatic thoughts* (Beck, Rush, Shaw, & Emery, 1979) and the sense of a critical reaction to threat (Eibl-Eibesfeldt, 1974; Lorenz, 1966). Pessimism would thus become hardwired with a quick trigger set off by emotional alarms, which are sometimes false alarms (see Hofmann, Moscovitch & Heinrichs, this book).

Epistemology of Pessimism

What will information be used for? Primitive pessimists are not interested in seeking out all information. They are primarily interested in information related to potential danger or loss. Thus, research on anxious and depressed individuals indicates selective attention to negative or threatening information (Gotlib & Neubauer, 2000). The information to be obtained must have pragmatic or action implications—that is, what will I do if there is a sign of a predator or scarcity?

Most models of behavior are based on probabilistic estimates—for example, Herrnstein's (1961) "matching law" suggests that the organism will match the rate of response to the ratio of rewards. These probabilistic models, based on a response-to-reward ratio, might be applicable in closed environments of learning. However, once the pessimistic schema or strategy is activated, the individual is less concerned with collecting information about probabilities and ratios over time. Taking too much time might kill you. The emphasis is less on probability and more on the chance, *any chance,* of a devastating negative (see Von Mises, 1957, on the distinction between probability and chance).

The imagination of a chance may be a sufficient guideline to step out quickly. Collecting a sequence of outcomes over a long period of "hands" may not be an option worth considering.

Pessimistic epistemology is not only in search of chance. It is also in search of examples, especially those that can be represented as images or narratives that can evoke emotions. This is why presenting pessimists with baseline information about abstract probabilities often seems so fruitless. We are asking people to consider the ratio of events to non-events at a time when they are looking for danger (these are the relative frequencies in probability statements). The primitive pessimistic mind is looking for sufficient evidence to escape or avoid—evidence that can be found in positive cases of danger, rather than non-events of non-danger. Thus, exposure to images or narratives of negative outcomes without distraction or escape can be an effective treatment for worry (Borkovec et al., 1998; Wells, 1997, 2000). The exposure allows the emotional processing of the negative image in the pessimism that is an important component of the pessimistic emotional process. Base-rate information leaves the anxious pessimist "cold."

An example of this search for chance is that worried pessimists often reject baseline information or probability statements by saying, "You can always be the one." The pessimist who focuses on the chance of being "the one" is emphasizing that, when it comes to predicting danger, false positives do not have much of a downside. If you think there is a tiger and you run, only to discover that there was no tiger, this produces only the sacrifice of the time and energy spent running. However, if you fail to predict a danger that is there (the false negative), then you are eaten by the tiger (see Hofmann, Moscovitch & Heinrichs, this book). As Gilbert (1998) has indicated, there is much in cognitive distortions that represents the better-safe-than-sorry strategy.

Anecdotes that represent images and narratives are often helpful in challenging pessimistic thinking since they are related to the level of emotional and cognitive processing of the pessimistic strategy. They make safety and optimism real by appealing to the emotional brain.

Investment Model of Depression

I have proposed that individuals differ as to their strategies in making decisions about how they will invest their behavior and resources (Leahy, 1997a, 2001a). In the primitive environment, the individual must contemplate a bet as to the payoff ratio for various risks. In an environment of scarcity, where the individual may have accumulated rather meager resources, risky decisions to pursue more might jeopardize the current limited resources for a low probability of obtaining meager payoffs. In such a gamble, a pessimistic strategy toward risk makes sense, in which one would minimize losses because the maximization of gain seems implausible. This may be similar to "protecting the nest egg," a concept applied in earlier research on risk behavior (Kogan & Wallach, 1964).

In contrast to the assessment that the environment contains few possibilities for reward, the optimistic (or manic) individual may contemplate high likelihood of highly valued resources (Leahy, 1999, 2000). In such an environment, the individual may be less concerned with protecting the nest than with building a new one. The investment model of decision making outlined below has implications for decisions made in variable environments with individuals perceiving themselves as having more or fewer resources.

Portfolio Theories

Markowitz (1952) proposed a micro-economic model of decision making that suggests different patterns of investment strategies for individuals who differ in their assumptions about current resources, time horizon, and risk tolerance. A portfolio is defined as a collection of various "investments" that one can make. In financial models, portfolios contain stocks, bonds, real estate, and cash. In an evolutionary model, a portfolio contains behavioral investments in searching for food, procreation, fidelity, and accumulation. In the financial metaphor, one considers a financial goal of accumulating capital in contrast potentially with protecting current assets. In an evolutionary model, the concern is whether one takes risks to obtain more food, territory, and mates, or whether one protects the nest egg that currently exists. The preference question is between maximizing gains against minimizing losses. Individuals differ as to the theories and strategies that guide their portfolios, with some individuals assuming that they have large current and future resources, a longer time horizon, and a greater tolerance for risk. I refer to this as an optimistic portfolio theory. Others view themselves as having few current and future resources, a short time horizon, and low tolerance for risk—a depressive portfolio theory (Leahy, 2001a).

It is the argument in the current model that maximizing and minimizing strategies may be flexible under different environmental conditions. Thus, depression, a minimization of loss strategy, makes sense in an environment of scarcity. Hypomania or mania may make sense in an environment of sudden increase of resources where these resources run the risk of rapid depletion. Given the considerably higher ratio of depression versus mania in the general population (with depression and anxiety occurring at rates about 50 times greater than manic states), one might infer that earlier environments were considerably more likely to be characterized by scarcity and danger than by opportunity and safety.

Resources and Predictability. Individuals will pursue a more risky strategy if they believe that they have high current and future resources (Leahy, 1997b). In times of scarcity, the most prudent strategy would be to protect the nest egg, especially if it is a diminishing resource. Gambles of the few resources left could lead to devastating losses. Reduced resources would likely result in decreased consumption and procreation. If future resources appeared to be unpredictable, the individual might opt for a bet on a smaller—but more certain outcome.

Time Horizons. The pessimistic investor views himself as having a limited time horizon. Rewards must be forthcoming immediately. This myopic demand for immediate payoff would be characteristic of deprived individuals in environments with instability and scarcity of resources. Limited time horizon and myopic choice would lead to binge eating, quitting early when frustrated, and choosing a small reward now rather than a larger reward later. As a procreative strategy, limited time horizon would reduce fertility, since the individual would be less likely to view the longer investment of childbearing as worth the risk. It should be noted that there is now considerable evidence that an early history of poor availability of resources (e.g., poor attachments to care providers) and/or high threats to a child (e.g., abuse) constitute powerful vulnerabilities to depression (Gilbert, 2001). Such findings may indicate that these early experiences tend to orient or shape the person's strategic focus to risk and threat sensitivity and pessimism. However, children who grow up in secure and resource-abundant environments may be advantaged by adopting more optimistic strategies for life. In other words early life experiences are informing psychobiological mechanisms what the likely life environment will be and how best to cope (e.g., be relatively more threat sensitive or reward sensitive).

Replications. Increased replication of investment of behavior increases the longer-term payoff. Repeating investment in a food or procreative source, along with an expanded time horizon, would imply that the individual could return many times to the investment to increase his holdings. Replication would be more characteristic of the "gatherer," who plants his seeds and waits to harvest. Depressive styles of investment are not based on replication. The worldview is myopic and focuses on the short-term payoff for immediate behavior.

Strategies of Risk Management

Threshold of Positives and Negatives

The depressive style maintains that only large positives count as gains, but small negatives are counted as losses. This asymmetrical definition of threshold reflects the belief that the environment has scarce and unpredictable resources and that becoming optimistic after a single positive may lead to disappointment and future risk. I have described this as the ambivalence about hope (Leahy, 2001b). By containing hope within the boundaries of a scarcity model, the individual reduces risk of overexposure. Primitive individuals utilizing this pessimistic strategy are betting that they would be wise to take the money off the table and cash in, rather than continue to play future hands and lose their small holdings. For example, a scavenging hominid, eating the carrion left behind by a satiated lion, would be wise to contain his hopes that he has found a free dining opportunity to which to return: better to eat and run.

Primitive pessimists would have ambivalence toward hope. Even if a positive event occurred, such as the discovery of a new food source, the pessimist might be afraid of getting hopes up too high. This is because the pessimist is guided by scarcity assumptions about resources in general. However, this ambivalence about hope, given the discovery of new resources, might be less if the individual has already accumulated significant resources. Thus, the willingness to count on the future might be predicated on having been successful in the past. Individuals who get their hopes up, and have few current resources, run the risk of increasing consumption and procreation only to find that they were basing it on fool's gold.

Hedging

Hedging refers to placing bets against yourself—one foot in and one foot out. In feeding behavior, animals will prefer to feed in areas that provide predictable and abundant supplies, but they will spontaneously alternate on occasion to other sites, as if they are collecting information about alternatives, should they need them (Krebs et al., 1978). Hedging is a strategy that is used in procreation as well. Females may hedge their bets against "inferior" male sperm by acts of infidelity with more intelligent, powerful, healthier, and more attractive partners, while attaching themselves to a partner who will supply them with food and protection (Buss, 1994). Males will utilize hedging by dispersing their sperm among many different partners, thereby using diversification as a bet against overexposure to females who may be hedging against them or whose offspring may not survive.

Depressed individuals may not view themselves as having a hedging alternative due to lower rank and attractiveness. Consequently, they will utilize a "lock and freeze" strategy of increased dependency and attachment demands, often characterized by jealousy and clinging behavior. By trying to "lock in" their investment with the partner (by eliminating the partner's alternatives), they may reduce the chances that their parental investment will be compromised.

Hiding

When all else fails, lay low. Hiding is a more likely strategy for pessimists fearing predators or attack from socially "superior" individuals. Hiding may take various forms including submissive posture, lowered eye gaze, softened voice, and escape from contact. Just as hiding reduces the likelihood of being attacked, either through inhibiting the aggressive behavior of others or through reducing opportunity (Eibl-Eibesfeldt, 1974), it will also dramatically reduce chances for procreation. This may also serve as a strategy to preserve resources that can be utilized at a more profitable time to bear young. Hiding can be utilized as a delay of appetitive behavior during seasonal fluctuations, most evident in hibernation, dormancy, and torpor.

Reducing Consumption

A common method of reducing the need for investment is to reduce consumption or demand. This takes the form of decreased appetite, lowered metabolic rate, decreased sex drive, and decreased fertility (ovulation, testosterone level, etc.). Primitive pessimistic investors might reduce the need for payoffs by lowering their expectations and drive level. Hibernation behavior is a prime example of this lowered consumption strategy. Lowered sex drive has the benefit of placing less demand on the individual to obtain partners, less risk of competition with dominant conspecifics, and less demand to obtain and protect food sources and nesting sites. Even where these rewards may be available, a lowered drive toward appetitive behavior provides the added benefit of increasing savings. We can refer to this as the "pessimistic budget," which is essentially lowered drive, lowered consumption, and increased savings through hoarding.

Focusing on a Single Figure

Although focusing on a single attachment figure may be viewed as a normal attachment development (Ainsworth, 1969; Bowlby, 1968), it can also serve the function of lowering the need for obtaining and consuming resources. During times of depression and anxiety there is often an increase of dependent behavior, which may appear in the form of clinging, demanding reassurance, or even agoraphobia. This reduces the opportunity for promiscuous pursuit of alternative attachment and sexual partners, and reduces the demand on the individual to obtain more. By focusing on a single figure during lean periods, the individual increases the likelihood that this single investment will pay off and the offspring will survive. Moreover, if the depression is a reflection of recent defeats and loss of resources, it may be the better strategy to consolidate investments in a single place. Of course, this nondiversified strategy creates a greater risk of abandonment and loss of existing opportunities, further adding to the apprehension that the attachment object will leave.

Parental Investment Strategies

Females have considerably greater investment in the consequences of sexual union than males do since the female will experience nine months of pregnancy followed by inhibition of fertility during lactation (Geary, 1998). Moreover, there is certainty for the female that the child is hers (Trivers, 1971). The male, however, may have very limited, if any, investment in the offspring. The male's investment in the sexual act may be limited to a few minutes, he is uncertain about paternity, and he does not bear the consequences of pregnancy and subsequent reduced fertility. Thus, in social contexts where males control resources, females will be more likely to select males who will provide these resources (wealth), who are generous, and who are ambitious, since this will increase the likelihood of access to resources to support the offspring. Males will be more likely to select for physical attractiveness and signs of health, since these may reflect the likelihood that the offspring will be healthy (Buss, 1994).

Do males and females differ in their tolerance of risk? First, there is considerable evidence that males are far more likely to take risks (see Slovic, 2000) and far less likely to be depressed. Females may prefer males who are ambitious, industrious, and assertive, as long as these traits imply that the male will be generous with his resources (Buss, 1994; Geary, 1998). Second, if females are more likely to be depressed—and to utilize a risk-averse strategy—there may be times when a "risk-loving" male may be less desirable. This reflects the different preferences that females have for short-term and long-term relationships. In the short-term, they may prefer the risk-taking, Don Juan type, but in the long-term, they prefer the more conservative investor who will replicate and protect investments and who has abundant resources. This latter type is neither depressed nor manic, rather, we might label him as *prudent*.

Portfolio Theory of Parental Investment

Why is there greater prevalence of depression in females than males? A well-established principle of evolutionary models is that females have a greater investment in offspring than do males (Geary, 1998). This *parental investment model* may help us understand why depression is a more useful strategy for females to employ for inhibiting procreative behavior. The female who views her current resources as low and anticipates deprivation is wise to inhibit sexual behavior until a time when investments that are more profitable can be secured. Males, on the other hand, because of their reduced parental investment in offspring, might be less affected by deprivation of resources since they can diversify their genetic investment with many partners. Males are more diversified in their portfolios than are females. Consequently, it may be that the reason females are twice as likely as males to be depressed is that depression is a preferred strategy to inhibit risky procreative behavior in females other than in males: females have more to lose by unrealistic optimism in procreating.

Promiscuity may be a hedging strategy that works better for males than for females. Promiscuous pairings by the nondepressed male allows him to diversify his sperm portfolio into numerous receptive and reproductive females. The promiscuous male employs a strategy of hedging against a single pregnancy. A single pregnancy may not succeed; the child may not live. Moreover, the male can never be certain of the paternity of the child, so diversification provides a protective insurance policy against false-positive pregnancies.

However, too much diversification by the male may result in none of the offspring living. Overpopulation, with limited food resources and competition with other males and their offspring, may render the overly diversified portfolio a waste of valuable resources. Consequently, the male who is inclined to overly diversify would contend with as strong a tendency to protect and nurture the sperm investments that he makes. This might produce strong monogamous attachments (especially during the early years of childhood of the offspring), jealousy (especially during the child-bearing years of the female), antagonism toward other males and their offspring, and accumulation of food resources that can be distributed to the offspring. A greater ability to inhibit behavior may prove adaptive in these situations, allowing longer-term investments in child rearing by the male (Bjorklund & Kipp, 1996). Inhibition may be an essential component in the ability to build up a larger portfolio of children who live by virtue of being protected, nurtured, and socialized by the familial unit (see Bjorklund & Kipp, 2002 on inhibition and evolution). Indeed, the ability to inhibit impulses may be an essential component in the formation of lasting families, expansion of kinship groups, and the development of rudimentary culture.

We can apply the portfolio theory to these different investment positions implied by parental investment theory (Trivers, 1971). Assume that the payoff is survival of offspring bearing direct genetic resemblance to the individual—that is, inclusive fitness will define the goal of behavior (Geary, 1998; Hamilton, 1963; Trivers, 1971). In order to pursue inclusive fitness, males and females would approach sexual behavior and childbearing with different portfolio theories, or strategies. These different portfolio strategies are shown in Table 4.1.

TABLE 4.1. Male and Female Portfolio Theories

Dimension	Female	Male
Replication	Low	High
Duration	High	Low
Diversification	Low	High
Threshold for positive	High	Low
Threshold for negative	Low	High
Stop-out/Quit	Low	High
Information demands	High	Low
Ability to absorb loss	Low	High
Regret	High	Low
Hedging	Low	High
Risk preference	Low	High

Given the time committed to each pregnancy and the lifetime limit on total possible pregnancies, females have low replication for pregnancies; they have less replication of pregnancy than males, who can possibly impregnate countless women. The female is committing her investment for a long duration, not only in pregnancy, but also in raising the child. Male investments might be quite short or transitory. Females, due to the limitations posed by pregnancy, are much less diversified than males are, given that males can pursue a Don Juan strategy of impregnating many women.

Because females have more to lose by choosing a partner who might abandon them, they would be expected to have a high threshold for defining a positive partner. Thus, females would be less likely than males to agree to sexual union and would require clear evidence of some commitment. Males would have lower criteria for defining a positive opportunity, since they are investing less and can replicate and diversify more readily. Similarly, just as females may have higher standards than males do, they would be more likely to define a negative as a reason to terminate an initial relationship. Thus, females would be more likely to consider "inappropriate behavior" as relevant; their standards will be higher than the standards held by males. Males, on the other hand, pursuing a strategy of diversification and opportunity, might be more tolerant of negatives in the initial interaction.

Females would be more likely to be pursued by males who are trying to demonstrate that they, the males, live up to these demanding standards. Given the different positions regarding parental investments, males might be more likely to appeal by displaying wealth, power, physical strength, status, and generosity, while females would be more likely to display physical attractiveness, youth, fidelity, and nurturance (Buss, 1994). Since females have more to lose, they would require greater information about the desirability and trustworthiness of their partners, whereas males might view partners in an opportunistic short-term frame, seeing the opportunity for a quick liaison as a chance for diversification at low cost and no commitment. For males, simple willingness to participate may be the only relevant information required. For females, a promise of commitment and fidelity and the chance for a longer-term partnership may be required.

Males and females would evolve points of equilibrium with relatively more conservative females and diversified and risk-taking male strategies. However, the relative points of these equilibria would change, dependent on current resources available and the pressure of competitors. Females would select for males willing to commit and males would select for females who are likely to bear and nurture healthy offspring.

Females are in a poorer position to absorb a loss of a child or the premature termination of a pregnancy, since they have lower replication, longer duration of investment, and less diversification. Males, because of their diversification strategy, can afford losses more readily and may view a loss as a sufficient reason to terminate a relationship. Females would exercise more choice over partners than males would. Females would be more likely to regret a poor decision; not only emotionally, but practically, since choosing the "wrong mate" may saddle them with long-term costs without a supportive partner. Females have more to regret since they have more invested and more to lose. Males would be less likely to regret since they can more easily focus on longer-term opportunities with many other potential partners. Although both males and females might use hedging strategies by pursuing out-of-relationship coupling, the male is more likely to utilize this strategy (Buss, 1994; Geary, 1998). Hedging for the female is not likely to produce a supportive new partner, since the hedging partner is likely to be a male seeking quick gratification and low-cost diversification.

The foregoing suggests that males and females will differ in risk preference of risk tolerance. Research on risky behavior and subjective perceptions of risk consistently indicate that males are far more risk tolerant than females are and underestimate risks for more often than do females (Slovic, 2000).

Competition Between Pessimism and Optimism

Given the case made for pessimism it might even seem to the reader that pessimism is an excellent strategy and, therefore, why not use it at all times? Consider several individuals playing close to an infinite number of hands of betting on "high card wins." Winner takes the entire pot. Two players use extreme strategies. One is a pessimist, the other is an optimist, and both are inflexible. The pessimist always bets that he will lose (and drops out on each hand) and the optimist always bets that he will win. Over a period of hands, the pessimist may not gain anything, but he will suffer only the losses of his "ante." Eventually he will be extinguished. However, some pessimists may be less rigid. In the event of an especially good deal of an ace (where he might be the high card), he will still have all his chips, so he can bet when the betting is good. The optimist may win some of the hands, lose some of them against the other players, but his eventual standing in the game will depend on chance. He will "take his chances." Along the way, he may accumulate some winnings. In the evolutionary model, his winnings may represent offspring who are somewhat optimistic but not as gung-ho as dad. The extreme optimist eventually will start playing "double-or-nothing," being carried away by the momentum of earlier wins. Eventually he will end up with nothing.

If the pessimist is so negative that he will not utilize any of his resources, then his extreme negativity will die off with him. But few pessimists will stay this negative forever and, perhaps through some adaptive impulsivity, may play a hand, or have a child. This may lead to some winnings, breaking some of the inflexibility of the pessimism. Interestingly, there is some evidence that lower-ranked individuals are more impulsive than higher-ranked individuals, perhaps because complete inhibition would lead to total loss, whereas some impulsivity might produce some gains and, in some cases, a change in a dominance hierarchy (Bjorklund & Kipp, 2002).

However, the optimist will have spread some of his winnings to offspring who have regressed toward the mean of more balanced ideas of card games. The pessimist may have utilized some of his resources to support a few somewhat pessimistic offspring of his own. Perhaps the offspring of these respective players will begin to mix their strategies and their genes with each other, producing "balanced" approaches. Balanced approaches, along with more extreme outliers of pessimists and optimists, will emerge in the mix of genes over many iterations of these hands. A normal distribution of outlooks will result, some of which we will label as "depressed," others as "manic," and a few as "normal." Pessimism will remain part of this "normal" distribution.

Conclusion

Currently, cognitive therapists tend to see cognitive processing (e.g., automatic thoughts) as arising from acquired schematic representations of the self and the world that can be addressed by appeals to logic and evidence testing. However, evolutionary considerations offer a different focus that suggests our brains evolved to select certain strategies for engagement with the world. The details for the selection of these strategies may or may not be consciously available to us (e.g., male and female reproductive strategies) or changeable through the logic of argument alone. Indeed, pessimism has a mind of its own. It can represent a strategic orientation to life, which a person may consciously wish he did not have. It is directed toward finding reasons to avoid or escape and is motivated by the desire to reduce risk. I have suggested that many universally manifested tendencies such as phobia, worry, depression, and mania may be understood as biologically preadaptive parts of the modular mind. This modular mind attempts to protect whatever "investments" in genes the individual will make.

Rather than looking at pessimism as a distortion in thinking, I have proposed that it is better conceptualized as an evolved bias toward the negative. In environments where there is scarcity, lack of predictability, and threat of annihilation, pessimistic strategies might be both realistic and ultimately rewarding. In environments with sudden-appearing opportunities, optimistic or even manic enthusiasm could prove advantageous. Evolutionary pressures and adaptations cover all of their bets by producing individuals who vary along these dimensions of pessimism and optimism or who have periodic remission of their pessimism. Rather than look at evolution as creating an optimistic individual who holds 1000 tickets with the same number in a lottery, the present model argues in favor of variation, covering a diversity of "lottery tickets." Variation of response is an adaptation to the pressures of natural selection.

The portfolio theory model is also relevant to the putative different strategies of males and females derived from parental investment theory. In considering opportunities for procreation, the female portfolio theory emphasizes reducing risk, increasing the quality and protection of the investment, and assuring security. In contrast, the male portfolio theory is more risk accepting and will attempt to diversify and, in some cases, escape from the costs placed on procreation. However, these two strategies serve to correct each other toward an equilibrium point, such that males that are too diversified will sacrifice fitness and males that are too conservative may find themselves without partners. These investment strategies reflect many of the differences between males and females in their cognitive schemata, resulting in increased vulnerability for females. Insofar as cognitive therapists are engaged in efforts to help people change the way they think and feel, we are also engaged in helping people change the activation of evolved strategic options. The therapeutic implications and possibilities for such change open challenging horizons.

References

Ainsworth, M. D. (1969). Object relations, dependency, and attachment: A theoretical review of the infant-mother relationship. *Child Development, 40,* 969–1025.

Alloy, L. B., Abramson, L. Y., Metalsky, G. I., & Hartledge, S. (1988). The hopelessness theory of depression. *British Journal of Clinical Psychology, 27,* 5–12.

Beck, A. T. (1987). Cognitive models of depression. *Journal of Cognitive Psychotherapy, 1,* 5–37.

Beck, A. T., Emery, G., & Greenberg, R. L. (1985). *Anxiety disorders and phobias: A cognitive perspective.* New York: Basic Books.

Beck, A. T., Rush, A. J., Shaw, B. F., & Emery, G. (1979). *Cognitive therapy of depression.* New York: Guilford.

Bjorklund, D. F., & Kipp, K. (1996). Parental investment theory and gender differences in the evolution of inhibition mechanisms. *Psychological Bulletin, 120,* 163–188.

Bjorklund, D. F., & Kipp, K. (2002). Social cognition, inhibition, and theory of mind: The evolution of human intelligence. In R. J. Sternberg & J. C. Kaufman (Eds.), *The evolution of intelligence* (pp. 27–54). Mahwah, NJ: Erlbaum.

Borkovec, T. D., Ray, W. J., & Stoeber, J. (1998). Worry: A cognitive phenomenon intimately linked to affective, physiological, and interpersonal behavioral processes. *Cognitive Therapy and Research, 22,* 561–576.

Bowlby, J. (1968). *Attachment and loss: Attachment* (Vol. 1). London: Hogarth.

Buss, D. M. (1994). *The evolution of desire: Strategies of human mating.* New York: Basic Books.

Chapman, T. F. (1997). The epidemiology of fears and phobias. In G. C. L. Davey (Ed.), *Phobias: A handbook of theory, research and treatment* (pp. 415–434). West Sussex, UK: Wiley.

Cosmides, L., & Tooby, J. (2002). Unraveling the enigma of human intelligence: Evolutionary psychology and the multimodular mind. In R. J. Sternberg, & J. C. Kaufman (Eds.), *The evolution of intelligence* (pp. 145–198). Mahwah, NJ: Erlbaum.

Darwin, C. (1871). *The descent of man and selection in relation to sex.* London: John Murray.

Dugas, M. J., Buhr, K., & Ladouceur, R. (2004). The role of intolerance of uncertainty in the etiology and maintenance of generalized anxiety disorder. In R. G. Heimberg, C. L. Turk, & D. S. Mennin (Eds.), *Generalized anxiety disorder: Advances in research and practice.* New York: Guilford.

Eibl-Eibesfeldt, I. (1974). *Love and hate: The natural history of behavior patterns* (G. Strachan, Trans.). New York: Schocken.

Geary, D. C. (1998). *Male, female: The evolution of human sex differences.* Washington, DC: American Psychological Association.

Gilbert, P. (1998). The evolved basis and adaptive functions of cognitive distortions. *British Journal of Medical Psychology, 71,* 447–463.

Gilbert, P. (2001). Depression and stress: A biopsychosocial exploration of evolved functions and mechanisms. *Stress: The International Journal of the Biology of Stress, 4,* 121–135.

Godfrey-Smith, P. (2002). Environmental complexity and the evolution of cognition. In R. J. Sternberg & J. C. Kaufman (Eds.), *The evolution of intelligence* (pp. 223–249). Mahwah, NJ: Erlbaum.

Gotlib, I. H., & Neubauer, D. L. (2000). Information-processing approaches to the study of cognitive biases in depression. In S. L. Johnson, A. M. Hayes, T. M. Field, N. Schneiderman, & P. M. McCabe (Eds.), *Stress, coping, and depression* (pp. 117–143). Mahwah, NJ: Erlbaum.

Graham, J., & Gaffan, E. A. (1997). Fear of water in children and adults: Etiology and familial effects. *Behaviour Research and Therapy, 35,* 91–108.

Gray, J. A. (1981). A critique of Eysenck's theory of personality. In H. J. Eysenck (Ed.), *A model for personality* (pp. 246–276). Berlin: Springer-Verlag.

Greenberg, L. (2002). Integrating an emotion-focused approach to treatment into psychotherapy integration. *Psychotherapy Integration, 12,* 154–190.

Hamilton, W. D. (1963). The evolution of altruistic behavior. *American Naturalist, 97,* 354–356.

Herrnstein, R. J. (1961). Relative and absolute strength of response as a function of frequency of reinforcement. *Journal of the Experimental Analysis of Behavior, 4*, 267–272.

Kogan, N., & Wallach, M. A. (1964). *Risk taking: A study in cognition and personality*. New York: Holt, Rinehart and Winston.

Krebs, J. R., Kacelnik, A., & Taylor, P. (1978). Test of optimal sampling by foraging great tits. *Nature, 275*, 27–31.

Leahy, R. L. (1997a). Depression and resistance: An investment model of decision making. *The Behavior Therapist*, 3–6.

Leahy, R. L. (1997b). An investment model of depressive resistance. *Journal of Cognitive Psychotherapy: An International Quarterly, 11*, 3–19.

Leahy, R. L. (1999). Decision making and mania. *Journal of Cognitive Psychotherapy: An International Quarterly, 13*, 83–105.

Leahy, R. L. (2000). Mood and decisions: Implications for bipolar disorder. *The Behavior Therapist*, 62–63.

Leahy, R. L. (2001a). Depressive decision making: Validation of the portfolio theory model. *Journal of Cognitive Psychotherapy, 15*, 341–362.

Leahy, R. L. (2001b). *Overcoming resistance in cognitive therapy*. New York: Guilford.

LeDoux, J. E. (1996). *The emotional brain: The mysterious underpinnings of emotional life*. New York: Simon & Schuster.

Lorenz, K. (1966). *On aggression*. New York: Harcourt-Brace.

Markowitz, H. (1952). Portfolio selection. *The Journal of Finance, 7*, 77–91.

Marks, I. M. (1987). *Fears, phobias, and rituals: Panic, anxiety, and their disorders*. New York: Oxford University Press.

Meyer, R. G., & Deitsch, S. E. (1996). *The clinician's handbook: Integrated diagnostics, assessment, and intervention in adult and adolescent psychopathology* (4th ed.). Needham Heights, MA: Allyn & Bacon.

Nesse, R. M. (2000) Is depression an adaptation? *Archives of General Psychiatry, 57*, 14–20.

Poulton, R., Davies, S., Menzies, R. G., Langley, J. D., & Silva, P. A. (1998). Evidence for a non-associative model of the acquisition of a fear of heights. *Behaviour Research and Therapy, 36*, 537–544.

Poulton, R., & Menzies, R. G. (2002). Fears born and bred: Toward a more inclusive theory of fear acquisition. *Behaviour Research and Therapy, 40*, 197–208.

Price, R. A. (2002). Genetics and common obesities: Background, current status, strategies, and future prospects. In T. A. Wadden & A. J. Stunkard (Eds.), *Handbook of obesity treatment* (pp. 73–94). New York: Guilford.

Ridley, M. (1996). *The origins of virtue: Human instincts and the evolution of cooperation*. New York: Penguin.

Riskind, J. H., Long, D. G., Williams, N. L., & White, J. C. (2000). Desperate acts for desperate times: Looming vulnerability and suicide. In T. E. Joiner

& M. D. Rudd (Eds.), *Suicide science: Expanding the boundaries* (pp. 105–115). Norwell, MA: Kluwer Academic Publishers.

Riskind, J. H., & Williams, N. L. (1999). Cognitive case conceptualization and treatment of anxiety disorders: Implications of the looming vulnerability model. *Journal of Cognitive Psychotherapy, 13,* 295–315.

Schacter, D. L. (1996). *Searching for memory: The brain, the mind, and the past.* New York: Basic Books.

Shettleworth, S. J. (1998). *Cognition, evolution, and behavior.* New York: Oxford University Press.

Slovic, P. (2000). Trust, emotion, sex, politics, and science: Surveying the risk-assessment battlefield. In P. Slovic (Ed.), *The perception of risk* (pp. 277–313). Sterling, VA: Earthscan Publications.

Sternberg, R. J. (2002). The search for criteria: Why study the evolution of intelligence? In R. J. Sternberg & J. C. Kaufman (Eds.), *The evolution of intelligence* (pp. 1–7). Mahwah, NJ: Erlbaum.

Stevens, A., & Price, J. (2000). *Evolutionary psychiatry: A new beginning* (2nd ed.). London: Routledge/Taylor and Francis Group.

Tooby, J., & Cosmides, L. (1992). The psychological foundations of culture. In J. H. Barkow & L. Cosmides (Eds.), *The adapted mind: Evolutionary psychology and the generation of culture* (pp. 19–136). New York: Oxford University Press.

Trivers, R. (1971). The evolution of reciprocal altruism. *Quarterly Review of Biology, 46,* 35–57.

Von Mises, R. (1957). *Probability, statistics and truth* (2nd ed.). New York: Macmillan.

Weissman, M. M., Bland, R., Joyce, P. R., & Newman, S. (1993). Sex differences in rates of depression: Cross-national perspectives. *Journal of Affective Disorders, 29,* 77–84.

Wells, A. (1997). *Cognitive therapy of anxiety disorders: A practice manual and conceptual guide.* Chichester, UK: Wiley.

Wells, A. (2000). *Emotional disorders and metacognition: Innovative cognitive therapy.* New York: Wiley.

Wilson, E. O. (1975). *Sociobiology: The new synthesis.* Cambridge, MA: Belknap Press of Harvard University Press.

Acknowledgment. I would like to thank Randye Semple for her tireless and diligent attention to bringing my chapter to fruition. Also, Paul Gilbert has been an encouraging voice and a supportive and critical ear.

Chapter 5

Evolutionary Mechanisms of Fear and Anxiety

Stefan G. Hofmann, David A. Moscovitch
and Nina Heinrichs

Introduction

Evolutionary psychology examines the role of evolved psychological mechanisms in shaping human behavior and experience. Evolved psychological mechanisms are understood to be a set of processes inside an individual, which have developed into their current form as a result of successfully solving specific adaptive problems for that individual's ancestors (e.g., Buss, 1999). Generally, an adaptive solution is one that increases the inclusive fitness of the individual, meaning that his or her genes have an increased chance of being represented in subsequent generations (Hamilton, 1964).

Fear and anxiety are commonly experienced by all human beings and are part of an elaborate menu of defensive, adaptive processes, which have evolved over millions of years in us humans and our mammalian ancestors (Gilbert, this volume; Panksepp, 1998). Thus, in considering the clinical expressions and treatment of these experiences and behaviors—namely, anxiety disorders and phobias—the role of evolutionary mechanisms should be addressed.

Before examining these mechanisms, our primary task will be to define the constructs of our discussion. Clinical scientists do not clearly distinguish between anxiety and fear, and often use the terms interchangeably. The DSM-IV (APA, 1994), defines anxiety as "the apprehensive anticipation of future danger or misfortune accompanied by a feeling of dysphoria or somatic symptoms of tension" (p. 764). No separate definition is given for fear, but the term is included in the many definitions of the DSM-IV anxiety disorders. For example, the diagnostic manual defines specific phobia as the "marked and persistent fear of clearly discernible, circumscribed objects or situations" (p. 405), and social phobia as a "marked and persistent fear of social or performance situations in which embarrassment may occur" (p. 411).

Contemporary emotion theorists characterize fear (but not anxiety) as a "basic" emotion. Basic emotions are believed to occur in all human beings, across all cultures. They fulfill useful, evolutionarily adaptive functions in dealing with fundamental life-tasks by mobilizing quick and adaptive reactions in response to threatening situations. According to this conceptualization, the primary function of fear is to cope with threats. Ekman (1992) posits that a feeling constitutes a basic emotion if: (1) it has a quick onset; (2) it is of brief duration; (3) it occurs involuntarily; (4) the autonomic appraisal of the event that triggers it leads to an almost instant recognition of the stimulus; (5) its antecedent events are universal (i.e., are not specific to one particular culture); (6) the feeling is accompanied by a unique pattern of physiological symptoms; and (7) it is characterized by distinctive universal signals in the form of singular facial expressions and behavior. Emotion researchers postulate that, in addition to fear, there exist approximately three to nine basic emotions (e.g., Ekman, 1992; Izard, 1992; Öhman, 1992; Plutchik, 1980; Tomkins, 1963).

In contrast to fear, anxiety is conceptualized as a cognitive association that connects basic emotions (such as fear) to events, meanings and responses (Izard, 1992). These cognitive associations are less "hardwired" than basic emotions and, therefore, vary widely depending on the individual and the situation. Although fear and anxiety are different, both are adaptive emotional responses to threat. If these emotions become maladaptive (e.g. excessive in intensity, frequency or duration), they may develop into emotional disorders, or anxiety disorders.

The DSM-IV category of anxiety disorders comprises a heterogeneous group of emotional and behavior problems. Using an evolutionarily based categorization system, Mayr (1974) distinguished between behaviors directed toward the living and nonliving world (communicative vs. noncommunicative behaviors). Within the communicative category, Mayr further distinguished between behaviors that are directed toward members of one's own species (intraspecific behaviors) and behaviors that are directed toward members of other species (interspecific behaviors). Specific phobias of heights, snakes, and social phobia, for example, correspond to noncommunicative, interspecific communicative, and intraspecific communicative behaviors, respectively.

Our discussion will include examples from all three of Mayr's categories. We will begin our discussion with a review of the prominent fear-acquisition models of specific phobias in the history of psychology, and their relationship to evolutionary theories. In the second part, we will focus more closely on the evolutionary significance of cognitive variables and their relation to the maintenance of anxiety disorders in general, and social phobia in particular. In the last part, we will discuss some of the implications of the evolutionary model for the treatment of anxiety disorders from a cognitive-behavioral perspective.

Learning Processes and Evolutionary Mechanisms

The predominance of behaviorism and learning theories in psychology in the early to mid-1900s limited research on fear and anxiety primarily to classical and operant conditioning paradigms. Mowrer (1939) hypothesized that fears are acquired through repeated presentations of a neutral stimulus (conditioned stimulus; CS) and a pain-producing or fear-eliciting stimulus (unconditioned stimulus; UCS). The strength of the fear response was assumed to be determined by the number of repetitions of association between the CS and UCS, and by the intensity of the unconditioned response. It was thought that a stimulus that resembles the original CS could acquire its fearful properties and become a secondary CS. According to Mowrer's model, once stimuli acquired fear-provoking properties, they acquired the ability to motivate behavior.

This model greatly influenced and dominated psychological research of human fear and anxiety for many years and there was, initially, little debate about its merit. However, numerous studies began appearing in the literature demonstrating that fears could develop even without temporal contiguity of the CS and the UCS. For example, a series of experiments conducted by Mineka and colleagues demonstrated that young rhesus monkeys will learn quickly to acquire a fear of snakes after observing another monkey respond fearfully to them. Furthermore, observing another monkey responding nonfearfully could effectively prevent the acquisition of this fear following later exposure to models behaving fearfully (see Mineka & Zinbarg, 1996, for a review). In response to these and similar findings, Rachman (1977) proposed a revised theory, in which he suggested that fear can be acquired through three different pathways: (1) classical conditioning (the pathway that is identical to Mowrer's model); (2) modeling; and (3) information transmission.

Although Rachman's "neoconditioning" model was able to account for many findings that were incompatible with the original conditioning model, it was still far from comprehensive. Its limitations were illuminated by several research findings. For example, retrospective and prospective studies often failed to identify a conditioning event in common phobias (Hofmann, Ehlers, & Roth, 1995; Menzies & Clarke, 1993), and many individuals who did experience such conditioning events did not develop fears (Di Nardo, Guzy, & Bak, 1988). Furthermore, common fears are not randomly distributed. For instance, cars are considerably more dangerous to pedestrians than are dogs or snakes. However, while most individuals do not develop a fear of cars, even after a car accident, many people are fearful of dogs or snakes, even without ever having had a negative encounter with them. Finally, we know that certain fears are clearly instinctual and innate. For example, rats born in the laboratory who never encountered a cat before show a freezing response when exposed to cat odors for the first time (Blanchard, Blachard, Rodgers, & Weiss, 1990). Similarly, most laboratory-born rhesus monkeys respond with inhibited or withdrawal behaviors when exposed to a snake for the first time (Nelson, Shelton, & Kalin, 2003). Interestingly, the latter study also found considerable individual differences in the responses to snakes, varying from orienting to wariness to fear.

These findings raise important questions about the validity of traditional learning models to explain the acquisition of fear responses. Some researchers therefore assume that animals and humans specifically acquire fears of objects that were once potentially harmful or dangerous (e.g., snakes or predators), and for which the capacity to recognize and respond quickly to this potential danger would be advantageous for one's survival and reproductive fitness. This "preparedness theory" (Seligman, 1971) was an early attempt to explain human fears in the context of evolutionary psychology. The preparedness theory (also known as the "selective association model") states that humans are biologically "prepared" to acquire the fear of certain objects or situations that used to threaten the survival of our species. This model was developed to explain the rapid acquisition and seeming irrationality of common phobias, as well as their high resistance to extinction. However, psychophysiological studies questioned certain aspects of it (McNally, 1987, 1995). Therefore, a number of alternative models were proposed. For example, Davey (1992) argued that cognitive biases could better explain why some stimuli, but not others, become associated with aversive outcomes. Specifically, Davey (1995) hypothesized that heightened expectations of aversive outcomes following the presentation of feared stimuli may generate and maintain a learned association between fear and expectation.

Menzies and Clarke (1995) further proposed that some fears in humans might be inherited ("nonassociative"), such that they appear without any relevant associative learning experiences, either direct, or indirect. Specifically, the authors suggested that fears are potentially nonassociative if the following conditions are met: (1) the fear represents a long-standing danger to the species; (2) possessing the fear has increased reproductive opportunities, possibly by extending the individual's life; and (3) avoiding the feared object or situation is partly under genetic control. The authors assumed that individual differences arise because of differences in the opportunity for exposure at critical points in development, and because of differences in the rate or speed at which habituation takes place. This theory could explain why phobias often emerge in the absence of direct or indirect conditioning. In fact, Menzies and Clarke (1995) argued that Darwinian natural selection seems to favor individuals who display fear on their first encounter with a certain object or situation, rather than individuals who acquire fears only after repeated learning experiences (Menzies & Clarke, 1995). For example, it is rather un-adaptive for individuals to develop a fear of heights only after having encountered a "traumatic" experience, such as falling from a high cliff (which would be deadly in most instances). According to this nonassociative model, the biologically relevant developmental fears serve to protect the individual from being exposed to the stimulus from the earliest possible encounter. Consequently, individuals with stronger fear responses are best protected from dangers associated with the feared object or situation across the lifetime. In the case of height phobia, such individuals would then generally climb to lower heights and place themselves in fewer risky situations. These individuals may then develop a height phobia despite a history characterized by less frequent exposure to, and fewer dangerous encounters with heights (Menzies & Parker, 2001; Poulton & Menzies, 2002).

However, after reviewing the empirical literature, Öhman and Mineka (2001) recently concluded that the nonassociative model does not provide a viable alternative to selective associations as explanations for the acquisition of fear and anxiety disorders. Instead, Öhman and Mineka (2001) present evidence for a selective associative model and the existence of an evolutionarily evolved fear module that shows four characteristics, each shaped by evolutionary contingencies:

1. selectivity with regard to the input (i.e., the fear module is sensitive to stimuli that have been correlated with threatening encounters in the evolutionary past);
2. automaticity (i.e., the evolutionarily fear-relevant stimuli can trigger the module in the absence of any conscious awareness);
3. encapsulation (i.e., the module is resistant to conscious cognitive influences); and
4. specialized neural circuitry (i.e., the module is controlled by a specific neural circuit that has been shaped by evolution).

The proposed characteristic of encapsulation is of particular interest for our discussion here because it is assumed that the fear module is impenetrable to conscious cognitive control. In other words, once confronted with a snake, the fear module of a snake phobic is activated and cannot be aborted easily by any cognitive strategies. Öhman and Mineka (2001) hypothesize that the fear module originated in primitive brains with limbic cortex rather than neocortex at the top of the stimulus processing hierarchies. Therefore, the judgment of the fear relevance is a "quick and dirty" process that rather risks false positive than false negatives by proceeding without neocortical influence (LeDoux, 1996). However, Öhman and Mineka (2001) caution that the encapsulation assumption should not be taken to imply that cognitions are unimportant in phobias. In fact, the amygdala, the neural node of the fear network in humans, is reciprocally connected with areas of the frontal lobe that serve to regulate emotion (Davidson, Putnam, & Larson, 2000).

Öhman and Mineka (2001) view cognitions as evolutionarily shaped mechanisms to assure that fearful individuals keep avoiding threatening situations, and are thus important in maintaining phobic behaviors. Moreover, it might be possible that the fear and anxiety response to some objects or situations are under greater neocortical (and therefore also cognitive) control than others. In terms of Mayr's category system, for example, we might assume that intraspecific communicative behaviors are under greater cognitive control than noncommunicative behaviors. An example of an intraspecific communicative behavior is social anxiety, which will be the focus of our discussion in the next section.

Cognitive Processes and Evolutionary Mechanisms

There is considerable support for the idea that certain cognitive processes are determined by evolutionary mechanisms (Beck, Emery, & Greenberg, 1985; Nesse, 1998), and based upon basic algorithms that enhance and maintain fear responses in all anxiety disorders. A number of factors must be considered when examining the evolutionary role of the anxiety response, including self-related processes, social relationships, and the cultural context. Social anxiety and its clinical expression (social phobia) include many of these factors and will, therefore, be the primary focus of the following discussion.

An integral part of social anxiety in humans is the evaluation of the self as a social object in comparison to others. Darwin (1955, reprinted) already recognized this when he wrote: "Why a proud man is often shy, as appears to be the case, is not so obvious, unless it be that, with all his self-reliance, he really thinks much about the opinion of others, although in a disdainful spirit" (p. 330).

He suggested further that shyness and fear are two separate constructs:

Shyness, as the derivation of the word indicates in several languages, is closely related to fear; yet it is distinct from fear in the ordinary sense. A shy man no doubt dreads the notice of strangers, but can hardly be said to be afraid of them; he may be as bold as a hero in battle, and yet have no self-confidence about trifles in the presence of strangers. Almost every one is extremely nervous when first addressing a public assembly and most men remain so throughout their lives; but this appears to depend on the consciousness of a great coming exertion, with its associated effects on the system, rather than on shyness; although a timid or shy man no doubt suffers on such occasions infinitely more than another" (pp. 330–331).

Darwin recognized that social anxiety is not simply a general expression of fear generalized to various social situations, but that it is closely related to self-evaluation and social comparison. Similarly, current evolutionary theories of social anxiety focus on the role of competition among individuals that is fueled by their desire to be viewed as attractive by others. In evolutionary terms, an individual's "attractiveness" is based on his or her ability to secure the interest and approval of others, and determines whether others are likely to invest their resources in that individual (Gilbert, 2001).

Social contact and affiliation are fundamental needs of essentially all species and are closely related to neurobiological function. For example, it has been shown that social subordinance is correlated with high levels of cortisol (a stress hormone) in free-ranging wild baboons (Sapolsky, Alberts, & Altmann, 1997), and elevated levels of oxytocin and vasopressin (two pituitary hormones) in prairie voles (Insel, 1997). In humans, social anxiety is correlated with levels of serotonin and dopamine (two common neurotransmitters) in the central nervous system (Stein, 1998).

Humans in particular have evolved high-level motivations to compete for the approval and support of others (Barkow, 1989). Modern humans need to be liked, valued, and approved of in order to elicit parental investment, develop supportive peer relationships, attract desirable mates, and engage successfully in many types of social relationships (Tooby and Cosmides, 1996). Our species is also highly dependent on the social support of others (Baumeister & Leary, 1995), especially during times of stress (Duck, 1998), and ostracism from the social group impacts negatively on a variety of health-related variables, including one's self-esteem and sense of belonging (Baumeister & Leary, 1995; Baumeister & Tice, 1990; Chartier, Walker, & Stein, 2001). Humans are, therefore, constantly engaged in a competitive bid for social resources, and failure in this regard is costly (Gilbert, 2001).

Because time and energy are precious commodities, humans choose to invest their resources in people who are likely to be useful to them and help them achieve their own self-interests (Barkow, 1975, 1989; Tooby & Cosmides, 1996). In order to draw potential allies toward investing in them, humans continually engage in a process of impression management (Barkow, 1989; Gilbert, 2001; Leary, 2001). In order to track successes and failures in this ongoing process, it has been proposed that humans have developed an adaptive internal cognitive-affective mechanism (Gilbert, 2001). This mechanism essentially keeps an estimated running tab of the amount of attention and interest one elicits for the self in others, or what Gilbert termed one's "social attention holding power," or SAHP. By monitoring and tracking one's own SAHP, one learns to conform to those standards that are valued by important others, to whom one wishes to appear attractive (Gilbert, 2001).

These processes require an ability to view oneself and one's social position from another individual's point of view and to have insight into how others think and feel. Byrne (1995) called these cognitive processes "theories of mind." These abilities probably evolved during recent primate evolution in order to help individuals understand how others think and to enable them to make predictions of how others will behave.

This biologically adaptive mechanism seems to be accentuated in individuals with social phobia, who take an observer standpoint when imagining or recalling social situations, leading to heightened self-focused attention and negative self-evaluation (Spurr & Stopa, 2002; Wells, Clark & Ahmad, 1998). Individuals with social phobia tend to construct negative images of how they look from another person's vantage point, assuming that others will view them at least as negatively as they view themselves. Successful treatment changes are highly correlated with changes in these negative self-focused thoughts (Hofmann, 2000), especially if the treatment includes cognitive intervention strategies (Hofmann, Moscovitch, Kim, & Taylor, in press).

Evolutionary psychologists conceptualize social anxiety as a form of competitive anxiety, triggered in social situations in which individuals would like to increase or defend their social standing (e.g. attractiveness/reputation) in the eyes of others. However, to do so runs risks that individuals with social phobia believe they are unlikely to surmount. Thus, they feel vulnerable to placement in an unwanted and involuntary low or subordinate rank position, which in turn will lead to exclusion, rejection being 'out of the game' when it comes to competing for (to be wanted by) allies, mates and chosen for valued social positions. This can trigger desires to increase social standing, setting up a vicious circle (Gilbert, 2001). Individuals with social phobia see themselves as inferior and undesirable (Clark & Wells, 1995; Hackmann, Surawy, & Clark, 1998), and fear that others see them in the same way (Hackmann et al., 1998; Rapee & Heimberg, 1997; Wells, Clark, & Ahmad, 1998) and will not be interested in investing their resources in them. As a consequence, people with social phobia exaggerate the cost associated with social mishaps. In fact, studies showed that changes in subjective cost estimates of an undesirable outcome of a social situation mediate treatment changes in social phobia (Foa, Frankin, Perry & Herbert, 1996; Hofmann, in press). At the same time, however, people with social phobia recognize that eliciting the investment of others requires a competitive venture. Due to their view of themselves as inferior, individuals with social phobia tend to respond to social situations by recruiting various defensive or submissive behaviors rather than the competitive, confident behaviors they desire to display (Gilbert, Price, & Allan, 1995). These submissive displays, such as evading eye contact, concealing one's face, limiting one's speech output, or engaging in outright behavioral avoidance or escape, are triggered automatically (Trower & Gilbert, 1989), in spite of the individual's own conscious wishes or attempts to resist or control them. The automatic recruitment of submissive responses in the midst of a competitive venture to garner the approval of others can be extremely interfering, and even sabotage the entire effort. For example, eye contact is viewed in Western cultures as an important sign of confidence and honesty, while avoiding eye contact is seen as indicating unattractiveness, low confidence, and untrustworthiness (Gilbert, 2001). In socially anxious people, who are particularly apt to frame social encounters in a competitive or hierarchical manner, such maladaptive defensive behaviors become activated and interfere frequently, often reinforcing in the minds of individuals with social phobia their already inferior hierarchical status.

Many of these submissive displays have been termed "safety behaviors" in the cognitive-behavioral literature (e.g. Clark & Wells, 1995; Rapee & Heimberg, 1997). Gilbert (2001) persuasively argues that this "submissive defensive behavior set" (which seems to be a more appropriate term for these behaviors; see also Gilbert this volume) is an evolved adaptive module that was once a necessary tool for survival, as it enabled our human ancestors to signal to dominant others that they did not intend to confront them or threaten their superior status (Keltner & Harker, 1998). In essence, the person with social phobia falls victim to a biological, internally generated defensive response set that was designed to inhibit subordinate animals from making up rank bids for resources, and to backoff and express submissive behaviors if challenged by more powerful others. This defensive set may be less than helpful if it becomes overly responsive (a state that, in social phobia, appears to result from the chronic presence of metacognitions of performing poorly, which may significantly lower the "response threshold" at which these defensive behaviors are triggered).

It has been proposed that evolutionary defense and safety mechanisms may strongly influence the assessment of costs and benefits in decision-making situations (Gilbert, 2001). Mineka (1992) discussed the possible existence of "evolutionary memories" in humans (and non-human primates). In contrast to memories that fade away with the passage of time, these memory processes are hypothesized to have evolved along evolutionary principles of "adaptive conservatism" (Hendersen, 1985). This hypothesis states that, for our ancestors, it was much more costly (for their own survival) to mistakenly assume that a situation was safe when it was in fact dangerous than it was to err on the safe side and assume that a situation was dangerous even if it was not (Buss, 1999; Gilbert, 1998). Therefore, a cognitive bias that favors false positives (incorrectly perceiving danger) over false negatives (incorrectly assuming safety) becomes evolutionarily adaptive. As a result, humans characteristically fail to adhere to rules of logic and mathematical probabilities, especially under conditions of uncertainty and when pressed for time (e.g., Tversky & Kahnemann, 1974), which leads to fast and frugal decision-making heuristics (Todd and Gigerenzer, 2000).

These heuristics are expressed as cognitive biases in anxiety disorders. For example, individuals with social phobia typically process information as follows:

1. scan the environment for socially threatening cues. If a potential social threat is detected, redirect attentional resources toward the potential threat;
2. recheck whether the cue is in fact socially threatening; and
3. selectively choose ambiguous or actual objects of threat for further information processing, including storage in memory.

A review of the literature provides preliminary support for some of these stages of information processing in individuals with social phobia (Clark & McManus, 2002; Heinrichs & Hofmann, 2001; see Gilbert, 1998, for a more detailed review of a variety of cognitive distortions in psychopathology and their evolutionary potential). Thus, from an evolutionary perspective, social anxiety has both adaptive (e.g., wary of those who could inflict harm on the self, attentive to social norms and rule etc.) and maladaptive features (e.g., interfering with competing for social resources and developing alliances). This balance then depends on the context in which social anxiety is triggered, its intensity and duration and (from an inclusive fitness point of view) its impact on reproductive success of self and kin. Individuals with an extreme form of social anxiety are less likely to marry than less anxious individuals, thus reducing their chances for reproduction, but may stay close to a family and become kin helpers. This example is consistent with the notion that all adaptations carry certain costs, and thereby impose constraints on their own optimal design and potential (Buss, Haselton, Shackelford, Bleske, & Wakefield, 1998; Dawkins, 1982; Williams, 1992). Moreover some of the benefits may fall on kin.

Implications for Therapy

Depending on the model of fear acquisition, different treatment implications can be derived. The nonassociative model predicts differential treatment effects, depending on the nature and origin of the particular fear (Menzies & Parker, 2001; Poulton & Menzies, 2002). Specifically, evolution-relevant fears, such as a fear of heights, should respond best to repeated and graduated exposure because the persistence of such fears are assumed to be related to insufficient opportunity to habituate to them. In contrast, evolution-neutral fears, such as dental phobias, should improve more from a combination of cognitive and behavioral interventions (Poulton & Menzies, 2002).

Öhman and Mineka (2001), who are proponents of the selective associative model, believe that "for the eventual success of the treatment effort (. . .) it is mandatory that phobics sooner or later confront their phobic stimuli to extinguish the autonomic activation of the fear module" (p. 510). In this model, cognitions are viewed as evolutionarily shaped mechanisms to assure that fearful individuals keep avoiding threatening situations. It is therefore important that the therapist identifies and challenges beliefs that are responsible for the maintenance of the disorders, especially the need to avoid the phobic stimulus/situation (e.g., 'I will die if I have to face this'), and engage exposure practices.

The role of cognitions might further depend on the type of anxiety disorder. As we noted earlier, some individuals with anxiety disorders might show more of a basic fear response, whereas others exhibit more of a cognitively mediated anxiety response. We further assume that Mayr's (1974) intraspecific communicative behaviors (i.e., behaviors toward other people) are under greater cognitive control than interspecific communicative behaviors (i.e., behaviors toward other species) or noncommunicative behaviors (behaviors toward nonliving objects). The efficacy of cognitive intervention in conjunction with exposure strategies is likely to differ accordingly.

From an evolutionary perspective (whether assuming an associative or nonassociative model), the goal of exposure practices is to modify the innate and maladaptive fear and anxiety response. The biological correlate of this effect remains uncertain but acts in part via structures of the limbic brain, such as the amygdala. Evolutionary models assume that the brain begins to relearn when to activate and deactivate these natural tendencies through repeated exposure and defensive response prevention.

Gilbert and Trower (2001) propose incorporating an explanation of the evolutionary model into therapy in order to provide patients with a context to help them make sense of their symptoms and their automatic nature. An examination of the evolutionary model may help normalize patients' fears. Indeed, patients may feel relieved to learn that their symptoms are rooted in a normal, adaptive system that once served an important self-protective function.

CBT therapists should also consider the possibility that the so-called "safety behaviors" of patients with anxiety disorders, are evolutionary-based automatic defenses rather than conscious attempts to avoid uncomfortable situations. In some cases it may, therefore, be more helpful and therapeutic to teach patients to tolerate and accept these behaviors rather than attempt to eliminate them at all costs.

In addition, Gilbert and Trower (2001) suggested that the treatment of socially phobic patients ought to include an exploration of their assumption that social relationships are hierarchically competitive. In doing so, the therapist should encourage patients to determine whether they tend to classify relationships in this manner, and if so, to engage them in the process of examining possible alternative ways of understanding and categorizing social encounters.

Final Thoughts

Three essential ingredients of Darwin's theory of natural selection—variation, inheritance, and selection—led to the development of a new species some 50,000 years ago, probably somewhere in Africa: the modern human. New mutations to the human genome led to changes in the human brain, which enabled our ancestors to have the capacity to make and use sophisticated tools. Members of this new species fashioned sophisticated weapons and invented new ways of hunting and gathering that allowed a much larger population of *homo* species to flourish than had ever previously existed. In addition, they created jewelry and clothing, and developed a complex social system and culture.

When evaluating the evolutionary mechanisms of fear and anxiety, it is important to consider human culture, the influence of which has been powerful enough to alter the course of biological evolution. Human invention has altered the environment in a momentous way. As a result of these environmental changes, human traits that were once beneficial in the context of biological evolution have become maladaptive in the context of cultural evolution, and vice versa. For example, in the absence of technological advances, humans would be unable to fly and would rarely confront extreme heights. Being afraid of heights may have been adaptive for our ancestors. However, in modern-day society, the demands of which require many humans to fly in airplanes or to live and work in skyscrapers that are hundreds of feet above the ground, being afraid of heights is maladaptive and can interfere greatly with a person's ability to function normally. Hence, what was once adaptive biologically for our ancestors is at odds with what is now adaptive in the context of modern-day culture.

Similarly, in social phobia, displaying submissive or defensive behaviors in the presence of dominant others may have been biologically adaptive for our ancestors, but now interferes and comes into conflict with what is considered appropriate and attractive by today's cultural standards.

Evolutionary mechanisms therefore provide an important dimension in the discussion of the nosology of fear and anxiety disorders. From an evolutionary perspective, some anxiety disorders may be viewed as overresponsive, evolutionarily adaptive but culturally maladaptive mechanisms rather than qualitatively different disease entities. This is inconsistent with the DSM-IV classification, which defines a disorder as a statistically improbable or intraindividual disease entity.

In sum, our inquiry into the evolutionary mechanisms of human fear and anxiety suggests that evolutionary psychology offers a number of novel perspectives with regard to the etiology, maintenance, and treatment of anxiety disorders. However, many questions still remain unanswered, while many have yet to be raised.

References

American Psychiatric Association. (1994). *Diagnostic and statistical manual for mental disorders* (4th ed.). Washington, DC: Author.

Barkow, J. H. (1975). Prestige and culture: A biosocial interpretation. *Current Anthropology, 16*, 533–572.

Barkow, J. H. (1989). *Darwin, sex, and status: Biological approaches to mind and culture.* Toronto: University of Toronto Press.

Baumeister, R. F., & Leary, M. R. (1995). The need to belong: Desire for interpersonal attachments as a fundamental human motivation. *Psychological Bulletin, 117*, 497–529.

Baumeister, R. F., & Tice, D. M. (1990). Anxiety and social exclusion. *Journal of Social and Clinical Psychology, 9*, 165–195.

Beck, A. T., Emery, G., & Greenberg, R. L. (1985). *Anxiety disorders and phobia: A cognitive approach.* New York: Basic Books.

Blanchard, R. J., Blanchard, D. C., Rodgers, J., & Weiss, S. M. (1990). The characterization and modeling of anti-predator defensive behavior. *Neuroscience and Biobehavioral Reviews, 14*, 463–472.

Buss, D. M. (Ed.). (1999). *Evolutionary psychology: The new science of the mind.* Needham Heights: Allyn and Bacon, Inc.

Buss, D. M., Haselton, M. G., Shackelford, T. K., Bleske, A. L., & Wakefield, J. C. (1998). Adaptations, exaptations, and spandrels. *American Psychologist, 53*, 533–548.

Byrne, R. (1995). *The thinking ape: Evolutionary origins of intelligence.* Oxford: Oxford University Press.

Chartier, M. J., Walker, J. R., & Stein, M. B. (2001). Social phobia and potential childhood risk factors in a community sample. *Psychological Medicine, 31*, 307–315.

Clark, D. M., & Wells, A. (1995). A cognitive model of social phobia. In R. G. Heimberg, M. R. Liebowitz, D. A. Hope, and F. R. Schneier (Eds.), *Social phobia: Diagnosis, assessment and treatment.* New York: Guilford Press.

Clark, D. M., & McManus, F. (2002). Information processing in social phobia. *Biological Psychiatry, 51*, 92–100.

Darwin, C. (1955). *Expression of the emotions in man and animals (reprinted edition).* New York: Philosophical library.

Davey, G. C. L. (1992). Classical conditioning and the acquisition of human fears and phobias: A review and synthesis of the literature. *Advances in Behaviour Research and Therapy, 14*, 29–66.

Davey, G. C. L. (1995). Preparedness and phobias: Specific evolved associations or a generalized expectancy bias. *Behavioural Brain Sciences, 18*, 289–325.

Davidson, R. J., Putnam, K. M., & Larson, C. L. (2000). Dysfunction in the neural circuitry of emotion regulation—A possible prelude to violence. *Science, 289*, 591–594.

Dawkins, R. (1982). *The extended phenotype.* San Francisco: Freeman.

Di Nardo, P. A., Guzy, L. T., & Bak, R. M. (1988). Anxiety response patterns and etiological factors in dog fearful and non-fearful subjects. *Behaviour Research and Therapy, 21,* 245–252.

Duck, S. (1998). *Human relationships* (3rd ed.). London: Sage.

Ekman, P. (1992). An argument for basic emotions. *Cognition and Emotion, 6,* 169–200.

Foa, E. B., Franklin, M. E., Perry, K. J., & Herbert, J. D. (1996). Cognitive biases in generalized social phobia. *Journal of Abnormal Psychology, 105,* 433–439.

Gilbert, P. (1998). The evolved basis and adaptive functions of cognitive distortions. *British Journal of Medical Psychology, 71,* 447–463.

Gilbert, P. (2001). Evolution and social anxiety: The role of attraction, social competition, and social hierarchies. *The Psychiatric Clinics of North America, 24,* 723–751.

Gilbert, P., Price, J. S., & Allan, S. (1995). Social comparison, social attractiveness and evolution: How might they be related? *New Ideas in Psychology, 67,* 23–36.

Gilbert, P., & Trower, P. (2001). Evolutionary psychology and social anxiety. In W. R. Crozier & L. E. Alden (Eds.), *International handbook of social anxiety: Concepts, research and interventions relating to the self and shyness* (pp. 259–279). Chichester: John Wiley & Sons.

Hackmann, A., Surawy, C., & Clark, D. M. (1998). Seeing yourself through others' eyes: A study of spontaneous occurring images in social phobia. *Behavioural and Cognitive Psychotherapy, 26,* 3–12.

Hamilton, W. D. (1964). The genetic evolution of social behavior. *Journal of Theoretical Biology, 7,* 1–52.

Heinrichs, N., & Hofmann, S. G. (2001). Information processing in social phobia: A critical review. *Clinical Psychology Review, 21,* 751–770.

Hendersen, R. W. (1985). Fearful memories: The motivational significance of forgetting. In F. R. Brush & J. B. Overmier (Eds.), *Affect, conditioning and cognitions: Essays on the determinants of behavior* (pp. 43–53). Hillsdale: Erlbaum.

Hofmann, S. G. (2000). Self-focused attention before and after treatment of social phobia. *Behaviour Research and Therapy, 38,* 717–725.

Hofmann, S. G. (in press). Cognitive mediation of treatment change in social phobia. *Journal of Consulting and Clinical Psychology.*

Hofmann, S. G., Ehlers, A., & Roth, W. T. (1995). Conditioning theory: A model for the etiology of public speaking anxiety? *Behaviour Research and Therapy, 33,* 567–571.

Hofmann, S. G., Moscovitch, D. A., Kim, H.-J., & Taylor, A. N. (in press). Changes in self-perception during treatment of social phobia. *Journal of Consulting and Clinical Psychology.*

Insel, T. R. (1997). A neurobiological basis of social attachment. *American Journal of Psychiatry, 154,* 726–735.

Izard, C. E. (1992). Basic emotions, relations among emotions, and emotion-cognition relations. *Psychological Review, 99,* 561–565.

Keltner, D., & Harker, L. A. (1998). The forms and functions of the nonverbal signal of shame. In P. Gilbert & B. Andrews (Eds.), *Shame: Interpersonal behavior, psychopathology and culture* (pp.78–98). New York: Oxford University Press.

Leary, M. L. (2001). Social anxiety as an early warning system: A refinement and extension of the self-presentation theory of social anxiety. In S. G. Hofmann & P. M. DiBartolo, *From social anxiety to social phobia* (pp. 321–334). Needham Heights: Allyn & Bacon.

LeDoux, J. E. (1996). *The emotional brain.* New York, NY: Simon and Schuster.

Mayr, E. (1974). Behavior programs and evolutionary strategies. *American Scientist, 62,* 650–659.

McNally, R. J. (1987). Preparedness and phobias: A review. *Psychological Bulletin, 101,* 283–303.

McNally, R. J. (1995). Preparedness, phobias, and the panglossian paradigm. *Behavioral and Brain Sciences, 18,* 303–304.

Menzies, R. G., & Clarke, J. C. (1993). The etiology of fear of heights and its relationship to severity and individual response patterns. *Behaviour Research and Therapy, 31,* 355–366.

Menzies, R. G., & Clarke, J. C. (1995). The etiology of phobias: A nonassociative account. *Clinical Psychology Review, 15,* 23–48.

Menzies, R. G., & Parker, L. (2001). The origins of height fear: An evaluation of neoconditioning explanations. *Behaviour Research and Therapy, 39,* 185–199.

Mineka, S. (1992). Evolutionary memories, emotional processing and the emotional disorders. *The Psychology of Learning and Motivation, 28,* 161–206.

Mineka, S., & Zinbarg, R. (1996). Conditioning and ethological models of anxiety disorders: Stress-in-dynamic-context anxiety models. In D. A. Hope, *Nebraska Symposium on Motivation, 1996: Perspectives on Anxiety, Panic, and Fear. Current Theory and Research in Motivation* (Vol. 43, pp. 135–211). Lincoln, NE: University of Nebraska Press.

Mowrer, O. H. (1939). Stimulus response theory of anxiety. *Psychological Review, 46,* 553–565.

Nelson, E. E., Shelton, S. E., & Kalin, N. H. (2003). Individual differences in the responses of naïve rhesus monkeys to snakes. *Emotion, 3,* 3–11.

Nesse, R. M. (1998). Emotional disorders in evolutionary perspective. *British Journal of Medical Psychology, 71,* 397–415.

Öhman, A. (1992). Fear and anxiety as emotional phenomena: Clinical, phenomenological, evolutionary perspectives, and information-processing mechanisms. In M. Lewis & J. M. Haviland (Eds.), *Handbook of the emotion* (pp. 511–536). New York: Guilford.

Öhman, A., & Mineka, S. (2001). Fears, phobias, and preparedness toward an evolvued module of fear and fear learning. *Psychological Review, 108,* 483–522.

Panksepp, J. (1998). *Affective neuroscience: The foundations of human and animal emotions.* New York, NY: Oxford University Press.

Plutchik, R. (1980). *Emotion: A psychoevolutionary synthesis.* New York: Harper & Row.

Poulton, R., & Menzies, R. G. (2002). Associative fear acquisition: A review of the evidence from retrospective and longitudinal research. *Behaviour Research and Therapy, 40,* 127–149.

Rachman, S. (1977). The conditioning theory of fear acquisition: A critical examination. *Behaviour Research and Therapy, 15,* 375–387.

Rapee, R. M., & Heimberg, R. G. (1997). A cognitive behavioral model of anxiety in social phobia. *Behaviour Research and Therapy, 35,* 741–756.

Sapolsky, R. M., Alberts, S. C., & Altmann, J. (1997). Hypercortisolism associated with social subordinance or social isolation among wild baboons. *Archives of General Psychiatry, 54,* 1137–1143.

Seligman, M. E. P. (1971). Phobias and preparedness. *Behavior Therapy, 2,* 307–320.

Spurr, J. M., & Stopa, L. (2002). Self-focused attention in social phobia and social anxiety. *Clinical Psychology Review, 22,* 947–975.

Stein, M. B. (1998). Neurobiological perspectives on social phobia: From affiliation to zoology. *Biological Psychiatry, 12,* 1277–1285.

Todd, P. M., & Gigerenzer, G. (2000). Précis of simple heuristics that make us smart. *Behavioral and Brain Sciences, 23,* 727–780.

Tomkins, S. S. (1963). *Affect, imagery, consciousness: Vol. 2. The negative affects.* New York: Springer.

Tooby, J., & Cosmides, L. (1996). Friendship and the banker's paradox: Other pathways to the evolution of adaptations for altruism. *Proceedings of the British Academy, 88,* 119–143.

Trower, P., & Gilbert, P. (1989). New theoretical conceptions of social anxiety and social phobia. *Clinical Psychology Review, 9,* 19–35.

Tversky, A., & Kahnemann, D. (1974). Judgment under uncertainty: Heuristics and biases. *Science, 185,* 1124–1131.

Wells, A., Clark, D. M., & Ahmad, S. (1998). How do I look with my mind's eye? Perspective taking in social phobic imagery. *Behaviour Research and Therapy, 36,* 631–634.

Williams, G. C. (1992). *Natural selection.* New York: Oxford University Press.

Chapter 6

The Inner Schema of Borderline States and Its Correction During Psychotherapy: A Cognitive-Evolutionary Approach

Giovanni Liotti

Research on early attachment shows that during the second year of life, most infants are able to organize their attachment behavior according to three patterns, called secure, avoidant, and resistant (Ainsworth, Blehar, Waters, & Wall, 1978; Main, 1995).

In low-risk samples, a substantial minority of infants—about 20% according to recent estimates (Lyons-Ruth & Jacobvitz, 1999)—are unable to give organization and orientation to attachment behavior. In samples at high risk for emotional disorders (e.g., mother-child dyads where the mother suffers from depression, mother-child dyads living in chaotic or maltreating families, or mother-child dyads characterized by prenatal alcohol abuse) disorganization of infant attachment is the rule: up to about 80% of the children in these samples proved unable to organize attachment behavior along any identifiable pattern (Lyons-Ruth & Jacobvitz, 1999).

In the *Strange Situation* (the experimental procedure for the assessment of attachment behavior during the first 2 years of life: Ainsworth et al., 1978), disorganized attachment shows up as incompatible responses emitted simultaneously or in quick sequence, or else as lack of orientation during attachment interactions (Main & Solomon, 1990).

Disorganization of attachment (hitherto called DA for the sake of brevity) has been empirically linked to unresolved memories of losses, abuses, and other traumas in the caregiver (Lyons-Ruth & Jacobvitz, 1999; Main & Hesse, 1990). If DA characterizes the interaction between a child and a caregiver in the *Strange Situation,* then it is highly probable that the caregiver will rehearse, in the course of a properly devised semistructured interview (*Adult Attachment Interview* [AAI]: George, Kaplan, & Main, 1985), memories of loss of an attachment figure or of traumas suffered at the hand of attachment figures (emotional, sexual, or other physical abuses). These memories, moreover, are narrated in such a way (lapses, serious space-time confusions regarding when and where the events happened, other cognitive distortions) as to suggest that they have not been elaborated and resolved. Caregivers of children who are organized (secure, resistant, or avoidant) in their attachment seldom report unresolved traumatic memories in their response to the AAI. The link between DA in the child and unresolved traumatic memories in the caregiver is a statistically robust finding that has been replicated repeatedly (for a review of these researches, see Lyons-Ruth & Jacobvitz, 1999). This link is explained as the consequence of the traumatized parent becoming unwittingly frightening to the child, either because of outbursts of aggression, or because he or she, due to the rehearsal of traumatic memories during caregiving, looks frightened to the child (Main & Hesse, 1990; Lyons-Ruth & Jacobvitz, 1999; Schuengel, Bakermans, Van IJzendoorn, & Blom, 1999).

Disorganized Attachment and psychopathology

DA is an interesting theme of inquiry for developmental psychopathology (Carlson & Sroufe, 1995; Dozier, Stovall, & Albus, 1999; George, 1996; Main, 1995; Schore, 2001). The mere fact that it is by far the most frequent (up to 80%) type of attachment behavior in families at high risk of emotional disorders, while it is observed only in about 20% of children in low-risk samples, would already suffice to justify this interest. Moreover, DA

1. provides us with an interesting model of dissociative processes (Carlson, 1998; Liotti, 1992, 1999; Main & Morgan, 1996),

2. suggests useful interpretations of the dynamics underlying ruptures of the therapeutic alliance (and other difficulties in the therapeutic relationship) during the treatment of severe dissociative and borderline personality disorders (Liotti, 1993, 1995, 2000; Liotti & Intreccialagli, 1998), and

3. is a putative risk factor for any emotional disorder implying experiences of uncontrollable anxiety. (Hesse & Main, 1999)

In order to understand the psychopathological implications of DA, it is mandatory to reflect on the cognitive representations of self and others that accompany early experiences of attachment.

Attachment theory holds that children build structures of implicit memory concerning the self and the attachment figure (internal working models [IWMs]) on the basis of their actual experience with the attachment figure (Amini, Lewis, Lannon, & Louie, 1996; Bowlby, 1969/1982, 1988; Bretherton & Munholland, 1999). The IWMs soon assume the control of the inborn system regulating attachment behavior, and are reflected in the behavioral patterns observed in the Strange Situation. There are important differences between the IWM of DA and the IWMs of the three organized patterns of attachment. The IWM regulating the infant's attachment behavior in the secure pattern, as inferred by the type of relationship between the infant and the caregiver, is unitary and coherent. It portrays the caregiver as trustworthy, and the self as the bearer of meaningful emotions and meaningful wishes for closeness and protection when in danger. In the other two organized patterns of attachment, the avoidant and the resistant, the IWM portrays a far less favorable representation of the self and the caregiver. The caregiver is likely represented as unavailable in the avoidant and as unpredictable or controlling in the resistant pattern (theoretical reflections and reviews of empirical findings on the representations of self and the attachment figure are offered in Bretherton & Munholland, 1999; Carlson & Sroufe, 1995; and George, 1996). However unfavorable the representations of self and caregiver in the avoidant and resistant patterns may sometimes be, they still do not exceed the infant mind's capacity of synthesizing relatively coherent and unitary meaning structures. By contrast, the information available to infants disorganized in their attachment behavior is such as to disrupt the construction of a unitary IWM of self and the attachment figure: the IWM of DA has been described as multiple, fragmented, and incoherent (Main, 1991; Main & Morgan, 1996).

It conveys representations of the self and of the attachment figure so contradictory or incompatible that they cannot be reciprocally integrated: they tend to remain dissociated, at least in the first steps of personality development, and may stay so even in adult life (Carlson, 1998; Liotti, 1992, 1995, 1999, 2000; Schore, 2001).

Dissociated Inner Schema in DA: Rescuer, Persecutor, and Victim

The IWM of DA is a cognitive structure, an inner schema of self and others, constructed on the basis of repeated experiences in which the infant is both comforted and frightened by the traumatized attachment figure, either simultaneously or in quick sequence. These experiences induce an oscillation of the representational processes, regarding both to self and the attachment figure, between the three dramatic representational stereotypes of the Victim, the Rescuer, and the Persecutor (Liotti, 1999, 2000). The attachment figure may be represented negatively, as the cause of the ever-growing fear experienced by the self (self as Victim of a Persecutor), but also positively, as a Rescuer (a parent frightened by unresolved traumatic memories may be willing to offer comfort to the child, and may be unaware of his or her facial expression and of its effect on the infant; the child may feel such comforting availability along with the fear). Together with these two opposed representations of the attachment figure (Persecutor and Rescuer) meeting a vulnerable and helpless self (Victim), the IWM of DA also conveys a negative representation of a powerful, evil self meeting a fragile or even devitalized attachment figure (Persecutor self, held responsible for the fear expressed by the attachment figure). Moreover, there is the possibility, for the child, to represent both the self and the attachment figure as the helpless victims of a mysterious, invisible source of danger. And finally, since the frightened attachment figure may be comforted by the tender feelings evoked by contact with the infant, the implicit memories of DA may also convey the possibility of construing the self as the powerful Rescuer of a fragile attachment figure (the little child perceives the self as able to comfort a frightened adult).

Descriptions of the shifts of a patient's self-representations between the poles of the Victim, the Persecutor, and even the Rescuer (while the therapist is represented, in sometimes very quick succession, as Rescuer, Persecutor, and Victim) may be easily found in the literature on the treatment of borderline and dissociative patients (Davies &

Frawley, 1994; Liotti, 1995). It is possible that similar experiences of multiple, incompatible, dissociated, dramatic representations of self and caregiver (Persecutor-Victim, Victim-Persecutor, Victim-Victim, Rescuer-Victim, Victim-Rescuer) lie at the heart of DA.

Metacognitive Deficits and DA

Research on attachment yields evidence that the development of the integrative functions of consciousness during childhood and adolescence is hindered if the attachment relationship to the caregivers remains disorganized. The integrative functions of consciousness are based on the capacity of momentarily suspending decision and action, so as to compare with each other different representations of self, of other people's states of mind, and of reality. The development of this capacity manifests itself during childhood and adolescence with the growing abilities to

1. distinguish between appearance and reality (Flavell, Flavell, & Green, 1983; Wimmer & Penner, 1983),
2. construct a theory of mind (Baron-Cohen, 1995),
3. reflect on mental states (Fonagy et al., 1995),
4. monitor thoughts, feelings, and language (metacognitive monitoring: Flavell, 1979; Main, 1991),
5. perform formal operations of thought, and
6. pay proper attention to external stimuli without being unwittingly absorbed in daydreams.

The development of all these abilities is hindered by insecure attachment in general, and by the persistence of that pattern of relationship whose early prototype is manifested by infant DA in particular. Preschool children who had been disorganized as infants in their attachment behavior rank very low, particularly if compared with formerly securely attached children, in the false-belief tests used for the assessment of the child's theory of mind (Fonagy, Redfern, & Charman, 1997; Meins, 1997). In a longitudinal study, children whose attachment behavior in infancy had been disorganized were judged by their teachers as significantly more confused and "absent minded" than their peers with a different attachment history (Carlson, 1998). Children 5 to 7 years old, judged disorganized in their response to the Manchester Child Attachment Story Task, show attentional problems in comparison to securely attached peers (Goldwyn, Stanley, Smith, & Green, 2000). Adolescents who had been fearful/disorganized children show marked difficulties in tests of formal reasoning when compared with peers who had different attachment experiences (Jacobsen, Edelstein, & Hofmann, 1994).

Metacognitive deficits during development yield concurrent difficulties in understanding, naming, discriminating, and therefore controlling, mental states in general and emotions in particular (Fonagy et al., 1995). Therefore, children with metacognitive deficits should have difficulties in controlling emotions and impulses. In accordance with this hypothesis, a number of studies provide evidence that disorganized infants tend to grow into children with difficulties in the control of anxiety (Hesse & Main, 1999) and aggression (Lyons-Ruth & Jacobvitz, 1999; Van IJzendoorn, 1997).

Finally, a metacognitive deficit implies a poor capacity to reflect on one's own mental representations. This capacity yields the possibility of integrating contradictory features (thesis and antithesis) in cohesive wholes (syntheses). It is therefore not surprising that children who have been infants disorganized in their attachments show negative and disorganized self-representations more often than controls (Cassidy, 1988; Hesse & Main, 1999; Main, 1995; Solomon, George, & DeJong, 1995).

All these findings suggest that the effects of early DA may extend into childhood and adolescence and may become a risk factor for psychopathological developments. As to the nature of these developments, the dissociative disorders and the borderline personality disorder seem likely candidates. Theoretical clinical considerations (Fonagy et al., 1995; Lichtenberg, Lachman, & Fosshage, 1992; Liotti, 1992, 1995, 1999, 2000, 2001; Main & Morgan, 1996) and the results of some empirical studies (Anderson & Alexander, 1996; Carlson, 1998; Coe, Daleenberg, Aransky, & Reto, 1995; Liotti, Intreccialagli, & Cecere, 1991; Liotti, Pasquini, & The Italian Group for the Study of Dissociation, 2000; Pasquini, Liotti, & The Italian Group for the Study of Dissociation, 2002) suggest that DA not only illustrates and contains, as in a nutshell, the dynamics of the dissociative processes, but may also be an actual risk factor in the development of borderline states.[2]

Disorganized Attachment and Borderline Pathology

The role of DA in the origins of the borderline states seems compatible with clinical observations stemming from two major theories of borderline pathology: Kernberg's (1975) psychoanalytic theory and Linehan's (1993) cognitive-behavioral theory.

The central theme of Kernberg's model of borderline states is the idea that many of the patient's disturbances are linked to the existence of split representations of positive and negative features of self and others. These representations are held to be present since infancy, and to remain in a split condition throughout personality development. Kernberg's thesis is readily matched with the idea that DA is linked to multiple and incompatible representations of self and the attachment figure. An important difference between Kernberg's idea of splitting and the description of a multiple IWM (Liotti, 1995, 1999, 2000; Main, 1991) is that the development of a multiple IWM does not necessarily imply defensive processes, and is therefore more in keeping with the basic tenets of cognitive approaches to psychopathology and psychotherapy. Moreover, the status of the nonintegrated representations in DA may be more similar to dissociation (i.e., multiple and incompatible) than to splitting (i.e., dual and contradictory: see Young, 1988, for differences between dissociation and splitting within the psychoanalytic theory of defense mechanisms; see also Ross, 1989, p. 151, for a rebuttal of such differences).

The DA model also acknowledges the importance of the dysfunction of the system regulating the emotions, which is emphasized in the cognitive-behavioral theory of borderline states advanced by Linehan (1993). The developmental defect in the integrative functions of consciousness (theory of mind, metacognitive monitoring, reflective-self capacity, formal or operational thinking) observed in relation to insecure attachment in general and DA in particular, may be linked to the deficit in the system regulating the emotions (the nuclear disturbance of BPD, according to Linehan). Linehan describes the functions of this system as the capacity to reflect on the emotions as discrete mental states; to name them properly; and to acknowledge their origin, function, and value, both in the inner and in the interpersonal life. Linehan's system of emotional regulation, therefore, is linked to the development of both metacognitive monitoring and an adequate theory of one's own and others' minds. Metacognitive deficits have been assessed in samples of borderline patients (Barone, 1998; Fonagy et al., 1995).

The DA model of borderline states not only acknowledges the importance of both the split self-representations and the poor metacognitive capacity of emotional regulation; it also explains how the affective instability, the dramatically mutable relational style, the self-damaging behavior, and the identity disturbance are related to the frantic efforts to avoid real or imagined abandonment. All these features of the borderline states are explained by the DA model as the consequence of the *recurrent activation of the attachment motivational system*. When active, the attachment system of these patients causes fear of abandonment and frantic efforts to avoid it, while the multiple, shifting representations of the IWM are responsible for the uncertain sense of self, the dramatically changing attitudes toward significant others, and the self-damaging behavior (self as Persecutor, deserving punishment). Paranoid ideation (self as Victim, others as Persecutors)—which is as transient as the representations of self and others portrayed by the attachment IWM are mutable—may also be related to the episodic activation of the attachment system within unfavorable interpersonal relationships. The dissociative experiences may also be explained as the outcome of the activation of the attachment system in interpersonal contexts that are particularly confusing. These experiences would then reflect the disordered state of a consciousness that is forced to deal with multiple and incompatible *simultaneous* self-representations (Liotti, 1992, 1999).

The idea that borderline symptoms and disturbances are contingent upon the activation of a control system mediating attachment, and that not only specific behaviors and emotions, but also specific cognitions are channeled into consciousness by the activation of such a system, may be understood properly only in an evolutionary perspective.

How Attachment Processes Become Disorganized: The Evolutionary Perspective

According to evolutionary psychology, the mechanisms whereby attachment behavior can become disorganized are linked to the simultaneous and conflicting activation, in the infant, of two evolved, inborn behavioral control systems: the defense and the safety system.

The Defense and the Safety Systems

From an evolutionary perspective, threat signals, whether they come from other sources or from a caregiver, activate defensive responses in the infant. Defensive responses have been classified by Marks (1987) and others (Gilbert, 1993) into a number of basic behavioral strategies that may be elicited by perceived danger in most vertebrate species: flight, freezing, defensive aggression, and submissive behavior. The similarities among specific strategies in the different species strongly support the idea that these defensive responses have been favored by natural selection and therefore are innately available in the brain of vertebrates. Taken together, the inborn algorithms for the processing of information related to defensive responses, and the neural structures upon which these algorithms operate, constitute the defense system (Gilbert, 1989, 1993; LeDoux, 1996). By contrast, all sensory information indicating absence of danger, and all the inborn strategies for seeking protection from danger, are related by Gilbert (1989, 1993) to the operations of a safety system.

In vertebrate species endowed with a well-developed limbic cortex (mammals in general and primates in particular), a peculiar inborn strategy adds to the evolved repertory of possible responses to danger; the active search for the protective proximity of a conspecific. This strategy (attachment behavior) is regulated by an inborn behavioral control system, called "attachment system" by Bowlby (1969/1982), and considered by Gilbert (1989) a part of the safety system. Finally, the evolution of the neocortex endows human beings with a further strategy in the face of danger, based on the symbolic rehearsal of information related to previously met dangerous situations. When the context of human behavior and experience becomes similar to past contexts of hurt or threat, not only feelings but also thoughts related to danger and defense automatically surface in the stream of consciousness. These thoughts may help in devising better strategies for coping with actual or immediately forthcoming danger, but they may also be utterly inappropriate to the present situation, as exemplified by the ruminations accompanying posttraumatic phobias (LeDoux, 1996).

Disorganized Attachment: Conflict Between the Defense and the Safety Systems

The coexistence in humans of different evolved, inborn strategies for coping with danger allows, in certain circumstances, for a peculiarly paradoxical relationship that gives way to disorganized attachment. Such a circumstance is created by the fact that the two more recently evolved strategies for coping with danger—the symbolic, intrapsychic one and the interpersonal one linked to the evolution of the attachment system—may seriously conflict with the evolutionarily older defensive strategies (freezing, flight, and defensive fight). Gilbert (1989) expresses this idea in terms of a conflict between the defense system and the safety system. Empirical research suggests, as has been stated above, that such a conflict tends to take place whenever infants are cared for by parents suffering from unresolved traumatic memories (Lyons-Ruth & Jacobvitz, 1999; Main & Hesse, 1990).

To suffer from unresolved traumatic memories means that fragments of past painful events emerge unpredictably in the stream of consciousness, and that these fragments cannot be integrated in any organized process of thought (Horowitz, 1986; Main & Morgan, 1996). From the point of view of evolutionary psychology, such a compulsive surfacing of traumatic memories is the outcome of the inborn tendency to rehearse dangerous events in the face of new situations that may involve similar dangers. Parents who were abused children, or who suffered the loss of an attachment figure or of another child, may tend, at some more or less conscious level of mental processes, to remember these events while taking care of their infants. Just as they did not receive adequate care, so they may fear this being repeated, which makes them unable to care adequately for their own children. When people experience an intrusion of unresolved traumatic memories in their stream of consciousness, they will unwittingly, and often unconsciously, express fear.

Main and Hesse (1990) originally formulated the hypothesis that infants whose caregivers are suffering from unresolved traumatic memories will quite often witness, in the caregiver's face, an expression of fear (together with expressions of frustration, hurt, and anger). Among the emotional signals related to the automatic surfacing of unresolved traumatic memories, fear is particularly important in the context of DA. To the infant, the expression of fear in an adult's face is in itself frightening; it is interpreted as a signal of danger and it activates the defense system (Fields & Fox, 1985; Main & Hesse, 1990). The activation of the defense system by the same source of signals that modulate safety-seeking behavior (attachment) creates the paradoxical situation underlying DA. In children of parents suffering from unresolved traumatic memories, the inborn strategies regulated by the defense system—flight, freezing, defensive aggression, or submission—conflict with the strategy regulated by the safety system (attachment behavior).

It is important to emphasize that—with the notable exception of violent, abusive parental behavior that directly frightens children while they are asking for protective proximity—no other pattern of caregiving induce over such a conflicting activation of the safety and the defense systems. Indifferent, dismissing, or even openly rejecting parental behavior discourages the infant's overtures aimed at proximity-seeking, but does not frighten the infant, and therefore does not summon defensive strategies together with attachment. Therefore, children of parents who are dismissing of attachment will be able to coherently organize their attachment behavior (they will come to use avoidance of the attachment figure as an organized strategy whenever the system controlling attachment is activated: avoidant pattern of attachment). Parental behavior, corresponding to the resistant pattern of attachment that unpredictably oscillates between acceptance and refusal of the infant's attachment overtures, may be disappointing or distressing but not frightening to the child. It may yield an abnormally intense activation of the attachment system, not the simultaneous, conflicting activation of attachment and defensive strategies that is necessary to seriously hamper the organization of attachment behavior.

In the face of the simultaneous activation of safety and defensive strategies—both elicited by the same social releasers (the caregiver's nonverbal behavior)—attachment behavior cannot be organized because the conflict is intrinsically unresolvable (George, 1996; Main & Hesse, 1990). The caregiver, who is the source of the infant's safety, appears *at the same time* to be a source of danger. The infant's inborn defense system, in such circumstances, is activated and directed toward the caregiver. Infants tend to defensively attack frightened/frightening caregivers, and/or to withdraw (through flight or freezing) from them. Withdrawing from the caregiver, however, means loneliness, and any threat of loneliness forces infants to approach the caregiver because of the inborn structure of the attachment system (Bowlby, 1969/1982, 1988). Caught in this unsolvable dilemma, infants display a disorganized admixture of approach and avoidance behavior toward the caregiver, or else freeze or display defensive aggressiveness in the middle of a friendly approach. This is the essence of disorganized attachment.

The link between unresolved trauma in the parent and disorganized infant attachment also helps in the understanding of those instances of DA in which an abusive (and usually traumatized) parent abruptly shifts from tender caregiving attitudes to violent outbursts of rage that directly induce fear in the infant. Here, even more obviously than in the case of frightened but not maltreating parental behavior, the attention of the infant shifts from safety strategies (active while the parent is expressing protection and care) to defensive strategies. Koos and Gergely (2001), making resort to contingency detection theory, have recently proposed that such a "flickering contingency switch" adversely affects the developmental unfolding of the infant's innate "contingency detection module," and leads to the fixation of a state of mind characterized by two competing targets of attentional and control strategies (a self-oriented strategy linked to the safety system and an other-oriented strategy linked to the defense system). This flickering contingency switch, in Koos and Gergely's hypothesis, is the cause of disorganized attachment behavior.

Disorganized Attachment: Disruptive Influence of the Inner Schema

The inner schema constructed and confirmed during repeated experiences of such "flickering contingency switches" exerts a disruptive influence over cognition, emotion, and interpersonal behavior throughout development. Whenever the child is facing danger or pain and searches for safety in the protective proximity of another human being, expectations of forthcoming further danger are brought on by this inner schema, and paradoxically activate the defense system even in what appears to be a safe interpersonal situation. Cognitions, emotions, and behaviors related to the defense system make their appearance in a context that nobody could appraise as dangerous or threatening. The unmotivated rage, the transient paranoid ideation, and the frantic fear of abandonment that are so typical of borderline patients can be thus related to the conflicting, simultaneous activation of the safety and defense systems due to the inner schema of previous DA.

Understanding the Therapeutic Relationship With Borderline Patients

The therapeutic relationship is by definition an interpersonal situation in which the patient's safety system is repeatedly activated. Because of their inner schema of DA, borderline patients will likely find in the therapeutic relationship repeated occasion for the activation of the defense system together with the safety system. Dramatic shifts in the patient's representations of self and/or the therapist are contingent upon this conflicting activation of the safety and defense systems within the therapeutic relationship. While the conflicting activation of the two inborn systems explains the peculiar difficulties of the therapeutic relationship with these patients, it also constitutes an opportunity for clinical interventions aimed at the correction of the inner schema underlying the conflict. In order to devise such interventions, the therapist should think of interpersonal exchanges and interpersonal motivation in evolutionary terms. More precisely, while dealing with a borderline patient the therapist should pay particular heed to the activation of the attachment system within the therapeutic dialogues, since signs of such an activation predict forthcoming dramatic shifts of the patient's way of perceiving self and the therapist. In order to detect the activation of the attachment system, the therapist should be able to distinguish clearly between interactions mediated by the attachment system and interactions mediated by other evolved systems.

A Reminder: The Modular Evolutionary Model of Social Motivation

In the evolutionary perspective, human interpersonal behavior is regulated by a number of control systems, each linked to a distinct brain module (i.e., to a distinct, ethologically defined "value" of the old mammalian brain: see Migone & Liotti, 1998). The development of each interpersonal control system during the personal learning history is based on a well-defined set of inborn dispositions. These systems evolved in mammals to pursue independent, even if interrelated, biosocial goals such as attachment, mating, ranking, and cooperation (Bowlby, 1969/1982, 1988; DeWaal, 1996; Gilbert, 1989, 2000; LeDoux, 1996; Liotti, 2001). In the therapeutic relationship, as in every human relationship of sufficient duration and meaningfulness, various types of interaction succeed and alternate, each regulated by one or the other of the basic interpersonal motivational systems: attachment, competitive, seductive, and cooperative interactions. The important theme to be emphasized here is that every interpersonal control system, when it becomes active at any given time in the therapeutic relationship, potentially affords to the patient's and the therapist's subjective experience two types of information: emotional information linked to the inborn operations of that system, and cognitive information linked to memories of previous activation of that system. In other words, distinct "mentalities," comprising cognitions, emotion, and behavioral propensities, are regulated throughought the life span via the activation of these inborn systems (Gilbert, 2000; cf. LeDoux, 1996, for a discussion of the representation of these functional systems in the brain).

The Therapeutic Relationship in the Evolutionary Perspective

Cognitive psychotherapists strive to shape the therapeutic relationship, from the very first session, according to the ideal of collaborative empiricism (Beck, Emery, & Greenberg 1985). This is performed through the active search for an explicit agreement on goals and rules of the therapeutic work. If the joint formulation of a shared goal for the treatment has been successful, the inborn motivational system mediating cooperative behavior is likely to become active both in the therapist and in the patient at the beginning of the treatment. Patients, however, do suffer. Since the beginning of psychotherapy, they are gradually disclosing their troubles to benevolent persons (the therapists) that they come to perceive as emotionally available and as "stronger and/or wiser" than themselves (Bowlby, 1979, p. 129). Disclosing one's suffering to an available person who is perceived as stronger and wiser than the self is the typical situation in which, "from the cradle to the grave" (Bowlby, 1979, p. 129), the inborn attachment system is activated. Therefore, in the course of psychotherapy, the cooperative system will give way to the attachment system.

The activation of the attachment system within the therapeutic relationship may be detected in a variety of ways: through an analysis of the patient's and the therapist's emotional reactions (see the concept of the therapist's emotions as "markers" of particular interpersonal cycles and schemata in Safran & Segal, 1990), or through the patient's representations of self and the therapist as they may appear during the therapeutic dialogue (the patient perceives the therapist as able to provide comfort from emotional pain and protection from danger). If the therapist responds properly to these signs of activation of the patient's attachment system, the defense system will not intervene in the regulation of the therapeutic dialogues, and the safety system will govern the patient's experience, cognition, and interpersonal behavior. Such a proper therapeutic response, however, is usually a difficult and sometimes an impossible goal to achieve *in any lasting way* during the individual psychotherapy of borderline patients because of the linking between the safety and the defense systems brought on by the IWM of DA.

Clinical Example

Eva, a borderline patient in her late twenties, was prone to self-destructive cognitions, suicidal ideation, and parasuicidal behaviors. She had accepted, at the beginning of treatment, a therapeutic contract based on an agreement not to commit suicide for at least one year, according to the prescriptions of the dialectic-behavioral model of psychotherapy (Linehan, 1993). She also agreed to participate in the individual sessions and the group therapy sessions (led by a different therapist) of dialectic-behavior therapy (Linehan, 1993).

During the first months of treatment, Eva seemed very compliant in the individual sessions, while her behavior in the group sessions was rather troublesome, full of critical remarks toward the group therapist (G), whom she compared unfavorably with the individual therapist (P). At the end of each individual session, while shaking hands with his patient, P reflected that Eva had been covertly very anxious during the dialogue: her hand was cold and moist, while it was warm and dry at the beginning of the session. P interpreted this observation in the light of the DA model of borderline disorders. Eva's attachment system became active during the individual sessions, which led her to perceive P through the lens of her dissociated inner schema of DA, that is, overtly, as helpful and well-meaning (the Rescuer) and covertly as potentially threatening (the Persecutor). Thus, the defense and the safety systems became simultaneously active during the individual sessions. In the group sessions, Eva's attachment system was dormant; she approached G through the operations of her competitive (agonistic) system, without any conflict between the safety and the defense systems.

During the sixth month of treatment, Eva firmly stated, during an individual session, that she meant to kill herself in the near future. P reacted by reminding her of the contract they had agreed upon at the beginning of treatment: if she did not immediately give up her intention, the treatment would be stopped. Eva became furious. She said that P was forbidding her to be frank and open in the therapeutic dialogues, and she did not think she would come to the next session. P replied that he considered himself still engaged in the treatment, and hoped that she would come to the next session with the renewed intention not to commit suicide.

During the following session, one week later, Eva still appeared very angry. She said that she was now very afraid to report her feelings to P, thinking that he would stop the treatment if she told him of her suicidal intentions. "Until now I felt very secure in our dialogues. I felt that I could tell you anything that came to my mind, but now I cannot be so open anymore. Now I am really afraid of your reactions to what I could say." Since she was not then openly declaring the intention to kill herself, P ended the session by confirming the next scheduled session, while shaking hands as usual with her. P noted that for the first time in months Eva's hand was warm and dry at the end of a session. He thought that she may have felt protected by his expressed intention to have her alive and present for the next sessions. P also thought that this feeling of being cared for that Eva experienced, notwithstanding her expressed anger, was reinforcing her perception of P as a Rescuer and correcting her alternative perception of him as a Persecutor. Her expressed anger was, then, to be understood as a protest linked to the operations of the attachment system, rather than as an attack linked to the activation of the competitive system.[3]

This therapeutic success was confirmed by Eva's spontaneous reporting, in the following session, of memories of her mother dramatically threatening to commit suicide when Eva was a child. P acknowledged the relevance of this information by commenting, "Thus, you learned from your mother that when one desperately needs help and is afraid help will not be provided, he or she can express the need and the fear by threatening suicide." This comment opened the theme of how and why people one may ask for help could either provide it or refuse to do so. The representation of other people and of self as negative and hostile (the form assumed by the Persecutor in the IWM of attachment) that so often appeared in Eva's consciousness, was gradually related to their (and her own) alleged unwillingness to provide help. Much therapeutic work was thus done on correcting Eva's tendency to extreme forms of dichotomous thinking (i.e., people being either good or evil, rather than more or less episodically, or more or less justifiably, available or unavailable to provide help and comfort).

This therapeutic success, however, was far from being resolutive. When the treatment was in its eleventh month, Eva stated that she was going to quit therapy because she felt depressed again, and felt that this time P could not be helpful as he had been in the past. She said that she knew how well meaning, understanding, and emotionally available P was; she believed, however, that her suffering was too overwhelming for anyone to be able to alleviate it. P listened, thinking that the Victim aspect of the IWM of DA was now shaping Eva's perception of both of them. Eva was perceiving herself as the helpless victim of an overwhelming illness, and P as a well-meaning, but equally helpless, attachment figure.

Oscillating attitudes toward self and the therapist are common in the therapeutic relationship with borderline patients, as they are in these patients' other relations. In a short span of time, even within a single session, borderline patients may dramatically ask for help, look distant and indifferent, state their wish to quit therapy because of the fear of being damaged, express the fear of being dangerous to beloved persons, and make the therapist feel important and loved but also threatened or oppressed. These shifts in interpersonal attitudes and representations of self-with-others may exceed the expert therapist's capacity of directing the therapeutic relationship.

One way of coping efficiently with the problems created by the activation of the attachment system within the therapeutic relationship with borderline patients is offered by models of intervention in which at least two different therapists are engaged in the treatment. The efficacy of two such models has been empirically assessed (Bateman & Fonagy, 1999, 2001; Bohus, Haaf, Stiglmayr, & Linehan, 2000; Linehan, 1993).[4]

The Usefulness of Having Two Therapists Engaged in the Psychotherapy of Borderline Patients

The positive effect of two different therapists, operating in two simultaneous settings in the treatment of borderline states, is well explained by attachment theory. The simultaneous existence of another caregiving relationship (e.g., with a group therapist) protects the relationship with the individual therapist from the consequences of too intense an activation of the patient's attachment system.

When the activation of the patient's attachment system within the individual setting brings on the expected propensity to dramatic shifts in the way of construing self and therapist, the situation leading to DA is repeated. To relinquish a relationship that alone appears capable of affording comfort from unbearable emotional pain is frightening, but to approach the attachment figure is equally frightening. *Each pole of this dilemma increases the intensity of the painful emotions implied by the other.* One of the likely consequences of this state of affairs is the patient's dropping out of treatment; another is a therapeutic stalemate. If, however, a second therapist is engaged in the therapeutic program, the patient may feel that there is another source of help available, and this perception may reduce the emotional strain on the first therapeutic relationship. Moreover, the borderline patient's metacognitive deficits are amplified by the activation of the inner schema of DA (see above, on metacognitive deficits). The therapist facing such an activation within the therapeutic relationship will find that, as long as the activation lasts, the patient is unable to reflect critically on his or her ongoing thoughts and emotional experiences. The same thoughts and experiences, however, can become the object of reflection with the second therapist, toward whom the patient's attachment system is less strongly and less promptly activated.

Eva's individual psychotherapist, P, did try to express his disagreement with the patient's idea that he could no longer help her. Eva, however, interpreted his assertion of feeling both willing and able to help her as only a sign of his well-meaning attitude: "I know that you don't really believe that you can help me. You did, and I relapsed," she sobbed. "You just want to comfort me by saying that you can cope with this relapse," she added, and she ended the session prematurely, leaving the room in tears.

A few days later, however, Eva was discussing in the group setting her belief that the individual psychotherapy could not be effective in alleviating her depression, since she had so badly relapsed. When G expressed a different opinion, and asked her to examine the evidence on which she based such a belief, Eva complied, and reached the conclusion that she had no evidence that a therapeutic intervention could be ineffective in the face of a relapse just because the relapse did occur. This led her to agree to examine with P the feelings and thoughts that she had had while stating, in the preceding individual session, her belief that the therapy was destined to total failure. Such an examination revealed that her assumption that an attachment figure would sooner or later prove vulnerable and inefficient (the Victim in the IWM of DA, used as a schema to construe the attachment figure's capacity for help) was based on her childhood experiences rather than on a current situation with a new attachment figure.

Concluding Remarks

Among the advantages of an evolutionary approach to psychopathology, the possibility of a better understanding of the developmental roots of abnormal interpersonal cognition (stemming from early infancy, when cognition, emotion, and behavior are obviously regulated by innately based, evolved systems) is particularly relevant. The case of borderline psychopathology exemplifies well the practical use-fulness of such an understanding when dealing with an adult patient. Besides illuminating various aspects of the patient's cognitive processes by linking them to the activation of inborn regulatory systems (in the case examined, the attachment system), the evolutionary approach outlined here provides a strong rationale for the usefulness of having two therapists simultaneously engaged in the treatment of these dif-ficult patients. Although such usefulness has been empirically assessed the authors of the therapeutic models so successfully tested did not provide a rationale linking the use of two (or more) therapists to the hypothesized developmental core of borderline states.

If one reason for the usefulness of two simultaneous settings in the treatment of borderline patients is the distribution of the patients' attachment needs over more than a single therapist, then such use-fulness should also appear with combined interventions other than individual and group (the combination suggested both by Linehan and by the Bateman & Fonagy models). Combined individual psychother-apy and family therapy, or even individual psychotherapy and pharma-cological therapy (if the drugs are prescribed by a psychiatrist who is well grounded in psychological treatments), could protect the individ-ual psychotherapy from dropouts and stalemates as well as individual and group interventions do. This prediction can be tested. To encour-age its testing by clinicians interested in the treatment of borderline patients is one of the hopes underlying the writing of this chapter.

Notes

1. For "borderline states" I mean, in this chapter, borderline personal-ity disorder and some other clinically related conditions that are often diag-nosed in the category of dissociative disorders (Buck, 1983; Marmer & Fink, 1994; Ross, 1989).

2. This assertion by no means implies that infants whose attachment behaviour is disorganized are inescapably destined to develop psychiatric disturbances as they grow up. A risk factor in the development of psycho-logical disturbances is not a linear cause of them. Children or adolescents whose attachment has been disorganized in infancy may gradually become capable of organizing their attachment behavior and the corresponding representations, either as a function of their parents' gradual elaboration of traumatic memories, or as a function of other, more positive attachment rela-tionships. Even if the attachment relationship with a caregiver suffering from

unresolved traumas persists unmodified throughout childhood and adolescence, other risk factors should usually add up to disorganized attachment if a serious psychiatric disorder (e.g., a dissociative identity disorder or a borderline personality disorder) is to be developed. Risk factors that very likely add up to disorganized attachment in the genesis of most dissociative and borderline disorders are unfavorable temperamental traits (e.g., emotional vulnerability according to Linehan, 1993) and repeated traumatic experiences (e.g., incest and other types of abuses within the family: Perry & Herman, 1993; Spiegel, 1984).

3. Anger, in the evolutionary perspective, may appear as an operation of the attachment system whose goal is to energetically ask for the attachment figure's attention, (e.g., the secure child protects during the separation from the mother in Ainsworth's *Strange Situation:* Ainsworth et al., 1978). Anger, however, may also appear as an operation of the competition system (e.g., ritualized aggression aimed at defining the social rank: Gilbert, 1989).

4. As far as I know, these are the only two models of treatment of borderline conditions whose efficacy has been empirically proved.

References

Ainsworth, M. D. S., Blehar, M. C., Waters, E., & Wall, S. (1978). *Patterns of attachment.* Hillsdale, NJ: Erlbaum.

Amini, F., Lewis, T., Lannon, R., & Louie, A. (1996). Affect, attachment, memory: Contributions toward psychobiologic integration. *Psychiatry, 59,* 213–239.

Anderson, C. L., & Alexander, P. C. (1996). The relationship between attachment and dissociation in adult survivors of incest. *Psychiatry, 59,* 240–254.

Baron-Cohen, S. (1995). *Mindblindness: An essay on autism and the theory of mind.* Cambridge, MA: MIT Press.

Barone, L. (1998, November 13–15). *Attaccamento e metacognizione nei disturbi di personalità* [Attachment and metacognition in personality disorders]. Paper presented at the IX Conference of the Italian Association for Cognitive Therapy.

Beck, A. T., Emery, G., & Greenberg, R. (1985). *Anxiety disorders and phobias.* New York: Basic Books.

Bateman, A., & Fonagy, P. (1999). Effectiveness of partial hospitalization in the treatment of borderline personality disorder: A randomized control trial. *American Journal of Psychiatry, 156,* 1563–1569.

Bateman, A., & Fonagy, P. (2001). Treatment of borderline personality disorder with psychoanalytically oriented partial hospitalization: An 18-month follow-up. *American Journal of Psychiatry, 158,* 36–42.

Bohus, M., Haaf, B., Stiglmayr, C., & Linehan, M. (2000). Evaluation of inpatient dialectical-behavioural therapy for borderline personality disorder: A prospective study. *Behavior Research and Therapy*, *38*, 875–887.

Bowlby, J. (1982). *Attachment and loss* (Vol. 1, 2nd ed.). London: Hogarth. (Original work printed 1969)

Bowlby, J. (1979). *The making and breaking of affectional bonds*. London: Tavistock.

Bowlby, J. (1988). *A secure base*. London: Routledge.

Bretherton, I., & Munholland, K. A. (1999). Internal working models in attachment relationships: A construct revisited. In J. Cassidy & P. R. Shaver, (Eds.), *Handbook of attachment* (pp. 89–111). New York: Guilford.

Buck, O. D. (1983). Multiple personality as a borderline state. *Journal of Nervous and Mental Disease*, *17*, 162–165.

Carlson, E. A. (1998). A prospective longitudinal study of consequences of disorganized/ disoriented attachment. *Child Development*, *69*, 1970–1979.

Carlson, E. A., & Sroufe, L. A. (1995). Contribution of attachment theory to developmental psychopathology. In D. Cicchetti & D. Cohen (Eds.), *Developmental psychopathology: Theory and methods* (Vol. 1, pp. 581–617). New York: Wiley.

Cassidy, J. (1988). Child-mother attachment and the self in six-year-olds. *Child Development*, *59*, 121–134.

Coe, M. T., Daleenberg, C. J., Aransky, K. M., & Reto, C. S. (1995). Adult attachment style, reported childhood violence history and types of dissociative experiences. *Dissociation*, *8*, 142–154.

Davies, J. M., & Frawley, M. G. (1994). *Treating the adult survivor of childhood sexual abuse: A psychoanalytic perspective*. New York: Basic Books.

DeWaal, F. (1996). *Goodnatured: The origins of right and wrong in humans and other animals*. Cambridge, MA: Harvard University Press.

Dozier, M., Stovall, K. C., & Albus, K. E. (1999). Attachment and psychopathology in adulthood. In J. Cassidy & P. R. Shaver (Eds.), *Handbook of attachment* (pp. 497–519). New York: Guilford.

Fields, T. M., & Fox, N. A. (1985). *Social perception in infants*. Norwood, NJ: Ahler.

Flavell, J. H. (1979). Metacognition and cognitive monitoring: A new area of cognitive-developmental inquiry. *American Psychologist*, *34*, 906–911.

Flavell, J. H., Flavell, E. R., & Green, F. L. (1983). Development of the appearance-reality distinction. *Cognitive Psychology*, *15*, 95–120.

Fonagy, P., Redfern, S., & Charman, A. (1997). The relationship between belief-desire reasoning and a projective measure of attachment security. *British Journal of Developmental Psychopathology*, *15*, 51–63.

Fonagy, P., Steele, M., Steele, H., Leigh, T., Kennedy, R., Mattoon, G., & Target, M. (1995). Attachment, the reflective self, and borderline states. In S. Goldberg, R. Muir, & J. Kerr (Eds.), *Attachment theory: Social, developmental and clinical perspectives* (pp. 233–278). Hillsdale, NJ: Analytic Press.

George, C. (1996). A representational perspective of child abuse and prevention: Internal working models of attachment and caregiving. *Child Abuse and Neglect, 20,* 411–424.

George, C., Kaplan, N., & Main, M. (1985). *The Adult Attachment Interview.* Unpublished manuscript, University of California at Berkeley.

Gilbert, P. (1989). *Human nature and suffering.* New York: Erlbaum.

Gilbert, P. (1993). Defense and safety: Their function in social behavior and psychopathology. *British Journal of Clinical Psychology, 32,* 131–153.

Gilbert, P. (2000). Social mentalities: Internal "social" conflict and the role of inner warmth and compassion in cognitive therapy. In P. Gilbert & K. Bailey (Eds.), *Genes on the couch: Explorations in evolutionary psychotherapy* (pp. 118- 150). Philadelphia: Taylor & Francis.

Goldwyn, R., Stanley, C., Smith, V., & Green, J. (2000). The Manchester Child Attachment Story Task: Relationship with parental AAI, SAT and child behaviour. *Attachment & Human Development, 2,* 71–84.

Hesse, E., & Main, M. (1999). Second-generation effects of unresolved trauma in non-maltreating parents: Dissociated, frightened and threatening parental behavior. *Psychoanalytic Inquiry, 19,* 30–61.

Horowitz, M. J. (1986). *Stress response syndromes* (2nd ed.). New York: Aronson.

Jacobsen, T., Edelstein, W., & Hofmann, V. (1994). A longitudinal study of the relation between representation of attachment in childhood and cognitive functioning in childhood and adolescence. *Developmental Psychology, 30*(1), 112–124.

Kernberg, O. F. (1975). *Borderline conditions and pathological narcissism.* New York: Aronson.

Koos, O., & Gergely, G. (2001). A contingency-based approach to the etiology of disorganized attachment: The flickering switch hypothesis. *Bulletin of the Menninger Clinic, 65,* 397–410.

LeDoux, J. (1996). *The emotional brain.* New York: Simon & Schuster.

Lichtenberg, J. D., Lachmann, F., & Fosshage, D. (1992). *Self and motivational systems: Toward a theory of technique.* Hillsdale, NJ: Analytic Press.

Linehan, M. M. (1993). *Cognitive-behavioral treatment for borderline personality disorder.* New York: Guilford.

Liotti, G. (1992). Disorganized/disoriented attachment in the etiology of the dissociative disorders. *Dissociation, 5,* 196–204.

Liotti, G. (1993). Disorganized attachment and dissociative experiences: An illustration of the developmental-ethological approach to cognitive therapy. In K. T. Kuehlvein & H. Rosen (Eds.), *Cognitive therapies in action* (pp. 213–239). San Francisco: Jossey-Bass.

Liotti, G. (1995). Disorganized/disoriented attachment in the psychotherapy of the dissociative disorders. In S. Goldberg, R. Muir, & J. Kerr (Eds.), *Attachment theory: Social, developmental and clinical perspectives* (pp. 343–363). Hillsdale, NJ: Analytic Press.

Liotti, G. (1999). Disorganization of attachment as a model for understanding dissociative psychopathology. In J. Solomon & C. George (Eds.), *Disorganization of attachment* (pp. 291–317). New York: Guilford.

Liotti, G. (2000). Disorganized attachment, models of borderline states and evolutionary psychotherapy. In P. Gilbert & K. Bailey (Eds.), *Genes on the couch: Explorations in evolutionary psychotherapy* (pp. 232-256). Philadelphia: Taylor & Francis.

Liotti, G. (2001). *Le opere della coscienza: Psicopatologia e psicoterapia nella prospettiva cognitivo-evoluzionista* [The works of consciousness: Psychopathology and psychotherapy in the cognitive-evolutionary perspective]. Milano: Cortina.

Liotti, G., & Intreccialagli, B. (1998). Metacognition and motivational systems in psychotherapy: A cognitive-evolutionary approach to the treatment of difficult patients. In C. Perris & P. McGorry (Eds.), *Cognitive psychotherapy of psychotic and personality disorders* (pp. 333–349). Chichester, UK: Wiley.

Liotti, G., Intreccialagli, B., & Cecere, F. (1991). Esperienza di lutto nella madre e predisposizione ai disturbi dissociativi della prole: Uno studio caso-controllo. *Rivista di Psichiatria, 26,* 283–291.

Liotti, G., Pasquini, P., & The Italian Group for the Study of Dissociation (2000). Predictive factors for borderline personality disorder: Patients' early traumatic experiences and losses suffered by the attachment figure. *Acta Psychiatrica Scandinavica, 102,* 282–289.

Lyons-Ruth, K., & Jacobvitz, D. (1999). Attachment disorganization: Unresolved loss, relational violence and lapses in behavioral and attentional strategies. In J. Cassidy & P. R. Shaver, (Eds.), *Handbook of attachment* (pp. 520–554). New York: Guilford.

Main, M. (1991). Metacognitive knowledge, metacognitive monitoring, and singular (coherent) versus multiple (incoherent) models of attachment. In C. M. Parkes, J. Stevenson-Hinde, & P. Marris (Eds.), *Attachment across the life cycle* (pp. 127–159). London: Routledge.

Main, M. (1995). Recent studies in attachment: Overview, with selected implications for clinical work. In S. Goldberg, R. Muir, & J. Kerr (Eds.), *Attachment theory: Social, developmental and clinical perspectives* (pp. 407–474). Hillsdale, NJ: Analytic Press.

Main, M., & Hesse, E. (1990). Parents' unresolved traumatic experiences are related to infant disorganized attachment status: Is frightened and/or frightening parental behavior the linking mechanism? In M. T. Greenberg, D. Cicchetti, & E. M. Cummings (Eds.), *Attachment in the preschool years* (pp. 161–182). Chicago: University Press of Chicago.

Main, M., & Morgan, H. (1996). Disorganization and disorientation in infant strange situation behavior: Phenotypic resemblance to dissociative states? In L. Michelson & W. Ray (Eds.), *Handbook of dissociation* (pp. 107–137). New York: Plenum Press.

Main, M., & Solomon, J. (1990). Procedures for identifying infants as disorganized/disoriented during the Ainsworth Strange Situation. In M. T. Greenberg, D. Cicchetti, & E. M. Cummings (Eds.), *Attachment in the preschool years* (pp. 121–160). Chicago: University Press of Chicago.

Marks, I. (1987). *Fears, phobias and rituals: Panic, anxiety and their disorders.* Oxford, UK: Oxford University Press.

Marmer, S. S., & Fink, D. (1994). Rethinking the comparison of borderline personality disorder and multiple personality disorder. *Psychiatric Clinics of North America, 17*(4), 743–771.

Meins, E. (1997). *Security of attachment and the social development of cognition.* Hove, UK: Psychology Press.

Migone, P., & Liotti, G. (1998). Psychoanalysis and cognitive-evolutionary psychology: An attempt at integration. *International Journal of Psychoanalysis, 79,* 1071–1095.

Pasquini, P., Liotti, G., & The Italian Group for the Study of Dissociation. (2002). Risk factors in the early family life of patients suffering from dissociative disorders. *Acta Psychiatrica Scandinavica, 105,* 110–116.

Perry, J. C., & Herman, J. L. (1993). Traumas and defenses in the etiology of the borderline personality disorder. In J. Paris (Ed.), *Borderline personality disorder: Etiology and treatment* (pp. 129–146). Washington, DC: American Psychiatric Press.

Ross, C. (1989). *Multiple personality disorder.* New York: Wiley.

Safran, J. D., & Segal, Z. V. (1990). *Interpersonal process in cognitive therapy.* New York: Basic Books.

Schore, A. N. (2001). The effects of early relational trauma on right brain development, affect regulation, and infant mental health. *Infant Mental Health Journal, 22,* 201–269.

Schuengel, C., Bakermans, M. J., Van IJzendoorn, M., & Blom, M. (1999). Unresolved loss and infant disorganization: Links to frightening maternal behavior. In J. Solomon & C. George (Eds.), *Attachment disorganization* (pp. 71–94). New York: Guilford.

Solomon, J., George, C., & DeJong, A. (1995). Children classified as controlling at age six: Evidence of disorganized representational strategies and aggression at home and at school. *Development and Psychopathology, 7,* 447–463.

Spiegel, D. (1984) Multiple personality as a posttraumatic stress disorder. *Psychiatric Clinics of North America, 7,* 101–110.

Van IJzendoorn, M. H. (1997). Attachment, emergent morality and aggression: Towards a developmental socio-emotional model of antisocial behavior. *International Journal of Behavioural Development, 21,* 703–727.

Wimmer, H., & Penner, J. (1983). Beliefs about beliefs: Representations and constraining function of wrong beliefs in young children's understanding of deception. *Cognition, 13,* 103–128.

Young, W. (1988). Psychodynamics and dissociation: All that switches is not split. *Dissociation, 1,* 33–38.

Chapter 7

Command Hallucinations: Cognitive Theory, Therapy, and Research

Sarah Byrne, Peter Trower, Max Birchwood, Alan Meaden, and Angela Nelson

C onsiderable progress in schizophrenia research has been made in recent years in understanding the psychological and interpersonal characteristics of hallucinations. In this context, one particular class of hallucinations, namely command hallucinations (CH) have become a focus of theory, research, and clinical intervention. Indeed the importance of CH has become clear both for theoretical reasons, in the light that these symptoms throw on the psychological nature of the positive symptoms in general, but also for practice reasons, since CH are one of the most high-risk, distressing symptoms of schizophrenia.

CH have long been recognized but little understood, with few effective interventions. The key feature that distinguishes them from ordinary hallucinations is that phenomenologically the voice is experienced as commanding rather than commenting. The perceived commands range from making a harmless gesture to behaving in ways that are potentially injurious or lethal to self or others. CH are also a relatively common form of hallucination. Between 40% and 60% of all voice hearers will report what they believe to be instructions and commands (e.g., Birchwood & Chadwick, 1997; Hellerstein, Frosch, & Koenigsberg, 1987).

While there are many reports of patients who act on command hallucinations with serious consequences (e.g., Jones, Huckle, & Tanaghow, 1992), particularly in forensic populations (e.g., Rogers, Gillis, Turner, & Frise-Smith, 1990), the presence of a command hallucination per se does not automatically elicit compliance (Hellerstein et al., 1987). Nonetheless, Junginger (1990) found over 40% reported compliance on a recent occasion, particularly with commands that do not imply a major social transgression; and, in the forensic population, Rogers and colleagues (1990) report that 44% responded to commands with "unquestioning obedience" (p. 1306).

In a critical review of the literature, Braham and Trower (in press) found that the relationship between command and compliance was mediated by a number of factors, including beliefs about the voice's identity, familiarity, power, and intent. The studies reviewed support the idea that the beliefs an individual holds about his or her voice will influence compliance, and that a cognitive model is required to explain the relationships and guide clinical intervention.

Birchwood and his colleagues (Birchwood & Chadwick, 1997; Chadwick & Birchwood, 1994; Chadwick, Birchwood, & Trower, 1996) have developed a cognitive theoretical framework and intervention for auditory hallucinations in general, that is equally applicable with adaptation, we propose, to CH in particular. They have demonstrated that the distressing affect and behavior arising from auditory hallucinations may be understood not simply as a function of the content or topography of voice activity, but voice hearers' appraisal of their meaning. The voice here is viewed as an "activating event" (Trower, Casey, & Dryden, 1988) whose significance has to be appraised by the individual. These authors have found evidence for cognitive mediation in the maintenance of beliefs about voices: in many cases, belief content was at odds with voice content, suggesting that meanings are constructed by individuals rather than directly voice driven (Chadwick & Birchwood, 1994). Indeed, participants in this study disclosed what was for them compelling evidence for their beliefs, which only occasionally drew upon voice content. These results were replicated by Close and Garety (1998).

While the above cognitive framework helps to understand the cognitive process of interpretation of CH, it does not explain with any precision why CH hearers have specific beliefs to obey the voice, that is, cognitive content, and is not able to predict and guide the therapist in the search for relevant beliefs. Generally speaking, CBT theory has little to say about the structure of inference chains. Usually inference chains are derived pragmatically with the downward laddering technique, for example, by asking the client to further describe what it is (in the present case) about the voice that is most distressing or compelling, thus aiming to obtain a series of inferences that are connected in the client's mind. A theory is needed that proposes a structure to inferences, a theory from which we can make predictions about the type of inferences and what form the chain of inferences will take. In other words, we need an account that can give an explanation for the cognitive content of CH hearers' specific beliefs.

One theory that can provide an understanding of these phenomena is social rank theory (Gilbert, 1992; Price & Sloman, 1987). This theory, based on evolutionary psychology, focuses on the role of dominance hierarchies as coordinators of social behavior and affect in group-living animals in general. It states that humans and other group-living animals have evolved neurocognitive mechanisms that shape this hierarchical pattern of social organization, essential for maintaining cohesion rather than dispersion of conspecifics. In these social hierarchies, those with superior strengths and skills were able to threaten, attack, or intimidate those less able, while those in subordinate positions could defend themselves by escaping or fleeing. But if they were to stay within the social group, they had to have ways of coping with and de-escalating that threat. A variety of interpersonal behaviors, loosely labeled as appeasement and submission, have evolved for this purpose. In other words the subordinate animal can reduce the threat directed to it by expressing submissive and appeasing behaviors. These behaviors normally have the effect of terminating the aggression of the dominant and stabilizing the relative rank differentials. Other subordinate characteristics include selective sensitivity to the commands of the dominant, a compulsion to obey such commands, and appeasement of the dominants when obeying is risky or dangerous but escape is impossible. This model has been developed to explain features of depression (e.g., Brown, Harris, & Hepworth, 1995; Gilbert, 1992), social anxiety (Gilbert & Trower, 2001; Trower & Gilbert, 1989) and postpsychotic depression (Rooke & Birchwood, 1998), and is especially relevant, we believe, to command hallucinations.

Put simply, CH are self-generated, but patients experience them as if they are generated by external others (voices). Moreover, the commands are seen as emanating from a powerful dominant (rather than a weak subordinate) who has the power to inflict harm if a command is not carried out. It is this power relationship (dominant voice-subordinate self) that is key to the felt need to obey commands, and at times a sense of being severely subordinated by them and thus a focus for therapeutic intervention. It is unclear why patients who hear psychotic voices experience the command or harsh criticism as externally generated rather than from their own thinking, as in depression. Bentall (1990) argues that people suffering from auditory hallucinations have problems discriminating internal (self-generated) signals from external ones. Baker and Morrison (1998) and Morrison and Haddock (1997) offer evidence that voice hearers have generalized problems in correctly identifying and attributing the source of internally generated signals. There is evidence that psychotic voice hearers can misidentify internal signals/speech as external, possibly related to problems in the connectivity of different brain areas (McGuire et al., 1996). Crow (1997a, 1997b) suggests that such difficulties may arise from disturbance in the hemispheric specialization that evolved with human language. However, whatever the sources of "hearing a voice," it is the dominant-subordinate relationship that we focus on here.

Recent research has found considerable support for social rank theory in hallucinations in general and command hallucinations in particular. We found empirical support for the predicted power differential between voice and voice hearer in the level of distress and also in coping strategies (Birchwood, Meaden, Trower, Gilbert, & Plaistow, 2000). We have also found that—be it in nonpsychotic depression, where people have self-critical thoughts ("I am bad and inadequate") and issue commands to themselves ("I should," "I must"), or in people who hear critical and commanding voices—the power and dominance of, and inability to escape from, the negative thoughts and hostile voices. are highly associated with depression (Gilbert et al., 2001). The theory thus has predictive power when considering the risk of compliance with command hallucinations. Junginger (1 990) found that recent compliance was more likely when the individual personified, or attributed an identity to, the voice. Over 85% of voice hearers see the voice as powerful and omnipotent, whereas by contrast, the hearer is usually perceived as weak and dependent, unable to control or influence the voice (Birchwood & Chadwick, 1997). It was found that the greater the perceived power and omnipotence of the voice, the greater the likelihood of compliance (Beck-Sander, Birchwood, & Chadwick, 1997). This relationship is not linear and was moderated by appraisal of the consequences of resisting the voice on the one hand, and the consequences of the social transgression on the other. Results showed that those with benevolent voices virtually always complied with the voice, irrespective of whether the command was socially innocuous or severe (Beck-Sander et al., 1997), whereas those with malevolent (hostile dominant) voices were more likely to resist severe commands but more likely to carry out appeasement behaviors, as is predicted by social rank theory. Furthermore, we have argued that the relationship with the voice is a paradigm or mirror of social relationships in general, such that individuals who feel subordinate to the powerful voice also feel subordinate to others in their social world (Birchwood et al., 2000). In other words, the perceived dominant-subordinate relationship between voice and voice hearer may be driven by individuals' core social rank schema.

In this framework, the key independent variable is the perceived power—indeed, omnipotence—of the personified voice: the greater the perceived power differential between voice and voice hearer, the greater the probability of complying with the benevolent voices, and the greater the probability of complying with, or resisting and appeasing the malevolent voices, depending on the nature (severity) of the command. Thus, the social rank account of command hallucinations proposes that high-risk behaviors of people with command hallucinations are a consequence of a rank-oriented belief system, namely a conviction in the absolute power (superiority and dominance) of their voices, and lack of power (inferiority and subordination) of themselves, a belief that they are compelled to comply with and/or appease these voices or be punished.

Following the principles of social rank theory, the authors have developed Cognitive Therapy for Command Hallucinations (CTCH). The aim of CTCH is to deconstruct the belief system that underpins the dominant-subordinate rank relationship between client and voice, thus enabling the client to regain control over his or her actions. One way this is achieved is by challenging the perceived omnipotence of the voice and the inferiority and weakness of the client, and further reducing compliance and appeasement by disconfirming the belief in severe consequences (e.g., belief that the voice will harm the client if s/he resists).

Cognitive Therapy for Command Hallucinations

Cognitive Therapy for Command Hallucinations (CTCH) is based on cognitive therapy for voices (Chadwick et al., 1996), adapted in accordance with the theory outlined above. Commands are defined as orders that the client experiences as emanating from a voice, and that he believes he must obey. Some clients hear commands directly, such as "set fire to the house," but, for others the command is interpreted indirectly from something the voice says, and the compulsion follows this interpretation. For example, one client hears a voice saying "you smell"; she interprets this as meaning that she should shower or bathe immediately; for another client, when the voice says "you will be on your way next week," he has packed a suitcase in preparation for the journey. Our definition of command, therefore, requires that the client interpret the voices as a command, not the clinical assessor or the therapist.

Stage 1: The Assessment Stage

We call this the assessment stage because assessment is the main overall function, but it includes a variety of tasks, namely engagement, assessment, formulation, promoting control and goal setting. We utilize social rank theory to guide these tasks. Although assessment is sequentially the first stage, the assessment process continues throughout therapy, and, as described below, forms part of an organic whole with intervention, since a major function of assessment is to evaluate the outcome of an intervention before further interventions are attempted.

Engagement. Engaging and retaining individuals who hear voices can be especially difficult due to the very subordination the client has to the dominant voice, which may marginalize the therapist; or in a different problem, the therapist herself may be seen as a hostile dominant. Consequently, there are particular as well as general principles that need to be deployed in the development of a sound therapeutic alliance. The therapist has to be especially careful to be accepting and caring, and, initially at least, be perceived as not competing with the voice. Key aspects of these sessions include:

- Establishing rapport and trust.
- Listening to and encouraging the client to give a detailed account of the experience of hearing voices and the accompanying beliefs.

- Emphasizing a commitment to the client and the client's priorities, especially helping the client to reduce the distress and disturbance caused by hearing voices.
- Anticipating some of the problems involved in engagement and weakening specific beliefs that could threaten the engagement process; for example:
  1. Clients may be concerned about the expectations and pace of therapy. The use of a symbolic "panic button" gives them control over the process of therapy, with the option to disengage.
  2. Clients may be unused to talking about their experiences and may feel anxious about doing so, expecting that the therapist will think it "crazy" to have a commanding voice. The therapist needs to put clients at ease by giving explicit permission to talk openly about any issue.
  3. Clients may be reluctant to continue therapy because their voices express anxiety about treatment or about the trustworthiness of the therapist. Anticipating that voices may comment adversely about the therapist will help the therapist develop strategies for keeping clients engaged.
- Socializing the client into the cognitive model: The idea here is to begin the process of helping the client to distinguish between facts and beliefs, and that beliefs, unlike facts, can be true or false, and can be changed, especially when they are unhelpful. So, for example, it can be pointed out that it is a fact that the client has a commanding voice, but it is a belief of the client, albeit strongly held, that the voice is omnipotent and must be obeyed. The therapist's aim at this point is to do no more than this, that is, to establish the principle of belief versus fact and that beliefs may be true or false. It is the first step in trying to weaken the social rank belief system. The value of this preparatory work at this early stage is to help the client gain some optimism for the possibility of change and motivation to continue to work with the therapist.
- Developing a rationale for questioning voice beliefs by considering the advantages and disadvantages of the beliefs being true or false: Once clients see that their beliefs can be true or false, they will be more open to the possibility that they would be better off if the beliefs were false, and motivation to proceed with therapy will be further increased.

Assessment and Formulation: Identifying the Power Beliefs. Assessment and formulation form the nub of stage 1, clearly preceding and giving direction to stage 2 intervention. However, in practice, assessment, formulation, and intervention form a continuing reciprocal and iterative process. In these early sessions, the parameters of the belief system relating to the commanding voice are identified and formulated (this will be modified in later sessions), and psychological origins and alternative formulations are explored, as suggested below.

Four core beliefs define the social rank, client-voice power relationship and are explored in the early sessions. These are:

- Power and control: the belief that the voice is powerful and superior, the voice hearer powerless and inferior, and relatedly that the voice hearer does not have any control over the voice.
- Compliance, resistance, and appeasement: the belief that the voice must be obeyed, and that, if resisted, the voice must be appeased, and if neither obeyed nor sufficiently appeased, can inflict harm on the voice hearer.
- Voice identity: the belief that the voice is a powerful, superior, dominant figure, such as the voice of God or the Devil.
- Meaning: the belief that the voice hearer is being punished by the voice for past behavior, and will be further punished unless obeyed.

The therapist uses these power belief concepts and the social rank theory framework to explore the client's beliefs about the voice. This assessment is carried out mainly by interviewing the client in the manner described earlier, and by means of relevant questionnaires, some of which have been specifically developed for this problem, and which are described in later sections of this chapter.

The therapist's next task is to help the client to see that these power beliefs are the client's own beliefs *about* the voice. In this way the process of socialization to the cognitive model, already started in the first phase of engagement, is elaborated and indeed continued throughout this assessment and the whole process of therapy. The therapist makes a careful distinction (for herself and the client) between the voice as an activating event (e.g., what the voice actually says), and the client's interpretation of it.

The therapist then develops a social rank formulation around the theme of the identity and power differential between client and voice, with the client's consequent need to comply, or appease if resisted, and the fear of punishment if the voice is not obeyed or appeased. Having arrived at this formulation, the therapist tentatively proposes it to the client (or preferably elicits it by Socratic questioning), with the aim of achieving a shared understanding.

If this shared understanding is achieved, therapist and client can then explore, perhaps at a later stage in therapy, the psychological origins of this power relationship, thus giving the client a convincing alternative formulation, which will further weaken the power of the voice. As this is as much an intervention as an assessment strategy, we describe its use later as part of stage 2. However, at this early stage the therapist may well be *reformulating* in her own mind, ready to use this strategy at the appropriate time. We can illustrate this point from one of our cases, David. Drawing on a social rank theme, the therapist hypothesized that David's beliefs about his voice arose from the trauma of a childhood rape. The beliefs were construed as reactions to, and attempts to make sense of, the hallucinatory experience. Associated evaluative themes related, on the one hand, to the client's sense of worthlessness and feeling that he deserved punishment and, on the other, to anger at the powerful and dominant abuser, whom he saw as abusing this trust. In addition, the therapist noted how the relationship with the voice was probably a reconstruction of a dominant abusing other to the self (as subordinate), forcing him to do things he did not want to do. The therapist kept this tentative reformulation in the back of her mind ready to use as an intervention strategy when the time was right.

The process of exploring and communicating the formulations—indeed the therapeutic process per se—involves utilizing the skills of collaborative empiricism and guided discovery long established in cognitive therapy (e.g., Beck, Rush, Shaw, & Emery, 1979), and didactic and Socratic techniques in rational emotive behavior therapy (e.g., Dryden, 1995).

Promoting Control. This is aimed at modifying the client's extreme subordination and helplessness beliefs. It involves developing or reinforcing a coping repertoire by enhancing the person's existing coping strategies for reducing distress and compliance, and introducing ideas that have been tried successfully by other voice hearers, such as learning to start and stop voices at will (see below). One useful strategy is to frame the voice and voice-hearer as in a kind of relationship in which the client can develop boundaries. The aim is to help the client have his own time (turn the voice off), turn his attention to or away from the voice, and make his own decisions, rather than always listening to and waiting for the voice to initiate decisions.

These coping strategies are used not only to bring some immediate relief and help to cement engagement, but to start the process of gently challenging the power beliefs. Promoting control is designed to:

- Emphasize client's strengths in coping with their voices, and start to build evidence against their powerlessness.
- Highlight client's ability to have some control over their voices, and thereby to build evidence against the voices' power.
- Develop an understanding of factors that increase or decrease the presence of voices.
- Underpin, develop, and deepen the therapeutic alliance.

Setting Goals for Therapy. The goals of therapy are to reduce the client's distress and compliance behavior which are deemed to be a consequence of rank-related, power-differential beliefs. The means to these goals is to identify and modify the power beliefs. This involves identifying clients' current beliefs about their voices and developing a rationale to question them. These two tasks will usually have been facilitated in the steps outlined above. However, a key task in setting goals is to develop alternative beliefs and to use them to replace the existing ones. See Table 7.1 for examples of current and alternative beliefs in one case.

Stage 2: The Intervention Stage

Stage 2 is the intervention stage, the aim of which is to explicitly deconstruct the social rank beliefs, that underpin the problem of compliance and distress that characterize command hallucinations. Specifically, the aim is to challenge the four power beliefs listed above, in order to

- Reduce the perceived power (high rank) of the voice and increase the perceived power (low rank) of the voice hearer.
- Reduce compliance and appeasement and increase resistance.
- Weaken the conviction about the identity of the voice.
- Weaken the conviction that the client is being and will be punished.

TABLE 7.1. Belief in Change

Current Beliefs	Alternative Beliefs
I must comply (at least partially) to prevent the voice harming me.	I can understand why I would be frightened if this is the case but what is the evidence that the voice can actually harm me? Has it ever actually done so? Maybe it is no more than a verbal statement of a threat that relies only on my fear. In fact, the voice cannot harm me, therefore, I can choose to resist or ignore its commands.
I have no control over my voice	I have learned to have control over my voice by using the following coping strategies. . . .
My voice is powerful and therefore should be obeyed.	My voice may be unpleasant and say some nasty things, which is distressing, but (as noted above) there is no evidence that it can actually harm me. Also my voice is not powerful, and so I do not have to obey it.

The general guideline is that the therapist does not challenge the client head-on but uses a variety of indirect tactics carried out in the spirit of guided discovery. Having sown the seeds of belief questioning during the assessment phase, the therapist can now draw on the client's own doubt, past or present, the client's own contradictory evidence and behavior, and the client's own concerns about the possibility that his or her beliefs about the voices may be wrong. The "Columbo" technique is a particularly powerful form of Socratic questioning with an emphasis on curiosity, pointing out inconsistencies in a gentle, curious way (Fowler, Garety, & Kuipers, 1995).

Challenging the Beliefs About Voices. Challenging the dysfunctional beliefs includes questioning the client's evidence for the beliefs, following a line of logical reasoning that exposes inconsistencies in these beliefs, reality testing in a bid to disconfirm the beliefs, "normalizing" the voice qualities, and responding more assertively (behaving uprank) to the voice.

Questioning Evidence. The routine procedure in cognitive therapy can be used here first to list evidence that supports, then evidence that disconfirms, the identified belief. Commonly, the client will find it easier to provide supportive evidence, and help is often needed to build evidence against the belief. Such disconfirming evidence can be constructed from anything the client has noticed in the past that seemed to be inconsistent with what the voices said, plus evidence that has been elicited during the course of therapy. The client is asked to rank order evidence for and against each belief, from the most to the least convincing. Evidence for the belief is questioned starting with the least convincing aspects, The client is then asked to consider alternative explanations, and weigh the evidence for and against the alternatives. For example one client, David, explored and was unable to find any evidence that the voice had ever harmed him, or indeed as a "spirit" could possibly physically do so. He slowly came to realize there was no basis for his belief that the voice could physically harm him and he could therefore ignore its commands without punishment.

Logical Reasoning. This step involves developing a line of argument that moves in small steps, leading to the final step, which firmly challenges the belief. An important part of this exercise is to establish each of the key steps of the argument before they are connected together.

Reality Testing of Beliefs. Behavioral experiments can be used to test the validity of a belief. This entails carrying out or withholding a behavior in order to test a prediction that something catastrophic will happen. This strategy is particularly useful for testing beliefs that the voice will punish the client if he or she does not comply. For example, as a consequence of their perceived low social rank, many command hallucinators develop appeasement strategies, that is, they resist more serious commands by enacting less serious behaviors. The use of the social rank theory concept of appeasement can also be viewed as a safety or defensive behavior (see Gilbert, this book) preventing the individual from testing out the consequences of full noncompliance. The person is encouraged to reduce the degree of appeasement hand in hand with the promotion of his or her own (up-rank) power and control, and to discover that the feared outcome does not occur, hence weakening the belief. For example, having doubted his belief that the voice could harm him, David put this to the test by ignoring the commands, and after several such tests, discovered there were no consequences.

"Normalizing" the Voices. The client has personified and idealized the voice, resulting in beliefs around omnipotence and omniscience. Therapy aims to "normalize" (i.e., down-rank) the voice. highlighting ways in which the voice is as fallible as any human being and therefore not, for example, Godlike.

Questioning the Voice's Command. This is an extension of the behavioral test. When clients feel more confident regarding their power-rank relationship with the voice, they may find it helpful to challenge the voice more assertively. For example, in response to a voice command, the client may ask "Why should I do that? Why don't you do it yourself?" Such behavioral responses are designed to get the client to act against the dysfunctional down-rank beliefs and in line with the new functional beliefs, thus further weakening the former and strengthening the latter.

Emphasizing Benefits of Resistance. It can be useful to normalize the patient's fear and empathize with it. For example, if there really were hostile voices that could inflict harm this would indeed be frightening. This helps to de-shame the appeasement and fear response and build the therapeutic alliance. The therapist helps the client identify the perceived consequences of carrying out a command compared with the perceived consequences of resisting it (e.g., short-term gains of reducing anxiety may be outweighed by long-term disadvantages).

In pursuing this goal the therapist explores and challenges with the client the inferences that make the idea of severe punishment seem so compelling and certain. For example, the therapist can explore the idea that obeying the command is a kind of safety/defensive behavior, that, although understandable in the light of the client's beliefs, is preventing disconfirmation, and that these beliefs can be challenged and tested by the techniques described above.

Switching Voices On and Off. Once clients are able to take a more detached view of their subjective experience they can achieve a greater sense of control over the voices—and thereby further change their relative social rank—by learning to initiate and stop voice activity using the following steps:

- Identify cues or strategies that increase and decrease the frequency and volume of voices.
- Practice the use of decreasing strategies within a session.
- Propose the notion that "control" requires the demonstration that voice activity can be turned on as well as off, the analogy of learning to drive a car can be used, such that feeling in control of a car involves starting and stopping the car.
- Encourage the client to either initiate or to increase voice activity for short periods, then reduce or stop it. These periods are then gradually lengthened. In the case of David, he learned to start and stop his voices at will. He could activate his voice within a session by reading a newspaper article referring to abuse (he had been abused as a child and the voice was activated by media

references to child abuse). He was then able to stop the voice by talking about other matters.

- Consider the implications for beliefs about the voices' omnipotence once the client has achieved some control.

Increasing the Perceived Power of the Voice Hearer. Here clients identify evidence of their own mastery and control and increased social rank. Most of the preceding interventions aimed at challenging the beliefs about the power of the voice will simultaneously and necessarily be proving that the client has mastery and control, not the voice. By Socratic questioning, the therapist can help clients discover they can ignore the voice's commands without punishment, can control the voice by switching the voice on and off, and can care for themselves and keep active in spite of the presence of distressing voices. The aim is to help clients endorse their sense of mastery and control.

Reformulation. Sometimes it is possible to reformulate the explanation for the commanding voice, not only in terms of the questionable power beliefs so far challenged, but in terms of the psychological origins of the voice and even its identity, as we outlined in stage 1. This reformulation, skillfully handled and timed, can be a powerful coup de grâce with which to finally deconstruct the power and identity beliefs. In the case of David, having reached the stage of weakening the power beliefs by the methods so far described, the therapist explored the idea that the voice might not be Mr X speaking today, but a psychological reaction to the traumatic rape, a kind of reliving of the original experience where he was down ranked by a hostile dominant relative. David slowly began to question his belief that the voice was Mr X, and to entertain the possibility that it was a response to difficult feelings triggered by specific events.

To illustrate some aspects of the above procedure, we provide below an illustrative case study.

A Case Study Ralph

Background

Ralph is a 33-year-old man who began hearing voices at the age of 16. He reported being sexually abused at 9 years of age. He was bullied by some of his peers, both physically and emotionally, and was tormented by them over the abuse. He became increasingly disruptive and difficult to manage, and was put into institutional care at 14 years as his mother was unable to cope. At 16 he received a youth custody sentence for stealing. It was during this time that he began to hear voices. From 22 to 25 years he experienced remission from the voices but since then, he has reported hearing them almost daily.

Stage 1: Assessment

During the initial assessment, Ralph reported hearing three hostile, dominant, male voices to which he felt extremely subordinated. The content of these voices was always in the nature of put-downs, including personal threats to self (e.g., "we are going to stab you"), personal verbal abuse relating to his self-concept (e.g., "you are a pervert, you are evil"), and commands to self harm and harm others (e.g., "kill yourself, you deserve to die," "go and get a hammer: kill X [Ralph's abuser]," "kill your dad"). As a result, Ralph described feeling extremely frightened, inferior, and weak. He said that he heard the voices at least once a day, particularly at night, often lasting for hours at a time. He felt that he had no choice but to listen to them. He coped by shouting and swearing at the voices, listening to the TV or radio, and drinking alcohol.

The Voice Power Scale (Birchwood et al., 2000) showed that Ralph believed that the voices were much more powerful, strong, confident, knowledgeable, and superior to him, and much more capable of harming him than he was of defending himself. He believed that the voices were very powerful because he had no control over them, they appeared frequently, they said things in a loud, persistent way, if they told him something, it must be true, and they had taken over his mind.

Beliefs About Identity. Ralph reported being 100% certain that one of the voices was that of his abuser, and that the other two were from the devil, because "they sounded like them."

Beliefs About Meaning. Ralph believed that he was being persecuted by people for bad things in his past: he had committed burglary and theft as a young adult; he felt responsible for his mother's death; and he believed the voices were a punishment because he was sexually abused, for which, he believed, he bore responsibility.

Beliefs About Compliance/Resistance. Ralph had a past history of taking two drug overdoses in response to the voices, and he had previously cut his wrists superficially in order to appease them. He reported feeling compelled to obey the voices but had resisted commands to kill others for fear of being put in prison; he feared acting on the commands if they continued to be so distressing. He acted on commands to get out of bed on the majority of occasions.

Beliefs About Control. Ralph believed that he had some control over the voices, but only occasionally.

Target Behaviors. The main compliance behavior targeted for intervention was acting on commands to harm himself or others, including wrist cutting (appeasement behavior).

Stage 2: Intervention

Challenging Beliefs About Control Over the Voices. Supported by the therapist, Ralph developed a range of coping strategies that helped him to have more control over the voices; he found talking to someone he trusted helped when the voices were distressing. Other helpful strategies included telling the voices to stop or go away in a firm voice (out loud when alone or to himself when in company), listening to the radio or watching football on TV, keeping active by meeting with friends, and taking regular medication. It was suggested that these strategies offered him some control, and they were reinforced.

Exploring the Evidence for and Against the Power of the Voices. Using the above coping strategies, Ralph began to believe that he had more control over the voices and was not a helpless victim. He used the evidence that he could cope to support an emerging belief that he had as much power and rank as the voices. Gradually, Ralph became aware that his voices often worsened (i.e., became louder, more frequent) when he was depressed or anxious. Learning strategies for coping with anxiety and depression also made him feel more empowered.

Challenging the Belief That the Voices Were Powerful Because If They Said Something, It Must Be True. The voices said, "You killed your mother." The circumstances of his mother's death were explored. Ralph had believed that he should have done something to stop his mother's cancer. However, he ultimately accepted the fact that he and his family had done all they could to help their mother. Ralph concluded that she had died of an illness and that he was in no way responsible for her death.

The voices called Ralph a pervert. However, there was no evidence to support this claim. Ralph had never taken advantage sexually of another person; moreover, he had been the victim of abuse as a child, not the perpetrator.

The voices also called Ralph evil. Ralph defined an evil person as someone who would not feel guilty about, but would enjoy, physically or emotionally hurting someone, and would not help other people in any way. There was no evidence that Ralph was evil but there was much evidence that he was kind and caring and disliked upsetting people.

Such evidence helped Ralph change his belief that the voices were powerful dominants. It cast doubt on the truth of what the voices said, leading him to conclude that the voices were liars and not to be trusted. Consequently, he realized that he did not have to believe the voices when they threatened or said unpleasant things about him or others.

Exploring the Belief That the Voices Saying Things Frequently, Sometimes Getting Louder, Meant They Should Be Obeyed. This was challenged by asking him to consider whether saying "you are a pink giraffe" to someone over and over again would make this statement true. Ralph concluded that just because something is said repeatedly does not automatically mean it is true or that he should act on it. Gradually, Ralph began to believe that he could choose whether or not to believe what the voices said, and he could choose whether or not to act on their commands.

Reducing Appeasement. Ralph chose to resist more serious commands to harm himself or others: but he did respond to the command to "get out of bed," which, though obviously totally innocuous, was viewed as an appeasement in social rank terms, and therefore as a safety/defensive behavior, stopping him from behaviorally testing the social rank beliefs. Having reframed in this way Ralph agreed he would resist even these minor commands to see if the supposed consequences ensued. They did not. We should note that often the best way of helping the client to reevaluate commands is by starting the process with innocuous commands of this type.

Exploring Beliefs About Meaning and Identity. Ralph believed he was being persecuted for past misdemeanors. An alternative explanation was proposed, namely that stressful events in childhood and adolescence had triggered the development of Ralph's mental health problems.

As found by Birchwood and associates (2000), the relationship between people and their voice(s) is often mirrored in dominant-subordinate relationships they have, or have had, with people in their lives. Working on these relationships can be important. Links were made between Ralph's relationship with the voices and his relationship with his abuser. As a child, Ralph had felt powerless to act against the abuser; similarly he had perceived himself to be subordinate to the voices, just like with the abuser. Ralph was able to use this social rank account of the early dominant-subordinate victimization to understand the later voice relationship. This in turn enabled him to become more assertive with the voices and with significant others. For example, Ralph was learning that he could make choices about his behavior that might contradict the voices' commands. He began to describe various situations with friends, family, and staff in which he had been able to assert himself. For example, he initiated a move from a flat into supported housing because he felt that this would be beneficial for his mental health; he began to actively seek support from trusted others whenever he felt distressed by the voices or other events; and he started to talk more openly about his experiences with trusted others, no longer feeling ashamed to do so.

Outcome

The Voice Power Differential Scale (VPD: Birchwood et al., 2000) and the control and distress scales of the Psychotic Symptom Rating Scales (PSYRATS: Haddock, McCarron, Tarrier, & Faragher, 1999) were administered before and after the intervention. The VPD measures the power differential between voice and voice hearer on five-point scales with regard to overall power and a number of related characteristics. The PSYRATS measures the severity of a number of dimensions of auditory hallucinations and delusions, including amount and intensity of distress associated with these symptoms.

A major reduction in distress was observed, accompanied by a shift in the power balance favoring Ralph, as shown in Table 7.2.

The results indicate that the majority of targeted beliefs about the voices had significantly changed by the end of therapy. Ralph believed that he had more control over the voices and was equally as powerful as they. He had not felt compelled to act on serious commands to harm himself or others, and he no longer believed that he was being persecuted. In addition, the findings indicate that Ralph was somewhat less distressed by the voices post-therapy, although he was still upset by the fact that he continued to hear malevolent voices. With regard to the voices' identity, some doubt had been cast on Ralph's belief that one of the voices was that of his abuser, although he remained partially convinced, Ralph felt that he had benefited from having the opportunity to talk about the voices in terms of learning how to cope with them, being able to question what they said, and standing up to them.

TABLE 7.2 Summary Comparing Pre- and Post-Therapy Measures for Ralph (1–5 scales)

Measure	Pre-Therapy	Post-Therapy
Power	5 (voices much more powerful)	3 (we have same amount of power)
Power Differential[1]		
Strength	5 (voices much stronger)	3 (we are as strong as each other)
Confidence	5 (voices much more confident)	3 (we are as confident as each other
Knowledge	5 (voices much more knowledgeable)	3 (we have same amount of knowledge)
Harm	5 (voices more able to harm me than I, them)	5 (voices more able to harm me than I, them)
Superior	5 (voices much more superior)	5 (voices much more superior)
Control over the voices[2]	3 (I have some control but only occasionally)	1 (I have some control to the majority of occasions
Distress[2]	1 (very distressing)	3 (neutral: neither distressing, nor comforting)

Beliefs	Pre-Therapy	Post-Therapy
Resistance/Compliance	5 Compel me to obey them	3 Fairly distracting
Identity of dominant voice (percentage belief conviction)	Voice of his abuser: 100%	Voice of his abuser: 50%
Meaning of the voices	Persecuted for past events	Voices mixing up his thoughts

[1] Voice Power Differential Scale (VPD)
[2] Psychotic Symptom Rating Scale (PSYRATS)

Research

The marked improvements in pre and post-scores in the case of Ralph is by no means sufficient evidence of the efficacy of CTCH, which, in common with any intervention, can only be demonstrated by means of controlled empirical studies. However the evidence base for cognitive behavior therapy for psychosis in general is reasonably encouraging. In a recent meta-analysis of trials that met required standards of scientific rigor, Jones, Cormac, Campbell, and Da Mota Neta (1998) found that CBT in addition to standard care (relative to standard care alone) has a beneficial effect regarding the positive symptoms of psychosis, though not the negative symptoms. The beneficial effects of CBT become apparent in the long term. However, none of the trials focused on command hallucinations, and the authors have therefore undertaken a randomized controlled trial, currently in progress, to test the efficacy of CTCH and to evaluate whether the theory is supported.

Discussion

In this chapter we have presented a development in the application of cognitive therapy to people who are distressed by and compelled to act upon commanding voices. In developing this intervention we have drawn upon traditional cognitive behavior therapy but informed by social rank theory. At its core are three propositions. The first argues that what governs the distress and behavior arising from voices is not the voices per se, or indeed necessarily their content, but patients' beliefs about them; this extends to whether the voice is interpreted as a command. The second suggests that these beliefs center around the personification of the voice and the nature of the interpersonal relationship with it. Finally, this relationship is usually perceived as one of subordination to and appeasement of a powerful dominant, as described by social rank theory. This theory has been drawn upon to help predict the specific beliefs that command hallucinators have, and to guide the type and sequence of cognitive interventions involved in these types of hallucinations. The aim of CTCH, therefore, has been to reduce distress and risk behavior (rather than the physical presence or frequency of voices) through intervention in the perceived power balance between voice and voice hearer.

In the case study presented, changes in power, compliance, and control beliefs were achieved, with consequent reduction in distress and risk behavior. In this case the beliefs were rated as delusional, though with partial insight. Though the client continued to hear voices, he experienced reduced distress and preoccupation. Other examples of cases conceptualized and worked with in this way are outlined in Birchwood, Meaden, Trower, and Gilbert (2002).

One possible criticism of CBT is that evidence shows it has limited impact on frequency of auditory hallucinations (Tarrier, et al. 1998), and thus may not be particularly effective for reducing the frequency of CH. However, cognitive therapy for psychotic symptoms focuses on beliefs and not on primary experience. CTCH similarly aims not to eliminate the primary experience, but to change patients' beliefs about them, although changes in perceived frequency may be a by-product (Birchwood et al., 2000).

In conclusion, we have proposed that beliefs about voices can mirror evolutionary forms of social role (e.g., dominant-subordinate) and that conceptualizing beliefs in this way has major implications for intervention. We believe that CTCH, targeted as it is to deconstruct precisely the belief system that maintains the problem, (e.g., by addressing the dominant-subordinate relationships with the voice and the person's ongoing social life) could be more effective in outcome and efficient in time than a more general CBT or other general psychotherapy approach.

References

Baker, C. A., & Morrison, A. P. (1998). Cognitive processes in auditory hallucinations: Attributional biases and metacognition. *Psychological Medicine, 28*, 1199–1208.

Beck. A. T., Rush, A. J., Shaw, B. E, & Emery, G. (1979). *Cognitive therapy of depression.* New York: Guilford.

Beck-Sander. A., Birchwood, M., & Chadwick, P. (1997). Acting on command hallucinations: A cognitive approach. *British Journal of Clinical Psychology, 36*, 139–148.

Bentall, R. P. (1990). The illusion of reality: A review and integration of psychological research on hallucinations. *Psychological Bulletin, 107*, 82–95.

Birchwood, M., & Chadwick, P. (1997). The omnipotence of voices: Testing the validity of a cognitive model. *Psychological Medicine, 27*, 1345–1353.

Birchwood, M., Meaden, A., Trower, P., & Gilbert, P. (2002). Shame, humiliation and entrapment in psychosis: A social rank theory approach to cognitive intervention with voices and delusions. In A. P. Morrison (Ed.), *A casebook of cognitive therapy for psychosis* (pp. 108–131). London: Brunner-Routledge.

Birchwood, M., Meaden, A., Trower, P., Gilbert, P., & Plaistow, J. (2000). The power and omnipotence of voices: Subordination and entrapment by voices and significant others. *Psychological Medicine, 30*, 337–344.

Braham, L., & Trower, P. (in press). Acting on command hallucinations and dangerous behaviors: A critique of the major findings of the last decade. *Clinical Psychology Review.*

Brown, G. W., Harris, T. O., & Hepworth, C. (1995). Loss, humiliation, and entrapment among women developing depression: A patient and non-patient comparison, *Psychological Medicine, 25*, 7–21.

Chadwick, P., & Birchwood, M. (1994). The omnipotence of voices: A cognitive approach to auditory hallucinations. *British Journal of Psychiatry, 164*, 190–201.

Chadwick, P., Birchwood, M., & Trower, P. (1996). *Cognitive therapy for delusions, voices and paranoia.* Chichester, UK: Wiley.

Close, H., & Garety, P. (1998). Cognitive assessment of voices: Further developments in understanding the emotional impact of voices. *British Journal of Clinical Psychology, 37*, 173–188.

Crow, T. J. (1997a). Schizophrenia as failure of hemispheric dominance for language. *Trends in the Neurosciences, 20*, 339–343.

Crow, T. J. (1997b). Is schizophrenia the price homo sapiens pays for language? *Schizophrenia Research, 28*, 127–141.

Dryden, W. (1995). *Brief rational emotive behavior therapy.* Chichester, UK: Wiley.

Fowler, D., Garety, P., & Kuipers, E. (1995). *Cognitive behavior therapy for psychosis.* Chichester, UK: Wiley.

Gilbert, P. (1992). *Depression: The evolution of powerlessness.* Hove, East Sussex: Erlbaum.

Gilbert, P., Birchwood, M., Gilbert, J., Trower, P., Hay, J., Murray, B., Meaden, A. Olsen, K., & Miles, J. N. V. (2001). An exploration of evolved mental mechanisms for dominant and subordinate behavior in relation to auditory hallucinations in schizophrenia and critical thoughts in depression. *Psychological Medicine, 31*, 1117–1127.

Gilbert P.; & Trower, P. (2001). Evolution and process in social anxiety. In W. R. Crozier & L. E. Alden (Eds.), *The self, shyness and social anxiety: A handbook of concepts, research and interventions* (pp. 259–279). Chichester, UK: Wiley.

Haddock, G., McCarron, J., Tarrier, N., & Faragher, E. B. (1999). Scales to measure dimensions of hallucinations and delusions: The psychotic symptom rating scales (PSYRATS). *Psychological Medicine, 29*, 879–889.

Hellerstein, D., Frosch, W., & Koenigsberg. H. W. (1987). The clinical significance of command hallucinations. *American Journal of Psychiatry, 144*, 219–221.

Jones, C., Cormac, I., Campbell, C., & Da Mota Neta, J. (1998). *Cognitive behavior therapy for schizophrenia.* (The Cochrane Library, Issue 4). Oxford, UK: Update Software.

Jones, G., Huckle, P., & Tanaghow, A. (1992). Command hallucinations, schizophrenia and sexual assaults. *Irish Journal of Psychological Medicine, 9*, 47–49.

Junginger, J. (1990). Predicting compliance with command hallucinations. *American Journal of Psychiatry; 147*, 245–247.

McGuire, P. K., Silversweig, D. A., Wright, I., Murray, R. M., Frackowiak, R. S. J., & Frith, C. D. (1996). The neural correlates of inner speech and auditory verbal imagery in schizophrenia: Relationship to auditory verbal hallucinations. *British Journal of Psychiatry 169*, 148–159.

Morrison, A. P., & Haddock, G. (1997). Cognitive factors in source monitoring and auditory hallucinations. *Psychological Medicine, 27*, 669–679.

Price, J. S., Price, J. S., & Sloman, L. (1987). Depression as yielding behavior: An animal model based on Schjelderup-Ebbe's pecking order. *Ethology and Sociobiology, 8*, 85–98.

Rogers, R., Gillis, J. R., Turner, R. E., & Frise-Smith, T. (1990). The clinical presentation of command hallucinations in a forensic population. *American Journal of Psychiatry, 147*, 1304–1307.

Rooke, O., & Birchwood, M. (1998). Loss, humiliation and entrapment as appraisals of schizophrenic illness: A prospective study of depressed and non-depressed patients. *British Journal of Clinical Psychology, 37*, 259–268.

Tarrier, N., Yusupoff, L., Kinney, C., McCarthy, E., Gledhill, A., Haddock, G., & Morris, J. (1998). Randomised controlled trial of intensive cognitive behavioral therapy in patients with chronic schizophrenia. *British Medical Journal, 317*, 303–307.

Trower, P,, Casey, A.. & Dryden, W. (1988). *Cognitive behavioral counselling in action.* London: Sage.

Trower: P., & Gilbert, P. (1989). New theoretical conceptions of social anxiety and social phobia. *Clinical Psychology Review, 9*, 19–35.

Index